Certain Admissions

A Beach, A Body And A Lifetime Of Secrets

Gideon Haigh

16pt

9781458765192

Read How You Want

LARGE PRINT BOOKS, BRAILLE & DAISY

Copyright Page from the Original Book

VIKING

UK | USA | Canada | Ireland | Australia
India | New Zealand | South Africa | China

Penguin Books is part of the Penguin Random House group of companies
whose addresses can be found at global.penguinrandomhouse.com.

Penguin
Random House
Australia

First published by Penguin Group (Australia), 2015

1 3 5 7 9 10 8 6 4 2

Design by Laura Thomas © Penguin Group (Australia)
Front-cover photography: images of John Kerr courtesy of Corrections Victoria
Back-cover photograph: Clocks of of Flinders Street Station by Mark Strizic
Typeset in 12/16pt Adobe Garamond by Laura Thomas, Penguin Group (Australia)
Colour separation by Splitting Image Colour Studio, Clayton, Victoria
Printed and bound in Australia by Griffin Press, an accredited ISO AS/NZS 14001
Environmental Management Systems printer.

National Library of Australia
Cataloguing-in-Publication data:

Haigh, Gideon
Certain admissions : a beach, a body and a lifetime of secrets / Gideon Haigh.

Includes bibliographical references.
Subjects: Williams, Beth, –1949. Kerr, John Bryan.
Murder – Victoria – Melbourne. Criminal investigation – Victoria – Melbourne.
Trials (Murder) – Victoria – Melbourne.

364.1523099451

penguin.com.au

TABLE OF CONTENTS

CERTAIN ADMISSIONS

Gideon Haigh has been a journalist for more than thirty years, contributed to more than a hundred newspapers and magazines, written thirty-one books and edited seven others.
He lives in Melbourne.

Also by Gideon Haigh

The Battle for BHP
The Cricket War: The Inside Story of Kerry Packer's World Series Cricket
The Border Years
One Summer Every Summer: An Ashes Journal
The Summer Game: Australian Cricket in the 1950s and 1960s
Mystery Spinner: The Story of Jack Iverson
One of a Kind: The Story of Bankers Trust Australia 1969–1999
The Big Ship: Warwick Armstrong and the Making of Modern Cricket
The Vincibles: A Suburban Cricket Season
The Uncyclopedia
Bad Company: The Strange Cult of the CEO
The Tencyclopedia
Game for Anything: Writings on Cricket
A Fair Field and No Favour: The Ashes of 2005
Asbestos House: The Secret History of James Hardie Industries
Silent Revolutions: Writings on Cricket History
All Out: The Ashes 2006–07
The Green and Golden Age: Writings on Cricket Today
Inside Story: Unlocking Australian Cricket's Archives (with David Frith)
The Racket: How Abortion Became Legal in Australia
Inside Out: Writings on Cricket Culture
Good Enough: The Ashes 2009

Sphere of Influence: Writings on Cricket and its Discontents
Out of the Running: The Ashes 2010–11
The Office: A Hardworking History
On Warne
The Deserted Newsroom
End of the Road?
Uncertain Corridors: Writings on Modern Cricket
Ashes to Ashes: How Australia Came Back and England Came Unstuck, 2013–14

John Bryan Kerr, 25 *[sic],* radio announcer, of Washington St, Toorak, had made **'certain admissions'** about the death of Elizabeth Maureen Williams, 20, at Albert Park Beach on Wednesday, police said in the City Court yesterday.

The Argus, Friday 30 December, 1949

1

MURDER ON A SUMMER NIGHT

Speak of meeting 'under the clocks' and no Melburnian mistakes your meaning. The indicator clocks over the archway entrance to Flinders Street railway station became a local landmark almost as soon as they were installed more than a century ago. As early as the 1920s, a contributor to a railways magazine was versifying of their romance: 'A thousand dramas had their birth/Upon that busy spot of earth/O'er which the clocks preside'. Wartime folklore was of American servicemen converging on the clocks, and leaving with a bathing beauty on each arm. A photo of the clocks adorning a 1949 *Argus* feature about the 'gateway to the metropolis' was wistfully captioned: 'Is this where you used to meet her?'

So when twenty-year-old typist Beth Williams arranged to rendezvous with twenty-year-old sailor James Stevens on the evening of Tuesday, 27 December of that year, 'under the clocks' was the natural first step to their night on the town. They had met the night before, not far away, at the Trocadero, a ramshackle but still popular dancehall; they had had supper afterwards in a Swanston Street cafe called A Little

Bit of Sweden. Depositing Williams at her Middle Park lodgings, Stevens had suggested they catch 'The Big Holiday Laugh Show' at the State Theatre the following evening: Bob Hope's new comedy *The Great Lover,* plus Betty Hutton in *Red, Hot and Blue.* Beth had given him her number – MX4983 – to confirm the date.

Their plans had gone astray. Stevens rang at 4p.m. to say he had been unable to book seats. They agreed to meet at 7.15p.m., twenty-five minutes before the show, to try for unreserved seating. Then, unbeknown to Beth, Stevens had been caught up. He had arranged to come into town with Rudolph Peterson and Ernest Fossberg, two fellow crewmen from his Norwegian merchant ship who had also been his companions the night before. Now the trio dallied in Elsternwick, and at 7.15p.m. were just boarding the train.

Beth was not wearing a watch, but a glance aloft at those clocks would have reminded her of the viscosity of time spent waiting. Did she experience a twinge of impatience standing amid the back-and-forth surge of travellers at the busy intersection? Had she done a little too much waiting lately? It was warm, it was bright, it was the holiday season. She was young and pretty; she wore a beret, a smart red stroller coat and black kid gloves. She had just hours to live.

***

The public would never learn much about Elizabeth Maureen Williams – murder victims are seldom other than the pegs on which to hang the stories of their killers. Her family in Tasmania gave no interviews, and only the one grainy photograph was ever published of her: a full-length image of Beth as a bridesmaid, usually cropped to the specifications of a head shot. She was small, plump, brown-eyed, educated at New Town's Sacred Heart Convent, schooled in typing and stenography at Hobart's Remington Business College, from where she moved to the secretarial pool at Tattersall's. She liked to dance; she liked the movies; her family's home had been across the road from Moonah's picture theatre. For the previous year she had let a small room in a double-fronted brick house at 136 Page Street with her twenty-two-year-old Tasmanian friend Patricia Street, and worked as a typist in 'A' block, Victoria Barracks, on St Kilda Road. Her shearer father had just visited Melbourne and bought a new house in Margaret Street, Werribee, with the intention of relocating the family to the mainland. When she had been unable to obtain Christmas leave, the Williamses had set aside a portion of their lunch to share with her when she visited Hobart for her twenty-first birthday on 15 January 1950. Pat Street thought Beth Williams 'a wonderful type of girl'. Neighbours described her as 'a charming young lady' and 'a real little lady to speak to'. A meagre biography – but, then, life aged twenty tends to be about the future rather than the past.

Housing was in short supply in Melbourne after the war – desperately so, at times. With Pat, who worked behind the counter at Trans Australia Airlines, Beth shared not only her clothes and belongings but the bed as well, while their landlady, Mrs Eva Burns, would not permit male visitors. Fortunately, an older widow, Mrs Madeleine Patrick, who lived ten minutes' walk away in Harold Street, fussed over them, mother hen-like. Occasionally, when daunted by the dimly lit local streets, they would stay with Mrs Patrick and her soldier son Stewart, who doted on Beth with awkward, tongue-tied fondness. In the course of their later investigations, police interviewed a Major Noel Adams, who had squired Beth for a couple of months after meeting her during a quartermasters social evening at the Engineers Drill Hall in Batman Avenue. His statement was a model of propriety: 'I took her home in a taxi that night. I have not been in her room. She has never been in my room'.

Their relationship foundered after he went to Sydney and failed to call her on his return. Beth was piqued; the Major speculated that 'she may have met someone else'. To the police, though, he loyally ratified her virtue: 'I do not think she is a loose type of girl. I believed she was well behaved. She drank a little but not to excess'.

As she dawdled at about 7.30p.m., Beth met someone else she knew, also using the clocks as a rendezvous point. She and Pat had previously bumped into William Grinsted, a concrete mixer, at a couple of Parkville keg parties hosted by the 'No Hopers Club' – the name was a jesting reference to the punting fortunes of the young organisers. Not that Grinsted was in a partying mood. He was awaiting someone from whom he'd borrowed money, intending to pay it back – their meeting was at 8p.m. So distracted was Grinsted that he mistook Beth for her roommate, and called her 'Pat'. Beth asked Grinsted if he was interested in going to a party, without specifying where; Grinsted pleaded shortage of funds. She walked a few steps to buy two PKs and a Juicy Fruit from a streetside vendor; he declined her offer of a piece. She was killing time. The night was in danger of slipping away.

In quick succession, separated only by minutes, Beth Williams had two other encounters. The significance of the first proved ambiguous. As what Grinsted called 'three young fellows' approached from Swanston Street, Beth moved a few steps in their direction and engaged them briefly in conversation. Grinsted was unable to describe the trio, beyond that one wore an 'ordinary light suit'. As he was recorded saying in the stilted evidentiary language of the time, he chose to look the other way.

> I was about six feet away but I did not hear anything – I did not want to listen. I did not know what they were talking about, and it was no business of mine. I was talking to her, she said 'just a minute', and she walked away ... She was talking to them for about a couple of minutes, then she walked back to me and was talking to

> me. As to what she commenced to talk about to me, she was asking me how Nellie was. She did not tell me anything about the three young gentlemen she met; she did not say one word about them. She was still talking to me when the gentleman came around with the case and overcoat.

The 'gentleman' in this second encounter met that description in every inch. Twenty-four-year-old John Bryan Wallace Kerr was immaculately groomed. He wore a well-cut, blue twill suit that sat evenly on broad shoulders. He shone from his oiled dark hair to his black leather shoes. He had just left the evening express from Warragul, where he had spent Christmas, and walked perhaps even more jauntily than usual: that afternoon he had enjoyed a healthy collect on the Arlington Handicap at Moonee Valley.

Beth Williams recognised him at once. Eighteen months or so earlier, they had met at Hobart radio station 7HO, where Kerr had been an announcer. She called his name, met his gaze with a smile, and walked towards him. Kerr, recalled Grinsted, 'beamed' back, showing straight, white teeth. Then he opened his mouth. Kerr's voice was his signature – deep, rich, well modulated.

By his own recollection, Kerr was, at first, only noncommittally polite.

'I remember your face and I recall you in Hobart,' he said. 'But I can't think of your name.'

'Beth Williams,' said the girl.

'Yes, that is right,' nodded Kerr. 'How are you?'

Beth explained that she was now living in Melbourne. Further nothings were exchanged. She was all dressed up. Kerr sensed that she was looking for somewhere to go.

'I was off home with this suitcase,' he said presently. 'As you can see, I have had rather a good day. What about dinner with me?'

Beth paused. 'Well, I have got a date to go to the State tonight and he's late,' she wondered aloud. 'He was to meet me here.'

Kerr took the initiative. 'If he is late, come and have dinner with me,' he said. 'Because although I was going home, I'd rather have dinner in town first. I backed Laimell today at 20 to one, so I'd rather stay in town and celebrate.'

If Beth hesitated, it can only have been for an instant. Grinsted put the exchange between the pair at 'not ... more than about a minute'.

'All right,' she said. 'He has my phone number anyway, so he can contact me later.'

As they headed up the station steps for the cloakroom where Kerr intended leaving his suitcase, Beth said to Grinsted over her shoulder, 'See you later'.

***

Crossing Swanston Street, the pair began strolling east along Flinders Street, their first objective being the lively Phoenix Hotel near the corner with Exhibition Street. They found it full to overflowing. Kerr's next suggestion was Mario's, Melbourne's original Italian restaurant, a couple of blocks away, its pale, illuminated façade standing out in the twilight near where Exhibition Street met Little Bourke Street, opposite His Majesty's Theatre. Kerr was a regular here, and probably aware that a bob or two in the right pocket secured attentive service; perhaps he also pinned a flower to Beth's frock from the supply kept for female guests in a bowl at the front desk. The *table d'hôte* menu was cheap and the wine rough at Mario's, but the company was usually convivial.

No sooner had they taken their seats than another regular, fifty-five-year-old salesman Leslie John Wood, sidled up, having finished his meal. Kerr asked Wood's intentions for later, suggesting he 'come out with us'. Wood said he would like to, except that he was meeting friends upstairs – he would check their plans, although he had a morning engagement and did not 'want a late night'.

Kerr nodded, 'Neither do I. I've got a ship early.'

As Wood moved on, Kerr explained to his companion that since returning from a short spell at 2QN in Deniliquin he had been working as a clerk for the State Immigration Authority, one of his responsibilities being to meet immigrant ships as they arrived. It was purely a temporary measure: after four years in commercial radio, he had applied for a job at the ABC, and confidently anticipated acceptance. Feeling expansive, he requested the *à la carte* menu, and ordered chateaubriand, at 37/6, to share.

On ascending to the dance floor, Kerr spied Wood in conversation with a burly, moustachioed figure he did not recognise. Wood explained that Edward Penno, a tailor, had invited a few guests to supper in Malvern: John and Beth were welcome to join them when they left. As the band struck up and the floor filled with couples, plans were laid. For the next hour, drinks were drained, tunes played and songs performed by a singing waiter.

At 9.30p.m., two cars set off for Penno's upstairs flat at 91 Station Street, near the railway line. The party was composed of Wood, John Kerr, Beth Williams, a man called McFarland and his fiancée, another couple from Elsternwick, and a statuesque blonde, twenty-seven-year-old Barbara Robertson. Travelling in Wood's Chevrolet, Kerr soon slipped into conversation with Mrs Robertson, a model for Georges and a cosmetics saleswoman at the Myer Emporium. This stirred some mild cross-currents.

Mrs Robertson lived with her husband William and two young children in Trinafour Street, Moonee Ponds, having moved from Tasmania four years earlier. But tonight, for reasons never elaborated, she was unaccompanied, and she responded to Kerr's attentions: not long into the party they were flirting noticeably, chatting, dancing and for 'a few moments' adjourning to Penno's bedroom, where she slipped him her telephone number. Such was the degree of mutual allurement that Penno felt obliged to interrupt, finding the young man sitting on the bed and the older woman applying make-up in the mirror.

'I think you two had better come back in,' he said stiffly. He was stiffer still under questioning later.

> A little incident occurred in regard to Barbara Robertson during the evening in which I had to intervene. There was talking and getting very friendly. I did not like the idea, I spoke to them and they broke – finished – that is all ... It was just a matter as things do happen at parties – they are inclined to get matey and affectionate. I did not like it, I called the parties to order, and that was the end of it. As to who was involved in the incident, it was Mrs Robertson and Mr John Kerr. I did not think it was a party like that and I do not care for those sort of things. As to what sort of things I mean, nothing, but Mrs Robertson is a friend and I did not like the idea. Mr Kerr was playing a fair amount of attention to her. He was neglecting Miss Williams.

Afterwards, everyone made nice. Penno recalled of Beth: 'She was quite respectable and sitting down on the lounge quite enjoying herself'. Quite: beer was drunk, supper consumed, and dancing resumed after 11.30p.m. to tunes on the radiogram from 3AK's 'Voice of the Night'.

Kerr spent some time on Penno's telephone trying to contact the State Immigration Authority so as to check on his ship for the morrow, to no avail. As the party concluded after midnight, Kerr also had no success scanning the streets for a taxi. With other guests in a similar predicament, Wood stepped in as driver – a generous gesture as not only was he 'very tired', but the couple were in Elsternwick, Beth Williams in Middle Park, John Kerr in Toorak and Barbara Robertson in Moonee Ponds. But on a weeknight two days after Christmas, the options were limited. After the first couple were dropped off on Gardenvale Road, Beth Williams and John Kerr shared the back seat.

It was not a comfortable journey. Conversation was minimal. And as the Chevrolet glided past the Maison dancehall, Kerr, by his own account, started feeling unwell. He had not, he thought, had terribly much to drink: he described his state as 'a little bit bright'. But he had, perhaps, been unsettled by the brush with Barbara Robertson and by his failure to get through to his superior, and now was in barely familiar company and territory. He decided to get out with Beth in Middle Park, while leaving the navigating to her. He was aware only of driving 'a fair way along'

Danks Street, and of Beth at last remarking, 'If you drop us here it will be all right'.

As the young pair stepped onto the kerb beneath a street light around 1a.m., Wood wound his window down.

'You'll be able to get home all right, will you, John?' he asked.

'Yes, I will be all right,' Kerr replied.

Farewells trailed away. The car disappeared into the night. The street stretched emptily in each direction. The earth might almost have been uninhabited.

***

About four hours later, Martin Crosbie, a clerk who lived with his wife Mary at 239 Danks Street, was taking his regular constitutional on Albert Park Beach when he glimpsed in the distance the outline of a dark shape on the water's edge, near a fallen date palm. As he approached, he realised it was the figure of a young woman, on her back, head towards the sea, water lapping her ears. Her face was blue; her body, cool to the touch, was caked in sand. Crosbie's first thought was of a drowning victim. Looking round anxiously, he spied another beach walker, about fifty metres away, and called out, 'There's a girl here. Go and get assistance'. But the walker hurried on.

Crosbie hastened to Albert Park Police Station on Danks Street, the other side of Kerferd Road. It was closed. From the nearby telephone booth, he asked the operator to connect him with South Melbourne Police Station, and two constables of the Mobile Traffic Police were detailed to attend Albert Park Beach near the bathing sheds at the end of Mills Street. Crosbie met them as they parked on Beaconsfield Parade at 5.17a.m.

'There's foam around her mouth,' he reported. 'I think she may still be alive.'

While his colleague radioed for an ambulance, Constable Lionel Nelson hurried down the sand to apply artificial respiration, although when no water came from the girl's mouth or nose, he feared the worst.

The scene was slashed with violence. The girl's blue dress had been torn from the top down the middle, almost to the waist. A brassiere strap was broken and her breasts were exposed. The skirt was up around her buttocks. One black ankle-strapped shoe lay near a red stroller coat and black handbag; the other lay in water five metres away. With the sea so close, Nelson initially adopted Crosbie's view that they were looking at a drowning. They moved the girl up the beach to continue the artificial respiration, and were still going when ambulancemen arrived at 5.45a.m., treating the event as a medical emergency. But the ambulance's efforts to find a mechanical respirator at Prince Henry's and St Vincent's Hospital were in vain.

After a half-hour's resuscitation efforts at Royal Melbourne Hospital, Beth Williams was declared dead.

In 1949, there was none of the rigmarole that today accompanies public death. Within half an hour of Crosbie's discovery, the patch of sand on which Beth Williams had been found had reverted to part of an exquisite Melbourne summer's morning, by a flat calm sea, beneath a cloudless sky. To the left sat a timber kiosk advertising Sennitt's Ice Cream, with its familiar logo of a polar bear; to the right stretched inviting sand all the way to Kerferd Road Pier; across Beaconsfield Parade rose the walls of the Convent of the Good Shepherd, whose steam laundries were being stoked for the day. The only speck on the scene was a soggy handbag, whose contents were itemised by the police as follows: a purse containing sixpence, a lipstick, a comb, a powder puff, two small brushes, chewing gum and wrappings, and an unfinished typewritten letter bearing the address '136 Page Street, Middle Park'.

Soon after, Patricia Street awoke to find Constable Nelson at her bedside bearing what she recognised as her handbag, which her roommate Beth borrowed freely.

No, Beth had not come home the night before. Yes, the light had been on in their room and the door ajar when Patricia had returned home just after midnight from her own evening with Tasmanian friends at the State Theatre and Victoria Coffee Palace, which she had noted as a little odd. Maybe, she had thought at first, Beth had come home and gone out again; maybe Beth was 'down the back' (using the outside toilet); eventually, after reading a while, she had concluded that Beth was staying the night with the Patricks, then dropped into a fitful sleep. Was something amiss?

The constable advised Patricia to brace herself for bad news.

***

Beth Williams' death officially became a murder investigation at 8.30a.m. when a Homicide Squad car pulled up on Beaconsfield Parade containing Inspector Hugh Donelly, and Senior Detectives Frederick Adam and Cyril Currer. 'Big Bill', 'Bluey' and 'Smugs', as they were known, shambled round the scene, three hulking figures in suits and pork-pie hats, dwarfing the trunk-clad youths and little boys who had already arrived for their morning swim.

There was actually not much for them to see – Nelson pointed out hollowed out marks diagonally across the sand suggesting that the girl had been dragged about eight metres from the concrete at the bathing sheds' northern entrance to between the tree stump and a concrete groyne. At one stage, according to Nelson, Adam, gazing intently at footprints in the damp sand, thought he had a clue. 'Looks like a man with rubber-soled shoes,' he mused aloud. Then, with a laugh, Adam looked down – the marks were of his own rubber-soled golf footwear.

The bathing sheds not being locked at night, the area had something of a reputation for 'undesirable' visitors: prostitutes drifting from their usual beats in St Kilda, young couples seeking intimate seclusion, voyeurs enticed by the whiff of salaciousness. Now it was journalists craning their necks for a view, remaining deferentially up the beach from the detectives but with ears cocked for confidences: the *Herald* reporter actually overheard the remark about 'rubber-soled shoes' and would include it in his report.

It had been a violent festive season: this was Melbourne's third murder in five days, a veritable bloodbath in a city that till then had gone the whole year experiencing only nine. Hours before Christmas, detectives had been called to an Abbotsford address to investigate the lethal shooting of a noted local gunman, George Pearson. On Christmas night itself, detectives had broken down a door at a city boarding house to find the body of fifty-six-year-old William Stewart mutilated by 'unnatural sexual interference': the victim had been smothered, pulverised with a tack hammer and had six candles shoved up his rectum. This new death also had sexual connotations. When Currer inventoried the girl's clothing at the City Morgue, he found no trace of stockings or underwear.

Shortly after 11a.m., Currer welcomed Dr Keith Bowden of the department of forensic medicine at

Melbourne University – it was the third time his Christmas holiday at Cowes had been interrupted by a duty call. Such was the fate of a surgeon gazetted to the coroner. Bowden had not long succeeded the legendary Dr Crawford Mollison, whose experience stretched back to the diabolical crimes of Frederick Deeming, killer of two wives and four children in the early 1890s. The morgue's methods still seemed late Victorian too. It had no laboratory; not even a microscope. The premises were so insecure that two drunken sailors, presumably in search of the nearby Seamen's Mission, had recently been fined for trespass after wandering in under the impression it was a church, and falling asleep among the bodies. The morgue did at least now have a telephone line: Central 13. Currer used it to advise Donelly, now at Russell Street police headquarters, about the absent underclothing.

In the presence of Currer and two medical colleagues, Bowden commenced a postmortem. First he audited the body's surface. It took him a page-and-a-half of foolscap to document more than a score of scratches, abrasions and bruises, especially across the chest, concentrated around the left nipple. He paid particular attention to a 'flood' of petechiae, tiny pinprick haemorrhages caused by vessels leaking blood as a result of physical trauma, sometimes associated with vomiting, coughing or crying.

Manual strangulation can kill three different ways: by causing the heart to stop via the vagus nerve, sensitive to pressure on the carotid arteries; by cutting off oxygen supply to the lungs; by cutting off blood supply to the brain. The petechiae were consistent with the last of these, as was an examination of the hypoid bone, which revealed the greater cornu on the right to have been displaced forward and broken. Exploring the abdomen, Bowden found surface haemorrhages on the lungs, and froth in the trachea and bronchi too. Everything was consistent with the girl being strangled to death after a brief but violent struggle.

When had she died? Rigor mortis was present but incomplete. Although the skin was now cold to the touch, Bowden felt 'a little warmth' within the abdominal cavity, and in the space of twenty minutes took three temperature readings, averaging 70 degrees Fahrenheit (21 degrees Celsius), some 28.6 degrees (16 degrees) cooler than regular body temperature. Applying his rule of thumb that a dead body could cool at no more than three degrees an hour, and usually less, the latest the victim could have been alive was 2a.m., although he believed it likelier she had died far earlier – between '10 and midnight of the previous day'. Bowden finally took blood and hair samples and bronchial and vaginal smears for Currer to convey to the government analyst Harold Wignall.

By around lunchtime, Russell Street's interview rooms were busy. First to give statements were Madeleine Patrick and Patricia Street. They had last seen Beth late the previous afternoon; she had advised that she was going to the pictures with a young man she'd met the night before at the Trocadero. Pat remembered mention of an Australian sailor called 'Steve', on perhaps a Norwegian or Swedish ship. Quizzed about their friend's other male acquaintances, Madeleine mentioned Major Adams, and Patricia referred to Norman Sharpe and Keith Jewell, two youths they had met at a twenty-first birthday party on Christmas Eve. Detectives were assigned to locate them.

Statements not then being taken verbatim, the exact to-and-fro of questions was lost, but the initial purpose was clearly to profile the victim. The respondents loyally stressed Beth's reliability and chastity – Madeleine called her 'a girl who was morally sound and was careful with whom she mixed'.

Then, of Pat, the enquiries grew more intimate. First, did Beth always wear stockings? The answer was no: sometimes she applied sun tan to her legs. Second, did Beth always wear underpants? A note taken by Currer was clumsily ambiguous: 'Miss Street states that it was not unusual for deceased to go without a singlet or petticoat but she usually wore some type of pants, usually briefs. No sign of these could be found'.

'Usually'? Was she wearing them? Was she not? The detectives were to conclude that Beth's underwear had been souvenired by her killer, but here originated a titillating rumour destined for wide circulation.

Homicide's best lead was now the sailor 'Steve', and Donelly despatched Adam to the waterfront. At the time, the Port of Melbourne laid claim to being the Empire's busiest, a record seven million tons of shipping having passed through it in 1949. But on this day only one ship flew a Scandinavian flag, the dark-hulled 2100-ton *Citos,* an oil-burning steamer of Norway's Wilh. Wilhelmsen group moored at 15 Victoria Dock. Adam found no 'Steve' on the crew manifest, but a second motorman called James Stevens had been paid off shortly after the ship's arrival on 13 December. From shipmates, Adam obtained Stevens' Elsternwick address, with which he returned to Russell Street at around 3.30p.m.

Other information had also come in. Major Adams stated credibly that he had not seen Beth for some weeks; the lads Sharpe and Jewell had given statements, rather more anxious, but believable. They told of meeting Beth and Pat at the party, bringing them home, then 'talking and cuddling' in Sharpe's car for three-quarters of an hour about 100 metres from Page Street – so as, presumably, not to incur landlady Burns' displeasure. Sharpe's statement was a model of decorum: 'I then got out of the car and walked to the gate of 136 Page Street with Miss Williams where I kissed her good night. There were no improper suggestions between us, and Miss Williams appeared to be a girl of good morals and very level headed'.

A doorknock of the vicinity had produced some intelligence too. About seven to eight weeks earlier, labourer Percival Richie, who lived at 134 Page Street, on the other side of the cobblestone sideway leading through to Danks Street, had come home about midnight and seen an unfamiliar loiterer dressed in a leather jacket and brown pants. Thanks to a nearby street light, Richie was able to give a detailed description: about twenty-four years of age, approximately five feet six inches tall, solidly built with a dark complexion and slightly wavy hair parted on the right, plus a 'high-toned voice when he spoke'. Richie noted that 'from the position on the sideway one can peep in the window occupied by Miss Williams and Miss Street'. For that, Richie suspected, was what the man had been doing, because on being seen he had 'hurried out into the street'. When Richie came out again shortly afterwards, the man was gone.

The results of the government analyst's tests were also intriguing in what they revealed and what they didn't. Beth's nails had been 'short and blunt', but there were traces of blood in scrapings from beneath the middle finger of the right hand. Beth's vaginal smears, meanwhile, had come back negative. There had been a lethal struggle, but as the press would coyly report, no 'criminal interference'. Homicide was all set to move on Stevens when the telephone rang in their squad room: *he* had rung *them.*

***

Afternoon in Melbourne in 1949 meant *The Herald,* then circulating 400,000 copies daily in a city of 1.25 million. And by the news values of an afternoon paper, the dawn discovery of a murdered girl was black-and-white gold: straightforwardly understood, enticingly sexual, and *not* in the morning papers. *The Herald's* version of events, therefore, would essentially be exclusive for the next twelve hours. That being so, it was accorded a three-deck front-page headline, and breathless retelling:

MURDERED GIRL ON ALBERT PARK BEACH
Disappeared Last Night
Man Sought

> The partly clad body of Elizabeth Maureen Williams, a pretty 20-year-old brown-eyed blonde, was found early today at the water's edge at Albert Park Beach.
>
> Police are convinced that from the nature of her injuries, she was murdered after a desperate struggle, lasting several minutes.
>
> Detective Inspector H.R. Donelly would like to hear from a man who met Miss Williams at the Trocadero dance hall, near Princes Bridge, city, on Monday night.

Pretty, blonde, partly-clad, desperate struggle, murder: this was grist for a tabloid mill, even if *The Herald* was still respectably broadsheet. And as they were distributed, copies began crossing paths Beth Williams had taken the night before, and came beneath the nose of the 'man' himself.

By late afternoon, young, tow-headed Stevens had been collected from his lodgings, cautiously bringing with him his Swedish shipmates Peterson and Fossberg. By their account, they had taken missing Beth Williams in their stride. Stevens had rung Beth's number, and been advised by a male voice that she had left some time earlier; the trio had then made a night of it at the Trocadero. Stevens claimed not to have thought of Beth again until he encountered her picture in *The Herald.* By this stage the trio had had nearly a day to get their stories straight, and the Homicide Squad might have probed more deeply but for an independent attestation.

At about 6p.m., the enigmatic William Grinsted returned to his old stamping ground 'under the clocks' at Flinders Street Station. Why, it was never clear: he explained no more than that he often had his 'tea' nearby. But he was spotted on this occasion by a sharp-eyed *Herald* newsboy, who alerted him to the front-page picture of the girl Grinsted had been talking to the night before.

'I wouldn't say anything if I were you,' the boy told him confidentially. 'Least said, soonest mended.'

Grinsted surveyed the story anxiously. The police did not seem to be looking for him specifically.

Nonetheless, he presented himself at Russell Street station's front desk, and his evidence, fragmentary and evasive as it was in certain respects, seemed on its face to exonerate Stevens and his friends.

The investigation now had a new focus.

***

John Bryan Kerr's day had begun abortively. Woken by his father at 5.45a.m., he had caught the Toorak Road tram to town, then taken a cab to the Customs House at Station Pier in Port Melbourne, just 2.5 kilometres from where he had been dropped the previous evening. Kerr was bemused to find the scene deserted; even the Sea Breezes Cafeteria was closed. Eventually he located a solitary customs official.

'What time does the migrant ship get in this morning?' he asked. 'I am due to work on it.'

The official was nonplussed. 'There was one here yesterday and there'll be one this afternoon,' he answered. 'But there's none due this morning.'

Kerr asked for the telephone and rang his superior, William Cummane, at home. 'Kerr speaking,' he said. 'What time is the ship in?'

It was 6.30a.m., but Cummane had half-expected the call. 'What ship?' he snapped. 'You were rostered on yesterday for the *Chitral.* Where were you?'

'I was still in the country,' Kerr replied. 'I did not know I had to be back.'

Cummane was not unused to this from Kerr, hardly the most diligent of immigration clerks, and told him to report to the authority's William Street offices: someone might be needed for the *Cheshire* when it arrived later that day. But feeling tired, Kerr decided he needed some sleep. He caught a bus to Flinders Street Station, where he collected his suitcase from the cloakroom, then cabbed back to Toorak.

'I don't have to go into the office till later,' he told his father. 'I'm going to take a nap.'

When at last he rolled into work at one, he found Cummane grumpily eating his lunchtime sandwich. 'Where have you been?' Cummane demanded.

'I didn't think it was necessary for me to come in,' Kerr said defensively.

'Go home,' Cummane sighed. 'I don't need you.'

Home for Kerr was 'Afton', 54 Washington Street, Toorak: a medium-sized residence and a tight-knit household in a choice location. John, an only child, occupied a cosy sleep-out at the rear. Donald Kerr and Rose, his wife of twenty-eight years, shared the house with her elderly father John McKenzie, and had the services of a spinster domestic, Miss O'Neill. Three days after Christmas, they also had a visitor, Keith McKenzie, whom John regarded as his 'favourite uncle'. It was with Keith and Donald that John Bryan Kerr went for 'three small beers' at the Toorak Hotel an hour before 6 o'clock closing.

After starting a browse of his father's *Herald* with the sport, Kerr lit on the same headline as Stevens and Grinsted. His reaction was different. He said nothing. For this, he would go on giving roughly the same explanation again and again – this version in court almost nine months later.

> When I read *The Herald,* sir, I looked at the back page first and a few other pages and I looked at the front page and I saw on the right hand side 'Mystery Death on Beach', and I read this, and after I read several lines I got a very great shock, because I then discovered that was the girl I had been with the previous night. I did not know that until I had read several lines of the paper ... I did not want to alarm my people at this stage unnecessarily until I had got in touch with John Wood ... I thought if I am involved in this it will naturally involve others, and I thought I would get in touch with him first, and do him the courtesy first, and we would then decide what we had better do about it.

The report had not specified that Kerr was a suspect, because at the time it had been written the police were unaware of his existence. But Kerr was sufficiently concerned to try telephoning Wood after dinner, at a time he put somewhere between '8 and 8.30p.m.'.

There was no answer. Kerr put this down to Wood's habit of dining in town. He was mistaken. Wood had also read *The Herald.*

***

Only hints have survived of how the police were led to John Bryan Kerr, and they go back to Edward Penno's party. Twelve years after events, they were recalled in *Truth* by the doyen of Melbourne police roundsmen, Alan Dower, in an article, 'THE NIGHT THEY CAUGHT KERR'. The son of a former CIB chief, Dower was a brazenly partial storyteller, heavily invested in the mystique of the Homicide Squad. His retelling of the story was breezy and deliberately vague.

> By late evening, the case was almost at a standstill, yet the air was charged with possibilities.
>
> Suddenly a telephone rang in the small Homicide Squad room.
>
> A man known to a senior detective urgently insisted on an immediate interview.
>
> From that moment the case made giant strides.
>
> They met a man who told them Beth and a young man John Kerr had been to a Melbourne

> restaurant the previous night and then driven to a private party in the Malvern district.
>
> After the party, a man had driven his partner to Moonee Ponds and then taken Beth and John to the Middle Park area.

The story is inaccurate in the final respect: Barbara Robertson was the last passenger dropped off. But the 'man known to a senior detective' was almost certainly Wood. At the inquest into Beth Williams' death, he responded evasively to questions about his police links.

> Asked whether I have been associating with certain members of the Police Force, I have been with one or two members of the Force. I have had friends in the Force for a few years. One is a member of the Homicide Squad. I have not entertained him. I have not had a meal with a member of the Homicide Squad but I have had a drink with one. That is some weeks ago now.

Assuming 'a man' was Wood, what might 'partner' mean in this context? What was Wood to Robertson, Robertson to Wood, and the both of them to John Bryan Kerr? Kerr may or may not have wished to do Wood 'the courtesy' of consulting him before speaking to police, but why did Wood not extend Kerr a similar courtesy? It may be, then, that the police were set on Kerr's trail in the first instance not because of male lechery but male jealousy, arising from peevishness about his conduct with Robertson the night before.

Whatever the case, Kerr was unable to find Wood in the evening because he was already being interviewed by Adam and Currer at Penno's apartment. That had another impact on the investigation. While the two senior detectives were out, the phone rang again in the Homicide Squad room: it was another *Herald* reader, waterside worker Albert Sievers. Sievers told Detective Sergeant William Tremewen that he and his wife Betty had gone to Hampton at 8p.m., attended separate functions, and due to his being late meeting her back at the station, found themselves walking Beaconsfield Parade at 2.30a.m. on their way to Port Melbourne. As they came abreast of steps leading on to Albert Park Beach, they saw a man coming out from behind bathing sheds. Tremewen's note, bearing the time '8.45pm', recorded:

> He [the man] came up on the footpath and dwelt a while and then walked along the footpath towards St Kilda. He [Sievers] saw no one else and heard nothing. He describes the man as about 26 years, 5'8" or 5'9", broad shoulders, 11 1/2 stone weight, no hat, fair hair and complexion, hair parted on side, wearing sports clothes, with light mackintosh over them.

Thanking Sievers, Tremewen passed Donelly the note. But the investigation had now narrowed to a single target.

***

At 11.15p.m. on Thursday, 29 December 1949, an unknown finger dialled BJ1189, the Kerr's Toorak residence. The household was asleep, but the hallway telephone rang long enough for Donald Kerr to pick it up and give a foggy hello.

'Is John at home?' asked a male voice.

'Yes,' answered Donald Kerr. 'He's in bed asleep.'

'Don't worry him now,' said the voice. 'I'll ring him tomorrow. It's just a friend.'

In fact, it was the police, checking the whereabouts of their quarry. They seldom had much reason to visit Toorak. Only two calls had been recorded in the preceding fortnight, to attend a robbery in St Georges Road, from which thieves had lifted a radio set and antique copper entrée dish, and a robbery in Irving Street, where items stolen included bed and table linen, a tartan jacket and a pair of 'pink satin scanties'. With Kerr's whereabouts established, two black Ford Mercurys left Russell Street containing five detectives for the most serious police work of all: the pursuit of a murder suspect. On arrival at Afton, Senior Detectives Jack Matthews from Homicide, and Reg Jackson and James McElwaine from South

Melbourne CIB were positioned at potential exits. A pyjama-clad Donald Kerr opened the front door to find it filled by the bulk of Senior Detectives Adam and Currer. They introduced themselves and their purpose, then followed him through the house to the sleep-out.

As the light went on, the son heard the tremor in his father's voice, 'John, there are some detectives here to see you'.

John Kerr looked at the alarm clock on his white dressing table, saw the time was 11.30p.m., then tried to focus on the figures now crowding the room.

'I suppose you know why we are here,' said one of them.

'Yes,' said Kerr. 'I think I do.'

2

CERTAIN PERSONS, CERTAIN ADMISSIONS

While the preceding chapter hews faithfully to facts contained in the file of *The King v. John Bryan Kerr,* it rather belied the file itself: shabby, in no sort of order, like stuff swept from a desk in a hurry, whether from satisfaction, exasperation or relief, by somebody with no plan or desire to consult it again. It was neither indexed nor sealed; it bulged from its box; it was also jarringly incomplete. There were statements, letters, telegrams, handwritten scrawlings; a lunch order or a dry-cleaning ticket would not have been out of place. But many documents and exhibits referred to elsewhere were missing, assuming they had ever been there.

I was lucky to be seeing it at all. Normally the annals of *The King v. Kerr* dwell in climate-controlled comfort among a hundred lineal kilometres of material at Victoria's Public Records Office. It had been made available to me by the kind consent of Victoria's Office of Public Prosecutions (OPP); likewise the bare conference room in which to peruse it. And one aspect of archives, I reflected, was always worth recalling: the materials are not originated for posterity's gaze, like one of those time capsules sealed in the cornerstones of great buildings containing a Bible, a *Collected Shakespeare* and copies of the newspapers of the day. To begin with, what become archival documents are prepared by the creators for their own use; their preservation just happens to be provided for out of caution, or custom, or statutory *fiat.* And separated from the understandings of their creators, they begin, subtly, to degrade.

Even where record and creators are reunited, that loss might be irretrievable. Much later, I would visit the veteran Homicide Detective Ron Iddles to discuss, among other things, the evolution of policework. He contrasted the now almost inconceivably voluminous criminal trial briefs with his early days as a detective. Recently, he had pulled a file from one of his early cases to refresh his memory about a peripheral matter he knew had been investigated. There was no trace of it: either nobody had bothered to write it down, or nobody had troubled to keep it. Because it had not been useful at the time, it had never occurred to anyone that it might be useful later.

The delapidation of the file of *The King v. Kerr* was also expressive of a world of shorter criminal cases and swifter justice, of simpler tools and ruder labors. About half the police material, for instance, was handwritten, scored in a great variety of inks and scripts. To one literary quaintness I alluded earlier: in place of actual verbatim transcription of police interviews and inquest testimony, many documents adopted a kind of catechismal compression. Thus this from the statement of Madeleine Patrick: 'Asked whether I said to anyone "it was a pity she ever went to the Trocadero", I say I did not but I think it was strange her going there'. Thus this pained protestation of innocence at the inquest by John Wood when it was inferred that he had been spreading rumours about Beth Williams' missing underwear.

> I have not discussed with anyone the disappearance of her pants. I definitely did not say to anybody she was not wearing pants that night. I have never said 'the papers say she was not wearing pants' ... There has been some suggestion, or veiled suggestion, put to me that I knew this girl had no pants on. I do not know whether she had any pants on or not at any stage during that night.

Although the voices of the past had to be heard through a white noise of archaism, the style had not effaced personality completely. I was intrigued, for example, by the studied inattention of William Grinsted, a man so eager to repay a creditor he arrived at the station clocks forty-five minutes early; a man so unobtrusive that Kerr failed to notice him standing a couple of metres away. The formal circumlocutions of his inquest testimony could not disguise Grinsted's unease:

> I did not meet the person I was waiting for. If you ask me who he was, I ask do I have to tell

> you that. It was a friend I borrowed some money off. I borrowed some money off this person and I had arranged to meet him at 8 o'clock that night. I was at the station at about a quarter past seven and I waited there until a quarter past eight but he did not arrive. I have since paid him the money.

When Grinsted tried describing what Beth Williams was wearing that evening, the result was a fog of indecision and contradiction.

> When I offered my services to the police they did not show me the clothing she had been wearing. I said she had on a red coat. One of the gentlemen – I could not tell you which – said 'Yes, that would be right.' To be honest I do not know what I told the police about the frock she was wearing. I do not remember what I said about that. I am certain about the frock. As to only becoming certain this morning, after having seen the frock the police are alleging she had on, I did not know they had alleged it. I did not tell you I did not know what description I gave to the police when I first offered my services to them. When I first went to the police I said she had on a red coat and she had one of those hats with no top on it. I said she had a purse about as long as I indicate, it was a zipp purse [sic] she had when she was with me. I hope that is the description I gave of her clothing – I am not

> trying to put anything over you or anything like that. I think that is as far as I can go concerning the description I gave to the police of what she was wearing that night...

Actually, he went on and on, without making very much more sense. And it was probably fortunate that Kerr never denied being with whom Beth Williams went off that night, given Grinsted's panic at the eventual police line-up:

> I never counted the number of people in the line-up because I could not get out of the place quickly enough. I just went in there. They said to me, 'Can you pick the man?' They said, 'Can you be certain of him?' I said yes. As soon as that was over I sort of went blind in the place and could not get out quick enough. I was first out when they opened the door.

Here lay another trap for the unwary, research of any thoroughness always throwing up enticing trifles that every so often prove not to be so trifling. But on these preliminary visits to OPP, how to tell what was what? Not that I had expected the experience to be like switching on the light in an elegant period room, but it certainly had more in common with shining a torch from the top of the stairs into a darkened basement, detecting the outline of an object here, a rustle of movement there.

After a time, I decided I could not afford to be further detained by William Grinsted, for off the edges of this ragged dossier dangled loose ends that would take a lifetime's tidying. Even some of the absences were pregnant with potential meaning. For example, in a sheaf of sworn statements presented by the Homicide Squad to the Crown Law Department, where was Bluey Adam's? A contents page listed it as running to nine pages; all that remained was its first page, ending in mid-sentence like an erotic instalment novel: 'The clothing was torn and the body was...'

And what to make of the most important pages of all, written by Adam in a fluent round hand on three sheets of lined paper? That is, the 'confession' of John Bryan Kerr.

***

With the arrival of the police at Afton at 11.30p.m. on 29 December 1949, *The King v. Kerr* became just that: evidence until then more or less uncontested gave way to two antagonistic accounts of the previous night's events. And where sometimes a little art can reconcile competing stories at least at intervals, the competing narratives of police and suspect still stood at arm's length, heckling each other.

The version of events retold by the detectives at the inquest, and stuck to more or less throughout, began in the sleep-out with Adam asking Kerr his name then inviting him to answer some questions.

'We want you to go into Russell Street detective office with us'.

Without enquiring why, Kerr replied, 'All right, I will get dressed'.

While Kerr was doing so, Adam asked him his whereabouts the previous evening.

'I got back from Warragul about 8 o'clock, came home and went to bed,' Kerr responded.

'How did you come?' enquired the detective. 'By train, tram or by car?'

'I came home by taxi,' said Kerr.

'What time did you get home?'

'About 8.30,' Kerr claimed. 'I went to bed as I had to work early on a boat at Port Melbourne in the morning.'

Asked for the clothes he had worn, Kerr surrendered a blue suit and black shoes. Recounting the story to the *Truth* journalist Alan Dower in 1961, Adam added an ornate flourish.

> When awakened, Kerr allegedly denied he had been away from the house after 8.30 the previous night ... He denied he had been near the beach.
>
> An oppressive silence fell in the room as Adam and Currer turned back the cuffs of trousers Kerr had worn that day and poured out – sand.

'John, put your clothes on,' said Adam. 'You must come to Russell Street with us.'

On the face of it, this seemed implausible. According to Adam, Kerr began his dealings with police by lying palpably – and ineptly too, given that, as he would have known, such untruths could be exploded by a dozen or more witnesses. Kerr would have been aware for at least six hours, and probably longer, that his conduct of the previous evening might be subject to inquiry. Would he *really* have begun with a falsehood so easily penetrated?

The next part of Adam's testimony was then, as the detective himself actually had to concede in court, simply wrong. Kerr did not hand over his clothes from the previous day; he put them back on, disrobing later at the police station. As for the sand, it was surely surprising that this coup of detection took twelve years to emerge.

Adam's version of events, then, had problematic beginnings. Were these simple misrememberings, tactful embellishments or outright lies?

Kerr's account of that first encounter commenced with Adam standing at the end of his bed, pursuing a somewhat gentler line of questioning.

'You were at a party with Beth Williams last night, weren't you?' Adam asked. 'Where was it?'

'I don't know exactly where it was,' Kerr replied. 'Except I know it to be in the Malvern or Caulfield district and I recall a sort of embankment on one side of the street as we got out of the car. The flat was upstairs.'

'Well,' said Adam, 'we would like you to get up and come with us and see if you can show us where it was.'

'Very well,' answered Kerr, 'if I can be of assistance.'

While he dressed, Kerr said, another detective, probably McElwaine, came to the sleep-out door, and said in a jesting tone, 'Ask him where the rubber-soled shoes are he had on last night'.

Adam said gruffly, 'Forget about that.'

Currer then pulled a pair of rubber-soled shoes out from under the wardrobe. 'Didn't you have these shoes on last night?' he asked.

'No, I didn't,' Kerr recalled replying. 'As a matter of fact they were in my suitcase at the station. Besides, I would not wear tan shoes with a navy blue suit.'

Small matters, but accumulating into greater differences. In contrast to the police portrait of Kerr as one who lied on reflex, Kerr portrayed himself as someone obliging the agents of law enforcement despite the hour, despite the inconvenience, and despite their false pretences – because they would shortly be conveying him not to 'the Malvern or

Caulfield district', but to Russell Street. Kerr further described asking for a moment to brush his teeth, and being told by another detective not to bother – he would be home soon enough. He opted for rinsing his mouth at the gulley trap.

So was *this* account convincing? The exchange Kerr reported overhearing about the 'rubber-soled shoes' had a ring of authenticity, for he could not have been aware of its provenance – Adam's joking exchange with Constable Nelson on the beach during the morning, which Adam claimed not to recall, but which Nelson was comfortable standing by.

As for the shoes themselves, Currer gave a slightly different version of his exchange with Kerr.

> When Kerr showed the black shoes and suit to Senior Detective Adam, I picked up a pair of tan shoes with rubber soles. There was what appeared to be a sandy type of soil or similar substance on the corrugations of the soles, and I asked Kerr were those the shoes he wore last night, and he said, 'Don't be ridiculous. Tan shoes with a blue suit?'

This too has an authentic ring – the stylish young man making a point at the expense of the dowdy police. And here perhaps was an evolving dynamic of the interaction.

Sixty-five years ago, confession was the prince of evidence. Judges and juries were leery of expert testimony. Forensic science was rudimentary: the quantity of blood beneath Beth's fingernail was too small to be tested against Kerr's blood type; her shoe, apparently flung aside, was never fingerprinted. When surgeon Bowden himself attended the crime scene, he was shown a spot on the beach some distance from where the body was actually found, and incorrectly advised about the tides. Police methods were geared in the first instance to loosening tongues and weakening backbones. By the time car 161 entered the north gate to police headquarters on Mackenzie Street, Kerr would have grasped the gravity of his predicament. He would have felt the hands of Adam and Currer on his sleeves as they ushered him through the station's self-closing double doors. He would have recognised from popular culture the scenario of police interrogation as he entered an airless room, nine feet square, with a single small high window.

Sat at a tiny table, Adam to his right and Currer to his left, Kerr knew himself to be getting 'the third degree'. Why did he collude in it? He had been conveyed to Russell Street under what he claimed were false pretences. Why did he not protest? Why did he choose to talk rather than maintaining a watchful silence, or at the very least requesting a lawyer?

Adam would have explained this simply. Killers, he claimed, were often 'relieved to be caught', and driven to confess: 'The theologians and philosophers may be able to explain it, but many murderers seem to want to be punished for what they did'.

Kerr's explanation, presumably, would have been that he was a man with nothing to hide, so eager to help that he was prepared to overlook irregularities in his treatment. There was a third possibility, independent of Kerr's guilt or innocence, that part of him was faintly exhilarated by matching wits with his uncouth and overbearing captors. And the same applied to his interrogators. Adam claimed afterwards to have had an 'open mind' about the case even after talking to Penno and Wood. But it was an open mind he very much wished Kerr to walk into.

***

Whom to believe? It was on the next hour-and-a-half, arguably even more than on the corresponding hour-and-a-half the previous evening, that *The King v. Kerr* would hinge.

In the police version of events, Kerr took no self-preserving steps at all. Adam commenced the interrogation with a digest of the murder: 'It is now Thursday, 29th December. Early yesterday morning, the dead body of a girl named Elizabeth Maureen Williams, who was also known to her friends as Beth Williams was found on the beach at Albert Park. Her face and body were bruised and her left breast was injured. A post-mortem examination revealed that she had been strangled and the death had occurred about 1a.m. What do you know about her death?'

'Only what I read in the paper,' replied Kerr. 'Why should I know anything about it? I was in bed.'

'We have interviewed certain persons,' Adam pressed on. 'And it is alleged that you went with the dead girl to Mario's for dinner and later left with her and went to a party. What have you to say to that?'

At this, said Adam, all Kerr's swagger vanished. He 'hesitated', then capitulated.

'I killed her,' Kerr conceded. 'I was with her on the beach. I wanted to "perve" her but she wouldn't let me. I had my hands around her throat. I choked her. I can't help myself. I must be mad. I get a turn.'

Adam continued with a proforma statement: 'You will be charged with the murder of Elizabeth Maureen Williams. It is my duty to warn you that you are not obliged to make any further statement or answer any further questions but whatever you say will be taken down in writing and may be used in evidence. Do you understand that?'

'Yes, I do,' said Kerr.

'Do you wish to make a written statement about what you have told us?' asked Adam.

'I get a neurasthenia and can't help myself,' Kerr continued. 'Let me take my time and I will tell you what happened. This will be the truth. You write it down if you wish.'

And on the file of *The King v. Kerr,* bedraggled and torn but still legible, the 'confession' began with Kerr's name and address, the time and date.

> I returned on the train from Warragul, it ran express to town. I left Flinders Street Station, and I saw Beth Williams there, she called to me John, and told me she had been stood up on a date. I asked her to have a drink, and she said I may as well, and I went to the Phoenix Hotel, in Flinders Street, but couldn't get in, so I decided to go to Mario's for dinner and a spot. I asked John Wood a chap I know to come home with Beth and I and have a spot, he said he would but later we went with some others in a car to an upstairs flat at either Caulfield or Malvern. We left there about 12.30 and some others were in John Woods[sic] car, there was a girl who works at Myers. They dropped Beth and I in Middle Park, near a street with the tram line in it. Beth wanted to go home, I can't remember much as I felt a turn coming on but I got her to go down to the beach, we were inside a wooden structure. I could hear the sound of the sea, it was dark there. I was in the Navy, I like the sound of the sea. I put my hands around her throat, I am strong, usually, I have big shoulders and don't wear padding in my coats. I am stronger when a turn comes on 5 men couldn't hold me. It doesn't

matter if I drink or not, the turns come just the same.

We were inside the wooden structure. I didn't have sexual intercourse with her, as I had a good session a week ago and didn't want it. I took her pants off, I wanted to kiss her on the privates. I don't think she wanted me to. She said, 'John John John.' I always kiss women on their privates with whom I have been with. I do it before and after sexual intercourse.

I remember a white path, that was when I was dragging her. I remember her shoes lying there, one shoe was lying on the beach near her. I saw her lying down after I had her by the throat. I strangled her. She groaned while I was choking her. I was playing with her breasts. I don't think I hurt her breasts. I played with her breasts in the car. She was lying there and I dragged her, why I don't know. After I left the beach the next I remember was that I was near South Melbourne Football Ground. There was bright lights there, I knew that I had a neurasthenia. I walked home. I had an awful desire to go back all day, and see what I had done. I didn't go back. I had no feeling of remorse. I have no feeling of remorse now. I was shocked a bit when I read the papers, but didn't expect the police to come out for me. I saw by the papers that it was Beth, who I

> choked on the beach. I expected to see an account of what I had done in the papers.
>
> When I get a turn of my head, I get the urge to hit and break and hurt something. That is what happened last night, something goes 'click' to me and that's what happened to make me grab her throat.

The 585-word statement was timed as concluding at '2a.m.' on '29.12.49'. Because the police by their account asked no questions, that made for a talking pace of six-and-a-half words a minute, which Adam would explain by saying that Kerr was 'very slow in his speech and would hesitate for some time'.

It was, to say the least, an uneven document. The voice veered from cocktail chit-chat ('I decided to go to Mario's for dinner and a spot', and there met 'a chap I know') to free association ('I could hear the sound of the sea, it was dark there. I was in the navy, I like the sound of the sea'), from pulp porn ('I always kiss women on their privates') to prim fussiness ('I didn't have sexual intercourse with her, as I had a good session a week ago and didn't want it').

There was contradictory jumbling ('I had an awful desire to go back all day, and see what I had done. I didn't go back') and tortured grammar ('There was bright lights there'). Even the 'turn of my head' was described in contradictory ways: first as something

Kerr 'felt ... "coming on"' while remaining capable of luring his victim to the beach, then as the matter of a 'click'. Finally, there was the curious technical terminology. 'Neurasthenia' had first been described in the middle of the nineteenth century as 'exhaustion of the nervous system', and elasticised to encompass phobias, anxieties, insomnia, panic, trauma and, above all, listlessness and fatigue. From the early twentieth century, when Sigmund Freud linked it to excessive masturbation, it had been gradually englobed by psychiatry, and was actually slipping from popular usage. Its deployment here, as synonym for a kind of psychotic episode, sounded like the clumsy reaching for a half-remembered, impressive-sounding word – the question was, whose incomprehension did it demonstrate?

The three foolscap pages concluded with an equally curious postscript, in slightly smaller writing: 'Was cautioned & asked to sign. Kerr said 'No, thats [sic] all true. I can't remember any more, you have enough there, but I will plead that I am insane'. The very foot of the document bore the signatures of the officers in different inks:

> F.J. Adam Senior Detective
> Cyril Currer Senior Detective

No wonder it looked like it had been carried round in a dog's mouth: it bore the weight of the life of one man and the careers of two others.

***

If Kerr ever committed his own version of events to paper, it has not survived. And paper was almost insufficient a medium: he stuck to his story as though it were engraved in tablets, remembering and reciting it in identical detail time and again. His account began with him outlining to Adam and Currer the course of the previous evening: his chance meeting with Beth, their glance at the Phoenix, their detour to Mario's, the party in Malvern. He told of feeling unwell when he and Beth Williams were dropped off, at what he was to put as the corner of Danks and Wright streets, and asked the girl if she knew of a nearby public convenience. They walked a block towards the beach then a block left where Kerr found toilets on the Esplanade at the end of Harold Street. At this point, Kerr recalled, Adam cracked a joke about the 'Mario's plonk' being a frequent cause of queasiness.

While Kerr was dry-retching, he told the police, Beth had walked down a ramp onto the beach and waited in a small wooden shelter, about twenty metres away. After a few minutes, Kerr had joined her and, although still feeling unwell, listened as she described her planned trip to Tasmania. He put his arm round her and kissed her a couple of times. Then, Kerr continued, he had experienced another wave of nausea, and hastened back up the ramp into the convenience. Sticking his fingers down his throat, he succeeded in vomiting.

By now, Kerr told the police, he was thinking about his early start at Port Melbourne. He explained how he had suggested he drop Beth home, to which she agreed. They continued along Danks Street, a block past where they had been dropped off, coming to the end of the cobblestone lane that came out between 134 and 136 Page Street.

'I will leave you here, John, and slip in the back gate,' Beth had said. 'Just follow the tram line down to the football ground and you will know where you are then.'

Self-conscious about his breath, Kerr said, he did not kiss her goodnight; he obediently followed the tram tracks as they turned into Mills Street, walked a short distance left along Canterbury Road, and ducked right beneath the railway bridge. There being no taxis on Albert Road, he kept going past the South Melbourne Football Ground, then MacRobertson Girls' High School on his right, to where Park Street met Toorak Road. The all-night tram, which he knew left the city on the quarter-hour, then conveyed him to Grange Road. He estimated his arrival home at 2.30a.m.

It was once he had recounted these events that Kerr would recall the interrogation commencing in earnest. At first, he claimed, the policemen tried to bluff him.

'I believe you have been quite open and frank up to a certain point,' said Adam. 'But it would be better for you to tell us the truth about the beach, because we know all about it.'

When Kerr insisted on the veracity of his account, Adam interpolated a mystery witness. 'You were seen leaving the beach by a Mr Peterson,' claimed the detective. 'We have seen a Mr Peterson.'

'I don't know any Mr Peterson,' Kerr replied. 'In fact, I don't think I know anyone in that district.'

'Well, he knows you,' Adam continued. 'He saw you leaving the beach, so you might as well tell us the truth.'

'What I have told you is the truth,' said Kerr adamantly. 'As far as I am concerned my activities are an open book for anyone to see. If there are any details that are not perfectly clear, such as conversations or times, well, I had had a few drinks, and I might not be absolutely perfect about these matters, because I had no reason for remembering all the small details.'

Adam, said Kerr, then took a different tack, and asked about his discharge from the services. Kerr cited a problem with neurodermatitis. Abruptly, he recalled, Adam became all charm and persuasion.

'You are a likeable chap, John,' said the detective. 'I will help you as much as I can. We don't often come in contact with your type. I will stick to you right through if you tell us the truth about the beach, and I always keep my word.'

'I have told you the truth, Mr Adam. I had nothing to do with that girl's death.'

'I still think you can tell us more, although I believe, as I said before, you have been telling the truth up to the time you took her to the beach. And another thing. I can help you if you make a statement, because there is a lot of difference between murder and manslaughter.'

'What do you mean by that?'

'Well, you might not have meant to kill her. After you had your hands round her throat you got frightened and left her near the sea and she could have been drowned by the rising tide. We have a right to say whether it was murder or manslaughter.'

'Whether it is murder or manslaughter cannot affect me because I had nothing to do with her death.'

Adam became solemn. 'It does so concern you. You killed her.'

Kerr responded hotly. 'I did not kill her and I don't like being accused of it.'

'It's no use adopting that attitude here, Kerr,' Adam snapped.

'Mr Kerr, if you don't mind, Mr Adam.'

Adam flushed, and growled, 'Kerr will do me.'

'I have told you I have nothing to hide and I have been telling you the truth,' the young man protested. 'I am not afraid of what will happen to me here either for that matter.'

Adam picked up the allusion to police methods of coercion, and looked at Currer. 'Nothing will happen to you here if you tell the truth.'

'I have heard stories about police methods, don't you worry,' said Kerr.

'Look, nothing will happen to you here,' Adam insisted. 'You don't want to believe all you hear about us.'

Kerr answered calmly. 'Well, if you want to ask me any further questions I will do my very best to answer them. But as I have repeatedly said I don't know any more. As a matter of fact I am sorry for getting a bit hot headed. I suppose you will understand that I naturally don't like being accused of something I didn't do.'

It was at this point, Kerr recalled, that Adam produced a sheet of foolscap and pulled a pen from his pocket. 'How long have you known Elizabeth Williams?' he asked.

'I met her, I think, on only two occasions whilst in Hobart,' Kerr answered levelly. 'Once she phoned me and asked if she could come and see over the studio. On another occasion she came to the studio with another girl and I took them home on that night and I have not seen her since, until the other night.'

Asked how he had met her, he repeated his story of the encounter beneath the clocks. 'I have told you all this already tonight.'

'But you have never told me about being in the shed with Beth Williams yet,' Adam insisted.

'I most definitely was not in any shed with Beth Williams and I can't tell you about something I know nothing about,' Kerr retorted.

Adam looked at Currer, and again adopted a tone of calm reason. 'Actually this case is not as bad as the papers are trying to make out,' he said. 'This girl has not been sexually assaulted or attacked as the papers said. Do you feel remorse?'

'No,' sighed Kerr. 'Why should I?'

Adam took a new direction. 'When did you know this girl had been murdered?' he asked.

'Not until my father bought *The Herald* when we were at the Toorak Hotel the next night.'

'Well, did you connect yourself with the girl or were you shocked when you read it?'

'Yes, I was shocked when I realised the murdered girl was Beth Williams,' Kerr said. 'I didn't realise at first, until I had read several lines.'

'Did you mention to your father that you had been with her?'

'No, I did not. The papers said the police were on the track of a man and they were investigating the matter of her associates. I thought there would be no point in saying anything at that time that might cause my parents any concern until I had got in touch with John Wood and decided what we should do about it.'

'Were you very worried?'

'Yes, to a certain extent. I think anyone would be in the circumstances, particularly when I had been with her part of the night.'

Adam asked if Kerr had intended contacting the police; Kerr said he had been waiting to speak to Wood.

'I think John would have come to see us, don't you, Cyril?' said Adam.

'Yes,' said Currer, 'I think so.'

After some innocuous questions about his clothing, Kerr recalled, Adam approached from another angle.

'Have you ever had any queer sexual desires like wanting to kiss a girl on the privates?'

Kerr was shocked. 'No, I have not.'

'Well, there is nothing wrong with that anyhow,' Adam responded airily. 'Isn't that why you took her pants off?'

'I did not take her pants off,' said Kerr. 'Neither do I know anything about her clothing.'

'You were playing with her breasts in the car,' Adam claimed.

'I was not playing with her breasts at any time,' Kerr countered. 'Besides, there was another lady sitting with us in the back seat of the car.'

'Oh yes, you played with her breasts in the car because Wood said you did,' Adam said confidently. 'You played with her breasts all right, and got excited and took her to the beach to have sexual intercourse with her, didn't you, John?'

Kerr stood his ground. 'No, I didn't. I had no such desire. As a matter of fact I had been in Barbara Robertson's company most of the evening and she gave me her telephone number on a slip of paper.'

'Yes,' Adam agreed. 'There was a Barbara Robertson.'

'That will show you then how much interest I had in this other girl.'

Adam was not so easily deterred. 'What did you do with her pants, John?'

'I never had her pants to do anything with.'

'Did you bury them near South Melbourne Football Ground?'

'Look if you like,' Kerr offered. 'I will show you the exact way I went home and you can see if they are anywhere about. I know I didn't ever have them or see them.'

'If you don't tell us where they are we will have to search your home and it will be very unpleasant for your parents,' said Adam.

'I am certain you won't find any girl's pants at my home. So there is no need to bother my parents any more than you already have.'

'Did you have intercourse with her?'

'No I didn't.'

'How do you know you didn't?'

'Look, it seems to me you're trying to make out I am some sort of idiot who doesn't know what he does.'

'You could have had a turn or something and not remembered.'

'No such thing,' Kerr said adamantly. 'What a lot of rubbish. I told you the only thing I have ever had was neurodermatitis in the navy.'

'Well it has been reported that no intercourse occurred,' Adam replied. 'And I think that is a strong point in your favour.'

There was a pause as Currer spied a hair on Kerr's coat, picked it off and put it in an envelope.

Adam continued doggedly. 'Look, you were lying on the beach with her when you suggested intercourse to her, weren't you?'

'Never at any time was I lying on the beach with her,' Kerr replied. 'And I never suggested any such thing.'

Adam took another direction. 'You were in the navy, weren't you, John?'

'Yes,' said Kerr, 'I told you I was in the navy and I have always been fond of the sea. But I am not fond enough of it to go roaming round the beaches at night time, if that is what you are inferring.'

'Is it not a fact that you persuaded her to go to the beach and suggested intercourse with her and she refused and you got wild and killed her?'

Kerr was tiring. 'Look, I have told you several times I didn't touch her or kill her nor would I make any suggestions to her,' he said. 'And certainly even if I did ask about intercourse, which I didn't, and she refused, would that make me kill her?'

'How was she dressed?'

'As far as I can recall she had on a black sort of dress – a dark colour anyway. With a coat and some sort of hat, but I didn't take a great deal of notice of that.'

'Do you remember what sort of shoes she had on?'

'I thought they were black or navy, but I could not remember if she had stockings or not. But I think she must have because when I met her she said she had been intending to go to the pictures.'

'She was not wearing any stockings.'

'Well, I would not argue about it. I am not really sure about that.'

'Did you take her home?'

'Not right home. I left her at the corner of the lane. We left the flat in Wood's car, dropped a couple off on the road. There were six of us at the start and eventually we drove across Fitzroy Street, St Kilda, and then Beth Williams told John Wood to follow the tram line, which she said ran along this street, whatever street it is. Then Beth said: "This will do us all right here." We got out of the car under a street light.'

Adam focused in again. 'When you were on the beach do you remember her screaming or moaning at all?'

'Nothing of the sort,' Kerr said.

'Did you put your hands around her throat?'

'No, I did not. How is she meant to have died, anyway?'

'The papers seem a bit confused. We are not quite sure yet but we think she was strangled.'

Adam continued matter-of-factly. 'Look, why keep fighting it, John? You killed her, didn't you. She was dead, you put her in the sea.'

'I certainly did not. I did not kill her or put her anywhere. When I left, that girl was quite all right.

Look at my shoes. You talk about putting her in the sea. Is there any salt water on them or on my clothes?'

'Oh you killed her all right,' Adam continued. 'You knew she was dead. Why don't you tell us the truth? It will be easier for you because we will find out sooner or later.'

'I have told you the truth all along and you won't believe it.'

Adam changed tack again. 'You are pretty strong, aren't you, John?'

'I suppose I am as strong as the average person,' Kerr replied.

'You have got big legs,' Adam noted. 'I noticed while you were getting dressed tonight.'

'I do a lot of swimming and I suppose that develops you pretty well.'

Adam leaned across and touched his shoulder. 'You are pretty broad in the shoulders too.'

'Yes, I suppose I am,' agreed Kerr. 'I am like my people in that regard. We don't wear much padding in our suits.'

Adam continued probing. 'Which way did you go home when you reached the South Melbourne Football Ground?'

When Kerr repeated his route, Adam asked, 'Didn't you look for a taxi on St Kilda Road?'

'Yes, I did,' said Kerr. 'But as luck would have it there was not one in sight, so I did not wait. I walked up to the corner of Park Street and Toorak Road to get that all-night tram.'

'The reason you didn't get a taxi was because you didn't want to be seen, was it not?' Adam asked rhetorically.

'I told you there was not a taxi about and that I got the all-night tram,' said Kerr. 'Which I would not have done, I don't think, if I did not want to be seen.'

At this point, a head poked round the door of the room, just behind Kerr, who would identify the visitor as Adam's superior, Bill Donelly. In a confident tone, Kerr would claim, Adam said, 'He says he put his hands around her throat.'

Kerr recalled responding furiously, 'I beg your pardon. I did not say any such thing.'

'Yes, you did,' Adam said coolly. 'I have written it down here.'

Kerr was adamant. 'I don't care what you have written down there – I did not say it.'

Adam stood up, walked out, and left Kerr with the inscrutable Currer. Silence fell, so deep that Kerr was surprised when the detective finally broke it.

'Don't you feel better after talking about it?' Currer asked at last.

'I do not know about feeling better after talking about it,' said Kerr. 'But you certainly seem hard people to convince that some people do tell the truth.'

'Not many people we meet tell the truth, John.'

'I have been telling you the truth. I certainly would not tell lies about something as serious as this.'

Currer then made for the door, just as Adam arrived with a pot of tea and a plate of ham sandwiches, freshly made at the milk bar on Mackenzie Street. Kerr was invited to partake, and also offered a blue boiler suit that buttoned to the neck and a pair of canvas shoes: his clothing was needed for examination. Adam stepped out while he changed, then Currer reappeared to collect the clothes, and to take scrapings from Kerr's fingernails.

As Currer left, Adam returned.

'We would like you to come for a drive with us to the beach,' he said. 'We think it will help you to recall more of last night.'

Kerr acquiesced. While they were on the way to the car, Adam asked him what sort of girl Beth had been.

'As far I knew her in Hobart, she was quite a nice girl,' said Kerr.

'Yes,' agreed Adam. 'And a good chap like yourself should not have killed her.'

Kerr, he claimed, said nothing.

***

Again, the foregoing was Kerr's gospel alone. The police denied every word. But again, it had a certain logical coherence: Adam's *idée fixe* with oral sex, for example, sounded suspiciously like an attempt to reconcile the absence of underwear with the absence of evidence of sexual penetration. The veering from indirection to accusation suggested an inquisitor not quite sure how to proceed – and Kerr was indeed a 'type' of which Adam would have had little experience in the context of murder.

In describing the visit to the beach, the parties again gave diametrically opposed accounts: they agreed only that it occurred, with the five in the car being Kerr, seated in the front between Adam and the driver Reg Jackson, plus Currer and Jack Matthews in the back.

In Adam's version, Kerr was a willing passenger, saying, 'I can never forget where it happened as I have had the urge to go back all the time.'

In Jackson's version, Kerr was the navigator, answering willingly when asked directions, and bringing them to a halt on the beach side of the Esplanade at Mills Street. In the cool of the morning, the police said, Kerr guided them through the sheds of his own volition, taking them first to the ladies' end of the shed, the north-western entrance: 'I think this is where I started to choke her'.

Then he indicated the date palm stump: 'I think this is where I dragged her'.

On the way back to the car, Kerr referred to a damaged path in front of the sheds, and said, 'I think that must be the white path I saw'.

The visit, the officers agreed, was over in minutes, and the group returned to Russell Street.

In Kerr's version, the whole journey was a mystery. He claimed to have no idea where they were going. They were approaching Middle Park from the city, the opposite direction from the night before. When Jackson slowed down on the way and suggested that Kerr give directions, the young man in the boiler suit demurred, 'I cannot show you. I don't think at night time I would have known where I was.'

'Drive on,' said Adam.

'Don't you want John to show us the way, Bluey?' asked Jackson.

'It doesn't make any difference,' Adam replied dismissively.

Walking down steps to the beach, said Kerr, Adam gestured to the structures. 'You commenced to choke her by one of these sheds,' he stated.

Kerr sighed. 'You're entitled to your opinion, I suppose.'

'Which shed did you choke her in?' Adam pressed.

'She was not choked by me anywhere,' insisted Kerr. 'I was never here with her. This is the first time I have ever seen this place.'

'Did you try to have intercourse with her in the shed or on the beach?' Adam demanded.

'I never tried to have intercourse with her anywhere. I was never here with the girl.'

After a few more indeterminate exchanges, Adam grunted, 'That will do. Come on.'

As they turned, he asked, 'Did you have any desire to return to see if the girl was all right?'

'Of course I did not,' argued Kerr. 'I knew she was perfectly all right when I left her.'

'You still won't admit to being here last night?'

'No, I won't, because I was not here,' Kerr repeated. 'And besides, I am glad now you have brought me here, because I know for certain this is not the part of the beach where I was with that girl. This whole area is unfamiliar to me.'

As they ascended steps through the sea wall to the level of the footpath, he added, 'And I am certain also that when we left the beach we went up a white ramp that was near a light'.

'These are the steps,' countered Adam. 'It was not up a ramp at all.'

'I am absolutely positive that when we left the beach we went up a white ramp,' Kerr repeated.

'You went up these steps.'

'I did not.'

'I tell you, you did. It was not a ramp at all.'

'I am positive when we went to the beach we did so by means of a ramp. It was near a light.'

'You did not,' Adam stated flatly. 'These are the steps you went up.'

He sounded annoyed, Kerr recalled, but said no more.

***

About the rest of the night, there was not so much dispute as ambiguity. After a silent return drive to Russell Street, Kerr was fingerprinted, given a towel and invited to use a washroom, then brought back to sign the fingerprint documents, which he did. To the police, this was evidence of Kerr's acceptance of his guilt. To Kerr, it affirmed his innocence. He voluntarily endorsed a document that bore his fingerprints, but shrank from a document that did not bear his words.

At about 3.20a.m., Kerr was brought in to the Homicide Squad room, desks scattered with typewriters and papers, at one of which sat Inspector Donelly.

'Do you have any complaints about the treatment you have received here?' asked the Homicide Squad chief – this was now a prescribed question. When Kerr said that he had been 'treated all right', Donelly inscribed the detention book accordingly.

Kerr would agree that he had made no complaint, saying that he thought the question was accented to any incidences of physical violence. And he denied saying what, according to Donelly, he added, 'I told them the truth. I am sorry for what I have done. I will have to take my punishment for it.'

Soon after, Adam bustled Kerr across Russell Street to the City Watchhouse. At the counter, the dustcoated officer-in-charge awaited, hovering over a ledger.

'What is the charge?' he asked.

'Murder,' said Adam.

Kerr, in his account, piped up. 'I thought you said before this was a case of manslaughter.'

'The charge is murder,' said Adam.

'Do they still hang people for murder?' Kerr asked.

'My word they do,' Adam replied.

'Well, I'm not afraid,' Kerr claimed was his reply. 'And if they *do* hang me over this case, I want you to be there to see it – and then you can think to yourself they are hanging an innocent man.'

***

I left the file of *The King v. Kerr* a little ruefully. It was not merely the content of these contending narratives that was so different; it was their length, detail and voice. The police stuck to the simplest possible account. Forced to revise it in a few respects, they did so with a minimal nod. They did not even admit to asking Kerr questions. According to them, with minimal prompting, their suspect had laid himself bare, acted as their guide, and even embraced penance. Apart from anything else, this was sound procedure. Juries grasped confession; science stretched them. And because judges frowned on police referring to notes, simple evidence that could be learned by heart was most robust in court.

Kerr's recitation was the opposite. It was lengthy, purportedly verbatim, powerfully adamant and undeniably dramatic. It had twists, digressions, sallies and countersallies. And it would endure, surviving numerous retellings without revision – a policeman could only have envied such a compendious memory. To commit to it was an act of confidence bordering on recklessness. There was no obligation on a defendant to testify in a murder trial; many preferred not to submit to cross-examination. Kerr never hesitated to put his story on the line.

At issue here, it occurred to me, was not just whom to believe, but how we believe, whether we find it easier to trust the basic, crude, unevolved story stolidly supported by like-minded sources, with the possibility this raises of collusion, or the complicated tale fluently and repeatedly retold by an individual, scaling such heights it can only be either gospel truth or virtuoso lying.

Early on 29 December 1949, the justice system made clear its preliminary preference: a stipendiary magistrate denied bail on the basis that, as he was advised by Senior Detective Adam, Kerr had made 'certain admissions'.

3

NERVOUS LIVES

Shortly after my appointments with the OPP, the response to a Freedom of Information application on Corrections Victoria brought the official prison photographs of '49194 John Bryan KERR': mug-shots on grey backing; a full-length image on his admissions card. In each, he wore a dark suit, from whose breast pocket a white handkerchief protruded. Newspapers would exhibit a fascination with Kerr's dress sense throughout the case, from the moment *Truth* described his remanding in custody while wearing a 'pale blue tie with Windsor knot and white shirt', all of a piece with his imperturbable demeanour: 'His dark handsome face showed no emotion as the charge was read'.

I pored over the lineaments of that face much as I imagined Melburnians had those many years ago: they say he's a murderer; but he doesn't *look* like a murderer; but what does a murderer look *like?* The insolence of the full lips, the hauteur of the chin, the suavity of the precisely parted hair – to the photographer, they seemed to say, 'What are you looking at, little man?' On the admissions card, Kerr stood beside a gauge registering his height at '5ft 9 1/2ins'. Otherwise, with his natty tailoring, he might have been Sir John Betjeman's Young Executive, all clean cuffs and slimline briefcase.

No wonder Kerr stood out at once from the run-of-the-mill desperados and deadbeats usually propped in courtroom docks. No wonder he left such an impression on those whose paths he had crossed. The first of these I met was Brian Bourke, elder statesman of the Victorian Bar, whom I had encountered some years earlier when writing another book and remained in contact with. Bourkey's door at Owen Dixon Chambers is ever ajar, his feet usually on the desk, his memory uncannily clear and generally at any visitor's disposal. On one wall is a portrait of Ronald Ryan, the last man hanged in Australia, whom Bourkey defended; on another is a photograph of Grace Kelly, film siren, whom Bourkey would have rushed to defend had the opportunity presented itself.

Over lunch I got him talking about John Bryan Kerr. Bourkey had come to know him on visits to Pentridge Prison in the mid-1950s. Oh yes, Kerr was something, all right. You never met a man less like a prisoner. He walked the gaol like he owned it. He stuck to his innocence like scripture.

Then one morning I popped in on Bourkey to find him in conversation with a petite, well-spoken, middle-aged woman, Denise Duncan, John Bryan Kerr's widow. Except that when they married, Denise explained, he was not John Bryan Wallace Kerr, but 'John Wallace', having by then lost his parents, divested himself of his former identity, and winnowed his age by ten nuisance years. Their daughter, Kate, had now been inducted into their father's story; their son, Nicholas, had not, having little apparent curiosity about his father.

'John Wallace' had divulged his real name to Denise early in their relationship, although virtually none of the hundred guests at their wedding were aware of his past, including the best man. The same was true at his funeral in 2001, with none of those who spoke mentioning that the dear departed had outlived a sentence of death passed on him fifty-one years earlier.

Denise thought her husband would have been content with that. The price of his successful career as a medical detailer had been an unending anxiety about the penetration of his secret. 'John spent his whole life looking over his shoulder, wondering if people had guessed who he was,' she recalled.

Such distance had he opened on his past that Denise was now in touch with only two people who had known her husband as John Bryan Kerr: Bourkey, and another friend, Jerry Hughes. Everything else had been rendered down to two cardboard boxes of personal effects – at which, she said generously, I was welcome to look.

So far I had been feeling around the edges of the story, for a sense of its essence and extent; it was about files and photos, transcripts and testimonies. I knew from experience that to go further was the critical escalation. Here was where the past blurred with the present, where one came into contact with the beliefs of the living and the reputations of the dead. I should, perhaps, have thought longer. But when Denise made her offer, there was no refusing. Such a gesture of trust had to be reciprocated. And in a sense the story demanded it because, to a great degree, *The King v. Kerr* hinged on *who* he was, rather than merely *what* he did or did not do. When it came to court, the Crown's only evidence of Kerr's guilt was a 'confession' that he had not signed; they set to proving that it bore his character if not his signature, that he was *the kind of man* who was capable of murder. In his prosecution, then, Kerr's whole prior life became an exhibit; there being such abiding dispute around the verdict, similar considerations applied to his life post-incarceration.

And this, I was about to find, was extremely complicated. The man dedicated to 'looking over his shoulder' had done his best to discourage those who might come up behind him posthumously, leaving only vestigial traces of his first twenty-five years, and what would prove deliberately confusing remnants of his last forty. The material was not anywhere near as substantial as the material gathered to establish his guilt, while recollection of him would be shaded by the historical fact of his conviction. But if we knew where stories would lead us, where would be the point in starting them?

***

The enigma of John Bryan Wallace Kerr began with his birth on 7 August 1925 at Avonhurst, on Queens Road, South Melbourne. Avonhurst, run by 'Misses Telleson and Moffatt', was one of a number of small private hospitals in the locale catering to the well-to-do – Rupert Murdoch would be born there six years later. But both Brian Bourke and Jerry Hughes, whom I was later to meet, were convinced that Kerr was adopted.

Why, they couldn't really say. He simply seemed so different from his quiet, respectable, hardworking parents. They both had blue eyes; he had brown. They were dour, strait-laced, self-contained; he was handsome, polished, garrulous. And the background was ever so slightly suggestive.

Both Donald and Rose Kerr were from large, well-established, Scottish Presbyterian families: Kerr's father, Donald, born at Snapper Point in 1893, was the fifth of eleven children; mother, Rose, born in Casterton in 1884, was the oldest of six. John Bryan Kerr's paternal grandfather, John James Kerr, proudly described himself as a 'gentleman' or of 'independent means', and accumulated like an archetypal Scot, owning on his death three houses in East Melbourne and one in Collingwood.

Kerr's maternal grandfather John McKenzie settled near Hamilton in western Victoria, serving as manager of Murndal, the estate of grazier and politician Samuel

Winter Cooke. Both Kerr's parents served, lengthily, in World War I. Aged twenty, Donald joined up within days of the declaration of war, and served in Egypt, then France, before being invalided home as a corporal with pulmonary tuberculosis. A military nurse based mainly at Rouen Hospital, Rose had risen to rank of Sister by the time of her discharge in July 1919.

Kerr would describe his father as a 'nervy' man who suffered 'neurodermatitis' – a vague term for chronic itching that in the absence of more obvious explanations was sometimes ascribed to stress. He was also told that his mother had suffered some form of 'breakdown' in her youth. Certainly, for the time, they married late. After a twenty-month engagement, twenty-nine-year-old Donald Kerr, commercial traveller, wed thirty-eight-year-old Rose McKenzie, trained nurse, in the Scottish Church in St Kilda, making their matrimonial home in Rose Street, Ivanhoe. That made Rose forty-one when John Bryan Kerr was born – again, late for a first birth. He occasioned no birth notices in *The Argus* or *The Age,* unusual in his class and caste. As far as establishing adoption was concerned, there were no records of handover to look at: another four years would elapse until the *Adoption of Children Act* made formal what had previously been done through private networks. At the time, Victorians simply had sixty days to register a birth under the antique *Registration (Births, Deaths and Marriages) Act* – plenty of time to quietly place a baby in the right hands if you knew the right people, as nurse

Rose Kerr would have. Five years later, the rules would be tightened somewhat by the *Birth Notifications Act,* requiring notifications of the local municipal clerk, and here was something allusive: the first prosecution for noncompliance with that act was of ... Avonhurst Private Hospital.

Partly as a result, I paid the family tree more attention than I otherwise might have – and it had its peculiarities. John Kerr's favourite uncle Keith McKenzie, for example, turned out to be his cousin. His birth certificate showed him as the son of Rose's sister Jane, born in December 1907 under the auspices of Warrnambool's Presbyterian Sisterhood, a 'shelter and help for friendless women and their infants' who were 'one false step from drifting into degradation': eighteen-year-old Jane was listed as a 'single woman', with the space left for the father's name reproachfully agape.

The July 1910 death certificate for Donald's older brother, twenty-five-year-old James Dawson Kerr, was then vividly inscribed: 'Haemorrhage from wound in the throat self-inflicted – suicide'. The inquest related the story of a gifted law student working at the Statist Office returning home from some months in a Carlton boarding house where he had been swotting for exams, and striking his father as being 'strange in his manner'. To the local doctor, the young man gave an 'incoherent statement', to the effect 'that some people had been setting traps for him'. A conference was arranged for the following morning with Melbourne's leading 'alienist' Beattie Smith, but James awoke 'clean off his head', took his father's razor, and slashed his throat from ear to ear.

Although the coroner toned down 'clean off his head' to 'whilst in a condition of temporary mental unsoundness', mental health a hundred years ago was unconstrained by euphemism. There was an Inspector-General of Lunacy, a Superintendent of the Insane, Idiot Houses, Imbecile Homes, and treatments barely more advanced than sedation for the docile and restraint for the resistant, as the Kerrs were to find. Because eleven years after her brother's death, pretty twenty-one-year-old Grace Kerr, who had been a bright schoolgirl, pianist, chorister and for three years a dressmaker at Ball & Welch, also began behaving strangely after a 'love affair with a man', which ended in quarrels, umbrage and finally complete silence.

This time, the Kerrs were disinclined to wait. They admitted Grace to the Royal Park Receiving House, effectively the triage centre for Victoria's sprawling asylum system: fifty beds, through which a thousand patients passed annually, the majority heading only one way. The 'diagnosis' was 'primary dementia', the ancient term for catatonic schizophrenia, while the 'cause of attack' sounded almost like a country and western song: 'Love, hereditary defect'. Nowadays, Grace Kerr would have been treated promptly with benzodiazepines. In September 1921 she was just another uncomprehending, incomprehensible hysteric.

The photograph on her admission card to Sunbury Hospital for the Insane was of a face weary with pain and terror – and such was the future yawning before her. For Grace Kerr never reentered the 'sane' world. In response to a Freedom of Information request, the Department of Health disgorged 150 pages of her medical records. They were almost too haunting to read.

> 13 February 1926: 'Keeps to herself, will occasionally speak, but often sings in an idiotic manner. Is a habitual masturbator.' 5 September 1940: '"How are you feeling?" No reply. "Where are you?" Remains silent. "What do you do all day?" Does not answer. She remains stubbornly mute. Occasionally sniggers to herself.'
>
> 29 September 1965: 'Cooperative. Looks after herself. Uninterested in her surroundings.'

By the time of this last entry she was at Beechworth Asylum, whose corridors she wandered on tiptoe, holding out her skirt like a ballerina. When she died of a myocardial infarction on 20 June 1974, nobody knew her parents' names or how to contact her family.

In the end, there was no proving John Bryan Kerr's parentage. You would want also more evidence before drawing conclusions about mental illness in the family: a gentle shake of any family tree will dislodge blemished, misshapen fruit. But here was a family with reason to be nervous about 'nerves', where at the time it was customary to imagine psychiatric disorders lodging, living in what Robert Musil called the 'nervous age', of 'nervous collapse', of 'nervous breakdown' and, indeed, of 'neurasthenia'. John Bryan Kerr's later travails, then, had for his family a discomfiting context.

***

When trouble came, the Kerrs also reproached themselves. They had spoiled their son, an only child, born into comfort if not into privilege, habituated to the company of the affluent and snug. If his parents were not themselves hugely wealthy, they ensured that John Bryan never went without. Because of his mother's strong ties to western Victoria, he was baptised on 8 November 1925 at the Coleraine and Tahara Presbyterian Church, and would retain fond early recollections of visits to Murndal, where John McKenzie worked until Cooke's death in August 1929, and Stoneleigh, a property in the nearby hamlet of Tahara that McKenzie bought with the help of a generous legacy from his old boss. Family resources were sufficient to see them through the Depression, when Donald's employment as a draper and salesman fluctuated.

John Bryan's schooling began at Christ Church, a Presbyterian schoolhouse in St Kilda about fifteen minutes' walk from their redbrick cottage in Wellington Street, Prahran; then in February 1935, aged nine, he was enrolled in Scotch College, *the* Presbyterian boys' school of Melbourne, purported at the time to be the biggest of its kind in the Empire.

The school's records reflected this. They were voluminous and zealously kept; 'Kerr, J.B.W.' lay rather lost within them. Unlike such contemporaries as Zelman Cowen, John Cain and James Balderstone, Kerr's school reports were perfunctory: 'Has ability but lacks perseverance. Character good'; 'Ability only fair. Good serious type of boy'; 'Yes the spirit is willing. A nice lad'.

Scotch's archivist Paul Mishura generously guided me towards surviving contemporaries from his house, Lawson, but the few gleanings were meagre: Kerr was tall for his age, a junior footballer, a senior swimmer; Kerr was fussy about his grooming; Kerr disliked having his hair cut. Scotch at the time was being steered in more liberal directions by New Zealander Dr Colin Gilroy, only the fourth principal in the school's history. Music, art, drama and debating were suddenly in favour. The library subscribed to both the Left and Right Book Clubs; it welcomed guest speakers representing the rights of indigenous people and the strivings of the International Brigades; in interschool debates, Scotch teams argued for Stalinism over Czarism, and against the proposition 'That the evils of Jazz and Swing should be crushed'. Kerr followed more predictably in the religious and martial traditions of the school motto *Deo Patriae Litteris* ('For God, for Country, for Learning'). He joined the school's Crusader Union, a Christian fellowship hosting evangelical speakers at lunchtime meetings, and the Cadet Corps, then so large as to comprise three companies. In 1941, his last year at Scotch, Kerr became corporal of the first company, entitling him to his own .303 and bayonet. By then, to go by his school report, the learning was a problem: 'Irresponsible. Unreliable. Work as NCO good. Class work poor'.

Nobody really seemed to know who his friends were. In later times, he cited only two childhood pals: John Gundersen and Teddy Buckland. Diminutive cream-haired Gundersen appeared with an unsmiling Kerr in two photographs of the Scotch swimming team, and the school's records for him petered out on his joining the Merchant Navy. Pursued along a daisy chain of records as exotic as immigration passenger manifests and as mundane as the Melbourne White Pages, Gundersen proved not only alive but kicking: pushing ninety, nearly blind, but still high up at Norway's biggest family-owned shipbuilder, after a career that had included being sunk three times.

Oh yes, Gundersen responded by email, he remembered John Bryan Kerr, but they had been 'good friends' rather than 'close friends', and after school had gone their separate ways. 'The bond was between our mothers,' he explained – and Kerr would indeed cite Lenna Eveline Gundersen as his 'second mother'.

Kerr's friendship with Teddy Buckland, meanwhile, was through his father, who worked at the Producers' Co-operative alongside Cyril Buckland, an auctioneer, in the late 1930s. Cyril's son Teddy Buckland, destined to be vice-captain at Melbourne Grammar, represented the *beau ideal* of educated youth: a versatile scholar, gifted athlete, and exemplary patriot, who left school for the Royal Australian Air Force. His death in September 1944, when the Wellington bomber he was piloting crashed near Lichfield Airfield in Staffordshire, was a crushing blow to his parents, which John Kerr also felt – for many years after, he noted the anniversary. Yet at the time they knew each other, Buckland's example could hardly have been said to have inspired Kerr in his grades and grain.

Just then, Paul Mishura introduced me to the historian Weston Bate, a Scotch Collegian a year John's senior, now a warm and lively nonagenarian. John Bryan Kerr?

Why yes, Bate remembered him, with melancholy vividness, not so much as a personality but as a type. Because Scotch was so big and streamed its classes so vigorously, Bate told me over coffee one morning in Brighton, it tended to encourage the excelling of a few while ignoring the struggles of the many. Some students were left behind altogether, without guidance, without assistance. 'John Kerr, I always thought, was one of these,' said Bate. 'A bit isolated, not sure of his identity. Slightly sneaky, slightly sleazy; not an aggressive rebel, just playing the bounds of law and order.' The kind of boy who would skive off to join the smokers at Gardiners Creek, be cited by prefects for flouting uniform regulations like forgetting his cap; the kind of boy resigned to being misunderstood.

By coincidence, Bate had also known Buckland. They had played sport against one another, then undertaken an RAAF training course together. Was Buckland as virtuous as he seemed, I asked? Bate paused, as if on the brink of something momentous. Perhaps honouring the memory of a young man dead seventy years is like that – you must get it *exactly* right.

'Teddy *was* a *most remarkable* young man,' Bate said finally, weightily. 'A person of *immense* poise. Open, clean, clear; reserved and polite but friendly to all; not the slightest bit judgemental. I admired him *enormously.* After the war his mother came to the school for a ceremony in Teddy's honour. I still remember how dignified she looked.'

What could have been the basis of the friendship between a boy as lost as Kerr seemed and a boy as accomplished as Buckland was? Was Teddy the boy John wished he could be?

Bate looked wistful. 'Teddy Buckland fitted perfectly,' he reflected. 'John Kerr looked like a boy who felt like he didn't quite belong.'

***

Did he? Much hinged on the question of what John Kerr would 'do with his life'. It was, in a sense, the next step in the family's progress. The Kerrs were steadfastly 'respectable'. Donald was a Freemason, Rose an adherent of the Presbyterian Church. Their residential trajectory betokened steady social advance: Ivanhoe, Fitzroy, Prahran and, at last, in 1939, Toorak. Their home at 54 Washington Street was a middling one, rented from a merchant who lived nearby. But it bore a sturdy Hibernian name, Afton, and their neighbours in the 1940s were very much of Melbourne's 'upper ten', from Rev W.L. Clarke, chaplain of Melbourne Grammar, to Aubrey Gibson, industrialist and philanthropist. There was even a whiff of the aristocracy, the Harkers at number 3 boasting a countess for a daughter when her husband, Major Galbraith Armar Lowry-Corry, became the seventh Earl of Belmore. Perhaps the foremost personality was the Kerrs' next-door neighbour, the socialite Zara Fell, owner of the popular local boutique Magg, privately the paramour of fast-rising conservative politician Harold Holt.

Early fantasies of a religious vocation having waned by the end of his schooling, John Kerr harboured only one ambition: a vehement enthusiasm for joining the navy. To his frustration, he was at sixteen too young to enlist, and had to settle for a temporary clerkship with the Harbour Trust. It seemed to unsettle him. In December 1941 he experienced what he would decorously describe, without further elaboration, as a 'near nervous breakdown'.

Near nervous breakdown: an expression both vague *and* precise, an assertion that whatever it was stopped exactly short of an acute phase. It savoured of the valetudinarianism of a 'nervy' family, with the son caught up in the hopes and fears of the parents, but some circumspection was advisable in the absence of better particulars. 'Nervous breakdown' sixty-odd years ago was a term nearly as fluid as 'depression' today, encompassing everything from exhaustion by overwork to extremes of bereavement. There was even an encouragement to self-diagnose. 'Are You Walking Around with a Nervous Breakdown?' asked a 1941 edition of *Ladies' Home Journal:* 'In the throes of an acute nervous attack, no matter how organically healthy the victim might be, the heart does beat abnormally fast, the hands do clench and stiffen, the breath comes with difficulty, and the brain may falter and go temporarily blank.' And where the modern paradigm is of permanent and chronic mood disorders, from a 'breakdown' one could be rebuilt; from a 'crack-up' one might be reassembled. That John Curtin was widely reported to have suffered a 'nervous breakdown' a year earlier, for example, had not stopped him becoming Prime Minister in October 1941.

But for the Kerrs, this was clearly an anxious time. As their son's schooling ended Donald was forty-eight, Rose fifty-seven – not best placed to be dealing with a brooding teen. Further frustration awaited the following year when Kerr tried to enlist and failed the seaman's eyetest. Not until June 1943 was *Probationary Supply Assistant Kerr, John Bryan Wallace, No. PM 6094* accepted into the Royal

Australian Naval Reserve, joining the cruiser HMAS *Adelaide.*

At first, the Kerrs were relieved – indeed, they glowed with pride. One of their most cherished items was a framed photograph of their son in his naval uniform, looking a little like Donald Sinden in *The Cruel Sea.* Nor need they have worried about the danger of his duties. Kerr liked to say that he had spent his eighteenth birthday 'at sea', but the ship's diary suggests that this was merely a gunnery trial on Port Phillip Bay. Apart from a couple of brief convoy assignments in the Indian Ocean, HMAS *Adelaide* had nothing very much to do, and Kerr's service went from uninvolving to uncomfortable. While in Perth, he was treated for 'neurodermatitis', the same condition as afflicted his father. It did not abate. Six months after joining the *Adelaide,* he was returned to shore duty; two months later, he was discharged as medically unfit, with an efficiency rating as 'inferior'.

Worse, at least for his parents, was their son's apparent coarsening by life in uniform, and his early brushes with alcohol. One in particular followed his returning home from catching up with former shipmates, when in his fury at a comment of his mother's he broke a chair and smashed two doors. His father was sufficiently alarmed to summon a family friend, Constable Tom Doig, from his home in nearby Tivoli Road – it's suggestive that he thought himself unable to cope alone. Kerr was later dismissive of the episode. 'I was drunk. That was the extent of it.' Doig was there 'more or less to give me a fright'. But the episode continued to reverberate within the household, playing upon its anxieties, and there would be more to be anxious over.

After treatment from a skin specialist, Kerr managed in June 1944 to join the Royal Australian Air Force. Yet *Aircraftsman First-Class JBW Kerr No.149942* made no better fit than he had in the navy. Five days after enlisting, he was given seven days' confinement to barracks in Shepparton for snapping at a guard on picket: 'You are nothing but a [expletive] blue orchid.'[1] Ten weeks later, he was fined 5/- for being drunk at an open house in Adelaide. Uncomfortable from a recurrence of his neurodermatitis and disturbed by 'noisy hammering', he failed to complete his trainee technician course, and the trade test board, assigned to find something else for him to do, were unimpressed with his impertinence: 'He was offered Trainee Equipment and was not very interested and therefore is not considered worthwhile putting on the course. In fact he has too much to say.'

Transferred to the RAAF training and stores base at Tocumwal as an office orderly, his service ended in the ultimate ignominy – a court martial for getting drunk on Armistice Day.

---

1 'Blue orchid' was a slang term for RAAF personnel used by soldiers and sailors, on account of their rarity, and their imagined glamour.

***

They weren't all sun-bronzed Anzac gladiators: the National Archives of Australia in Canberra holds almost 600 lineal metres about servicemen behaving badly, leading to courts martial. And applications for the escapades of Aircraftsmen Kerr and Leslie Irwin, his eighteen-year-old hutmate, returned fat brown files with some pretty typical features. An hour after the commemorative silence on 11 November 1944, Kerr and Irwin slipped out of camp using borrowed leave passes, and at Tocumwal's Tatts Hotel spent about four hours drinking twenty 10oz glasses of beer and two gins. 'After we got a bit full,' admitted Irwin, 'we could have been drinking anything.'

They probably had a bet on the Melbourne Cup, being held, as in the previous two years, on a Saturday. They certainly started to spar, half in jest, on the way back to camp late in the day. As they rolled in the gates, it became a full-blown fight, although this was less a problem than that when a zealous superior officer interposed they turned their attentions to him. This brought several other airmen who struggled at length to subdue the pair.

So far, so foolish. But at a certain point, their misdemeanours became distinguishable. Irwin's language to his escort was assessed as pretty fruity ('Get stuffed you rotten bastard. Try to make me move you rotten cunt'). Kerr's language so shocked another witness that he preferred to write it down (exhibit J of the court martial was a card on which was handwritten 'I will fight you, you fucking bastard. You are a greasy cunt fuck you, or words to that effect').

Where Irwin's misbehaviour was treated as the case of a straightforward skinful, Kerr's was made more serious by his riotous behaviour under restraint. Conveyed in a fire tender to a treatment room in the medical hut, he shattered windows and scattered vessels all round, and lunged at the orderly with broken glass in his hand. One witness could 'smell the intoxicating liquor' on Kerr but thought he was 'very excited, uncontrollable' rather than 'drunk'; a second thought he 'would not say he was acting sanely'; a third 'would not say he was acting like a normal man'; a fourth recalled him swearing 'in a quick gasping breath, like a person under nervous tension'; a fifth reported that it was only by means of a fire extinguisher that he was subdued.

And while Irwin's court martial was held within a couple of weeks, with a sentence of thirty-five days' detention imposed, Kerr's needed to wait until he had spent six weeks in Heidelberg Repatriation Hospital recovering from a broken jaw. Whether it was of his own volition or agreed in advance with his defence counsel, Kerr was candid.

> Kerr: AC1 Irwin wanted to have a spar with me, we often used to spar at night in the gym. He wanted to spar and I said 'no, not here – we'll

get into trouble'. He said something to me and hit me, I retaliated and hit him back. This went on for about five minutes and someone came along, I did not know who it was. Someone intervened. I still went on fighting and after that I do not recollect anything until I went to the medical section. I have a vague recollection of going in a car up to the medical section and being in a room, then, for no apparent reason, I was throwing my hands around and racing around and thought, 'This is not right – I should not do that.' But I could not stop myself. I kept on doing it until I was hosed in the face...

Judge Advocate: You were seized with a complete blackout, so to speak.

Kerr: Comparatively. I knew I was running around but I did not know what I was doing. I had no control ... I stopped when the water hit me in the face. I was punched and held. I have had these attacks before in civilian life when everything antagonizes me.

Judge Advocate: Do you go into these conditions of lapse of consciousness or conscious volition as a result of drinking or if you are thwarted in any way?

> Kerr: I get very nervy. I do not go into these conditions unless I drink. I get very upset. I do not go silly unless I have been drinking.

The court martial did not accept that Kerr had merely gone 'silly'. They imposed 140 days' detention, while allowing this to be settled by the payment of £5 11s damages.

Kerr was luckier than he knew. Because a medical board had already declared him medically unfit, his departure from the services on 16 March 1945 was deemed 'honourable'. A grumpy group captain left a complaint on his file that 'justice has been defeated in this case as undoubtedly this airman should have been given a disciplinary discharge', regreting it was 'too late to rectify this mistake', and insisting that a minute be 'placed on the airman's Personal File' for 'future reference' – *my* future reference, it had turned out.

What else might a future referencer infer from Kerr's brush with military justice? Under the Judge Advocate's questioning, he had not only described himself in a state we would now call dissociated, involving behaviours beyond his control, but admitted prior instances of same ('I have had these attacks before in civilian life when everything antagonizes me'). Alcohol ingested, dander up, the teenage Kerr was a risk to friends as well as family – and he knew it. Because when later it was brought up in a criminal court, Kerr anxiously played down his court martial, to the extent of insisting, pedantically and erroneously, that he could not have been 'court martialled' because his discharge had been honourable. That reticence was understandable. The question was: were these the squirmings of a guilty man, or of an innocent man?

4

STAR PUPIL

The John Bryan Kerr who left the services was handsome, confident, even stylish, but there was a strain involved, for he could also be moody, argumentative, petulant. He was polished and charming, vain and superior – a precocious snob aware of good grooming, conscious of social niceties, pedantic about correct English usage. Alcohol made him still more labile. But he was also only nineteen, young enough that this might all be a stage, providing he found a good guide. And to an extent he did.

One of few distractions from the rather dreary duties at Tocumwal had been a camp radio station run by Bill Bowie, who before the war had worked at 2UW and been part of the stable of radio actors known as the Lee Murray Players. Whether this played a part was unclear, but John Kerr was shortly to come under the influence of the tall, commanding and charismatic Murray, one of the medium's first and most successful entrepreneurs. Born Horace Mason in Collingwood in 1900, the son of a painter and decorator, he had no similar aptitudes, explaining later that he had attended Collingwood Technical School for exactly one day: 'They gave me a hammer and a piece of wood and I left'. Saving money from a decade's clerical work, he tried acting in Sydney with J.C. Williamson and Pat Hanna, crossing paths with a young Errol Flynn. He also formed part of a consortium luring to Australia the American wrestler Ad Santel, who for a few years wowed stadium crowds with his Boston Crab and Short-Armed Scissors.

Yet it was radio that proved the metier of Lee Whitehall Murray – the euphonious stage name he assumed. The trick to the new medium, Murray grasped, would not be in originality, but in presenting the already half-familiar. Thinking that many of the old dramas to which Williamson owned rights would work well on the air, he began adapting and producing them for 3AW, then 3XY. The Lee Murray Players toured far and wide, with a variety show starring soprano Gladys Moncrieff and baritone John Fraser. Also into his radio stable came comedian Roy Rene, alongside young straight man Lloyd Lamble, and ventriloquist Mal Verco, with his ebullient alter ego Ginger. By World War II, Murray was Australia's nearest thing to a commercial radio guru.

Then, in 1943, Murray took a different direction, as a trainer of aspiring radio talent. It began informally when a young Canadian, John Ford, on the way to a successful career with 3KZ, approached him for advice. Pretty soon, Murray had rented rooms at Kelvin Hall on Melbourne's Exhibition Street, gathering classes of about a dozen at a time reading scripts and reciting advertisements into a dummy microphone.

Murray had clear tenets of correct vocal production. You had to perfect the enunciation 'New Pwa'. You had to project *into* the microphone. 'Not from the back of the throat, young man!' he would insist. 'Project from the tip of the tongue. The tip of the tongue!'

But Murray's ambitions went further. He sought to impart a whole ideal of professional living – of diligence, of reliability, of sartorial excellence, and preferably of the Collingwood Football Club. And he wanted to spread his message as widely as possible. His thirteen-week course cost a trifling £10, and young triers he would train for nothing – he welcomed anyone with an interest in improving their voice, or themselves. One student was a young Italian train driver, who strove valiantly but seemingly to no avail. Another student could not help asking: why did Murray spend time with him? Murray answered with emphasis: 'Because it will make him *a better man'.*

This had a personal pay-off. In January 1945, the management of Russell Manufacturing, a subsidiary of Repco, installed a new public address system at their factory, and wanted to train their switchboard girl to use it. Esme Hollonds, known universally as Lynne, was eighteen. Forty-four-year-old Murray courted her assiduously. They would marry in November 1951, although never become parents. 'Lee's pupils are his children,' Lynne would say – and none became more fully his proxy son than John Bryan Kerr.

For on Kerr nature had bestowed a deep, arresting, memorable voice – the register lowered slightly, perhaps, by all those juvenile cigarettes. Murray liked it at once, and Kerr liked that he liked it. Murray was a stickler for correct usage, which appealed to Kerr, and for sobriety, which appealed to the Kerrs.

The family welcomed Murray in their circle; Murray's circle of radio personalities welcomed a bright newcomer. Kerr was soon socialising with the likes of 3AW's Norman Banks, 2CH's John Mahon, Professor William Osborne, the caustic polymath of 3DB's panel quiz 'Information Please', and Lt-Col Leonard Thomas, the ABC's Victorian manager. He followed his father into Freemasonry, joining Elliott Memorial Lodge No.613, an order favoured by old Scotch Collegians. He attracted young women: to his first radio ball he chaperoned a pretty twenty-year-old radio actress June Clyne. At last, Murray recommended his protege for work at a new regional radio station: 3CS needed replacements for two announcers who had enlisted. So in June 1945, the fresh-faced ex-serviceman moved into Colac's rambling Victoria Hotel on Murray Street, and reported for work.

Of the next year or so of Kerr's life, relatively few traces remained. He appeared twenty-third on a historic roll of 3CS employees. He also appeared in the verdict books for Colac Petty Sessions, which bore witness to his nautical vocabulary. On 1 August 1945, John Bryan Wallace Kerr pleaded guilty to a breach of the peace, and was fined 10/- for using indecent language in a public place: the Victoria Hotel's publican, Harold Thom, took a dislike to his guest's city slickness, and they clashed repeatedly, Kerr being disinclined to bear any provocation silently. But this did not prevent his moving to a bigger role at a larger station, 3UL in Warragul, early in 1946. And although he stayed here at Gippsland House, the town's biggest boarding house, he was also befriended by the Nash family: Peter and Margot, who ran the local mixed business store and milk run, and their teenage children Frances, Patricia and Walter. Kerr in turn was solicitous of Frances, two years' his junior, a beautiful, delicate girl afflicted by chronic nephritis – they were regarded, in hushed tones, as courting. With Kerr apparently settling, life calmed down at Afton too. Now a widower, Rose's father John McKenzie moved in. Now semi-retired, Donald took a new job as a temporary clerk in the accounts branch of the Navy Department at Albert Park, as part of a scheme under which war veterans replaced young female clerks. After the Kerrs' troubles, this would have been a hopeful period. Perhaps things would work out after all.

***

Two steps forward, one back. That temper again: towards the end of 1946, Kerr was involved in another incident, vague in cause and extent, at 3UL. A Crown Law Department file note in *The King v. Kerr* referred only to a 'clash' with a station manager, sufficient to cost him his job. Kerr returned to Melbourne, and for a time taught alongside Murray at Kelvin Hall. But his mother was now anxious enough about her son's patterns of behaviour to organise for him to see a 'nerve specialist', Dr Henry Stephens of 85 Spring Street. In fact, Dr Stephens was a psychiatrist, but in May 1947 there was little distinction between the designations; Stephens was simply an experienced physician who had just finished a diploma in psychiatry then become one of a dozen practitioners forming the Australian Association of Psychiatrists.

The appointment was inconclusive. When Kerr realised to whom he was talking, his gorge rose. What did he need to see a 'psychiatrist' for? The doctor mollified him: he had many clients, some of them top businessmen, who found it helpful to talk. Kerr thawed sufficiently to impart a little personal history, which went into Dr Stephens' files on little library cards: 'Single. No siblings. Mother and father alive and well. Paternal aunt [Grace Kerr] psychotic. Occasional excesses of alcohol at parties. Smokes rather excessively now he thinks. Sociable. Likes company, male and female. Many friends, usually older than himself. Dances occasionally – Mario's'. The doctor summed the patient up succinctly: 'Precise, superior, elated and rather euphoric'.

Under 'present complaint', Stephens put: 'Sudden outbursts of rage – about five to date. Attacks others. Always an incentive, broke a window at home in an argument with mother'. Without her son's knowledge, Rose herself visited Stephens soon after. It was not much for the doctor to work with – not that there were ready solutions anyway. While more advanced than in the 1920s, psychiatry in the 1940s remained accented to organic diagnoses and solutions, and treatment options were minimal if no physical cause proclaimed itself. So when Stephens submitted Kerr to a 'full examination of the central nervous system' on 17 June and found nothing amiss, twenty-one-year-old Kerr embarked on the next frontier of his career with the reassuring verdict of 'no abnormality detected', and wondering, perhaps, what the palaver was about.

For by now, the loyal Murray had recommended his protege to 7HO Hobart station manager Eric McRae. This was the brink of the big time: 7HO formed part of Hugh Denison's Macquarie Broadcast Network, a nationwide chain of stations including Melbourne's 3AW and Sydney's 2GB, featuring stars such as Harry Dearth and John Dease. Pretty soon, Kerr had an overriding goal: a job on 'Star Pupil', a top-rating talent parade in which music teachers showcased their best untried performers. 'Star Pupil' had begun in Melbourne and Sydney, spread to Adelaide and Brisbane, and was about to become national by staging shows in Perth and Hobart. Kerr saw the role of host for the Tasmanian link-up as a shortcut to mainland recognition.

It was a big moment, so big that it stayed with Kerr even after the dissolution of his ambitions. Among the leaves of a short correspondence course in journalism that he undertook in prison was a poignant memoir of the night in March 1948 when he reached his biggest audience, and when his hopes must have seemed close enough to touch. Among all the materials I examined, it was unique: a personal account of an occupational accomplishment, told in his own voice:

> In 1947, after being in Tasmania for some time as Chief Announcer for the Macquarie Broadcasting Services in Hobart, the news came that Tasmania had been granted its first National Radio Programme. To the Radio World this was news indeed! It meant that Tasmania could originate its own Australia-wide 'hook-up'.
>
> The following weeks were packed with interest. Producers and radio technicians flew in from Sydney ... Radio men from other local radio stations volunteered assistance ... Business men and public officials combined their efforts for the success of the broadcast.
>
> It had been agreed that the show would be part of the national 'Star Pupil' broadcast, and that the best vocalists discovered in Talent Quests would be featured. So the stage was being set, not for just another routine radio show, but for a publicity campaign advertising Tasmania to the rest of Australia.

> My own moment came when the organisers announced my selection as Compere ... and the weeks of rehearsals sped by until the show was passed as 'satisfactory for broadcast'.
>
> The gala night arrived. An hour from broadcast time – 8 o'clock – the auditorium was full. The orchestra tuned up. Vocalists revised introductions back stage. Technicians and producers checked final details. At last there were only two minutes left before Tasmania greeted Australia.
>
> Slowly I walked front stage and announced – 'Please stand-by to broadcast.' That final minute seemed an eternity. Excitedly I fingered the script, knowing that this show must be successful. The signal came that John Dease, in Sydney, had commenced his introduction. A nervous cough resounded in the hushed auditorium. Off stage the indicator light flickered on and off expectantly. Then, amidst a crescendo of applause, I spoke ... and to this day I can't recall exactly the next thirty minutes. I do know that the show was a success, and Tasmania justified her claims as a Musical State.

It was tempting to analyse the prose closely, in search of the personality delineated by Dr Stephens: 'Precise, superior, elated and rather euphoric'. Perhaps you could find traces of it in the arbitrary capitalising of 'Compere' and 'Radio World', in the jubilation of 'my own moment' and the 'crescendo of applause'. Yet a scarcity of material is ever an invitation to exaggerate the significance of a discovery. This was not a disclosing document. Actual emotion was recessed behind a veneer of pride, disappearing completely at the decisive moment ('I can't recall exactly'); it kept things perfectly superficial. Not that Kerr misremembered the response: 'Black Note', talent parade correspondent of the *Listener-In,* thought Tasmania's sopranos, contraltos and baritones had provided an 'entertaining experiment', and praised their poised young host for having 'capably handled the situation'.

At this time, John Kerr would have radiated success, complemented by the comely brunette on his arm: twenty-two-year-old Betty Smith, a typist and part-time mannequin from South Hobart whom he had met in Kingston six months earlier. But even then, Kerr's 7HO experience was souring. McRae never warmed to his chief announcer, finding him boastful, bumptious, rude to colleagues and contemptuous of Tasmania. And from an annexure to *The King v. Kerr* came two statements, never entirely deployed by the Crown, though they would have shored up the beliefs of their readers.

***

The first statement was by pretty Betty Smith, so charmed by Kerr at first, but also finding him possessive, jealous and sexually demanding. The statement concluded with the note that a policewoman had been present during questioning because 'this matter was one in which sexual intercourse between parties [was] concerned'. For the 1940s, the detail was, indeed, uncomfortably intimate:

> He was not satisfied with the usual position during sexual intercourse (to explain, me on my back facing him) and would want me to try other positions such as leaning over a chair or bed with my back to him. He was always wanting to touch my breast with his mouth but I could always manage to resist him. On several occasions he has bitten me on the mouth or neck. I always had to use force to stop him from behaving in this fashion. I usually had to resort to pushing or slapping his face ... His temper was uncontrollable and my opinion is that he was over-sexed. By this I mean not like a normal person should be. He possessed almost unnatural strength and did not seem to know how strong he was as I was often left with bruise marks on my arms and shoulders.

Here, I reflected, was the raw material for a veritable thesis on 1940s sexual manners, on what was 'usual' and 'normal', the active role in relations a man was assumed to take, the civilising influence on men that women were expected to exercise. Readers of Kerr's 'confession' would have found the depravities it described – 'I always kiss women on their privates with whom I have been with' – all the more believable after perusing Betty Smith's sexual cameo.

The other statement, later the subject of limited questioning, was signed by thirty-seven-year-old Winifred Metz, briefly Kerr's landlady. In early June 1948, a Tasmanian constable, Trooper G.A. Lynch, visited Loina Street, New Town, to serve a summons. Passing number 7, he noticed damage to its front door, then discolouration of owner Metz's right eye. She explained with chagrin that one of her three lodgers, a man called Kerr, had put on 'one of his insane acts'. Lynch asked if she wished to take action; she said he would be moving out anyway. But when a police inspector returned two years later, by which time her former lodger was a great deal better known, she recounted Kerr's brief stay in detail.

Tensions had arisen, she said, almost as soon as he had moved in. Metz and her two other young male lodgers, Harry Jones and Adrian Grayley, found their new guest conceited and humourless.

> He told us that his aunt thought he was very handsome and at least three times a week he would tell us that he had no padding in the shoulders of his coats and he would take his coat off on occasion and make us feel that in fact there was very little padding.
>
> Adrian Grayley said to him one day, 'You are the man who carries 7HO on his shoulders', and Kerr

replied 'Those words were spoken in jest, but nevertheless they are true.'

There were also hints of a smouldering temper. One day, Kerr asked for Metz's tweezers to pluck his bushy eyebrows, and when a hair would not come dashed them into the fire. When Metz refused him another pair, he visibly fumed.

Another day, disagreement broke out between Grayley and Kerr about the meaning of the word 'agnostic', and a dictionary was fetched, proving Grayley correct.

'The dictionary is wrong!' Kerr roared, seizing the book and hurling it across the room.

Kerr had been resident only eleven days when matters came to a head. Returning from a Saturday evening out with Betty Smith and Harry Jones to find his landlady playing cards with two girlfriends, he pulled up a chair and turned the conversation to himself.

'What is your opinion of me on the air?' he asked one of the women.

She replied cautiously, 'I suppose your voice is good but it is not one that I care for.'

Kerr flushed with anger. 'Fancy me wasting my time and talents in Tasmania broadcasting to animals of your type.'

Not surprisingly, the woman was taken aback. 'Why do you remain in Tasmania?' she asked.

'Because of that girl there,' Kerr replied, pointing at Betty.

Winifred Metz had had enough of her lodger's moods. 'You can leave in the morning,' she said to Kerr. 'I will not have my guests insulted.'

'But she insulted me,' Kerr protested.

'Constructive criticism never hurt anybody,' said the landlady primly, and adjourned to the kitchen to prepare supper. Kerr followed to propitiate her, and she accepted his apologies; in fact, when Kerr asked if he could invite over Studley Ruxton, a 7HO colleague who finished on air at 11p.m., she said yes.

Ruxton arrived just as Grayley returned from the pictures, and supper passed pleasantly enough. But about midnight, Kerr began bickering with his colleague – Ruxton had apparently asked if Betty would like to come to a dance. Suddenly the pair were peeling their coats off and shaping up. Metz tried to interpose and Kerr slapped her three times across the face. When she slapped him back, he went 'absolutely mad'.

> He grabbed hold of the kitchen table with both hands and pushed it over, breaking four Shelley cups and saucers, a quantity of other cups and saucers, eight sherry glasses, which had been set to drink the bottle of sherry that had been sent ... After that he picked up a bottle of Tomato Sauce, which had the top off, and swung it around

his head, so that everyone in the room had tomato sauce thrown on them, and sauce was also thrown on the walls and floor.

By this time, Jones, Grayley and Ruxton were trying to hold him, and Kerr was roaring like a bull, completely out of his mind. When I got close to try and knock him out, I received a black eye.

Ruxton rang for the police, and we shut him in the kitchen by holding the door closed against him, but he forced his way out, and with Grayley, Jones, Ruxton and I all trying to hold him, he took the lot of us straight up the passage. We were literally swept up the passage as we tried to restrain him.

Kerr had absolutely no control over himself, and on reaching the front door, he smashed the lead light out in the front door, and finished up by putting a slight cut on his elbow from a piece of the broken glass.

As soon as he saw blood on himself, he broke down altogether, and cried (just simply blubbered) and cried out to me not to lay a charge against him, not to let the Police take him.

He said I have these turns and I don't know what I am doing, and seeing him blubber for mercy, I

> took pity on him and told him he was not safe to be at large.

When the police arrived, Metz recalled, she suggested that an ambulance was required, and in due course Kerr was whisked to Royal Hobart Hospital for sedation. He returned with a recommendation that he re-establish contact with Dr Stephens. Metz decided she was 'sorry for the boy' as she listened to his faltering explanations.

> Kerr told me the following day that he took those sort of turns, and said 'I'm strong then, and five men could not hold me.' He said he didn't know what he was doing, and I do know that he in fact did know what he was doing but just could not control himself.

'Uncontrollable temper'? 'Over-sexed'? 'Turns'? 'Five men could not hold me'? And again the dissociated state, where Kerr 'didn't know what he was doing'. These were powerful echoes of the Kerr 'confession'. In the event, the statements arrived after Kerr's first trial, and were too prejudicial for the Crown's direct use. They went instead, more generally, to the Crown's composite sense of a defendant who was sexually voracious, apt to 'perve', and physically explosive, eager to 'hit and break and hurt something'.

Actually they admitted of more doubt than their readers probably allowed. Would the possessor of a sex drive so allegedly insatiable merely have ripped a victim's clothes? Would one susceptible to rages so chaotic simply have strangled and scratched a victim? No mention from Betty Smith of a partiality to oral sex; no sense from Winifred Metz that Kerr's rage focused on any individual, as distinct from whatever was in range. And another shadowy influence on Kerr's behavior may also have lurked, just out of sight.

When Ruxton recounted the evening to McRae, the station manager at last had the pretext for dismissing his overweening chief announcer. After another week, Kerr went slinking back to Melbourne, where his mother was predictably devastated. She posted Metz a cheque to cover her damages; she rang Dr Stephens to make an appointment for her son. But when the psychiatrist asked what had gone wrong in Tasmania, Kerr was evasive. He admitted to weeks of feeling 'strange' – enraged, confused, 'physically and mentally exhausted', to have been losing weight and going without sleep. Then into further depth he would not go, because his mood since coming home had been increasingly buoyant. Stephens quoted him as saying, 'I feel exceptionally well'.

It was at this point that Stephens deemed Kerr to be suffering cyclothymia – abnormal mood swings, although not so abnormal as to constitute manic depression – and to now be in a hypomanic state. But his volatility may have been aggravated by another factor. McRae mentioned to police two rumours about Kerr, possibly related: that he had spent time at Milbrook Rise Receiving House, a psychiatric hospital in New Norfolk set up in the 1930s for shell-shock victims, and that he used Benzedrine. When I searched Millbrook Rise's admissions register, Kerr's name did not, in fact, appear. But as an outpatient he might well have been supplied with Benzedrine, an amphetamine applied at the time rather indiscriminately for everything from lethargy to constipation.

The drug had first been described by the *British Medical Journal* in 1938 as giving 'confidence', increasing 'initiative and promptitude in reaching decisions' and aiding 'convincing, fluent speech'. Ten years on and the American Medical Association was associating 'the bennies' with 'malnutrition, poor judgment, impaired self-control', while noting abiding popularity among 'students' and 'entertainers'. Most Australian states now had Benzedrine on their poisons lists, restricting its access, but it remained in wide circulation as a pick-me-up. The lost weight and sleep Kerr complained of in Tasmania were consistent with its use; escape from the influence of its febrile highs and paranoid lows might well have conduced to a feeling of wellbeing. And Kerr had certainly bounced back.

***

Stephens had a point about the cycles in John Bryan Kerr's young life nonetheless. The standard one was initial competence and success, gradually compromised by bad temper and personal antipathies.

It would be repeated once more. Kerr told his parents he was eager for Betty Smith to come to Melbourne. They were reluctant, but found it difficult to deny their son anything, and so consented. She was referred to euphemistically as John's 'friend', and officially lived with a neighbour, Amelia Meagher, at 47 Washington Street. Lee Murray, meanwhile, had secured Kerr an attractive announcing vacancy at Geelong's 3GL, Victoria's second-oldest regional radio station owned by Australia's oldest regional newspaper. A 500W transmitter carried its signal deep into Melbourne.

Station manager Reg Gray wanted his recruit for a new show, 'Solomon's Family Quiz', a general knowledge quiz pitting teams of families against each other. It was sponsored by one of the town's most prestigious citizens, draper Loris Solomon, a certified war hero who saved Lord Louis Mountbatten during the 1941 sinking of the *HMS Kelly,* a story stirringly retold in Noel Coward's *In Which We Serve.* Kerr exhibited all the charm he often showed elders, engaging Solomon as one naval man to another. A surviving publicity photograph showed a cheerful Solomon presenting a winners' cheque to a beaming family as a fresh-faced, bow-tied Kerr looks on.

Again, it was not to last. Kerr had difficulties with his co-workers, and with boarding in Geelong during the week. Separated much of the time from Betty, he began calling Afton to ascertain her whereabouts ever more often. These apprehensions were not assuaged by the announcement of their engagement on 7 April

1949: he took a fortnight's leave for an indeterminate illness.

Was he drinking? Was he taking Benzedrine? Whatever the case, he returned to work, and took the microphone for the Associated Public Schools' Head of the River on the Barwon River in an agitated mood. This 'Australian Henley' was a big deal, relayed through 3KZ, 3AW and a host of regional stations. Kerr's airs and pretensions now irritated some listeners as well as colleagues. At 11p.m. in 3GL's James Street studio, Reg Gray summoned him. He was fired.

'What for?' asked Kerr.

Gray said that 3GL was 'not satisfied with his work'.

Kerr was wan, subdued. 'That's a surprise,' he said, and asked if he could ring his parents.

Kerr had experienced embarassments before; this was abject humiliation. At home he moped, brooded and at times lashed out. Betty Smith described coming home in a taxi with him from an evening at Mario's soon after, and his strange question as they alighted, 'Where's my bloody money?'

When she said she did not have his money, he punched her 'on the chin near the mouth'. And among his effects turned up a melancholy letter, dated 11 July 1949, from Rose Kerr to Henry Stephens, preluding another appointment.

'John asked me to see you, but I think it better to explain in writing,' Rose began. Her son, she said, had been 'very enthusiastic and good at his work at 3GL'. Then there had been 'friction at the station', culminating in his sacking. 'He will tell you of that,' she wrote. 'He never seems to have fully recovered from that and speaks threateningly of settling with Gray.' Her own tale was more graphic.

> Saturday night was the worst break since being back from Tasmania. He came in from the football, we were having dinner, he immediately questioned where Betty (his friend) had been, and when he knew she had called in at a neighbours [sic] where there is a young man we know, he decided to go and settle him. He behaved so strangely that I said, 'Oh send for the police'. He then pulled the phone off the wall, broke glasses, lots of other things. It took his father, my brother and self all we knew to hold him down, he spoke of killing, but I don't think that meant much. Betty ran away to Mrs Meagher's with whom she stays at night. He said to Betty later 'I've nearly killed my darling mother'.
>
> Betty told me there was a similar occurrence in Tasmania. It always occurs when he has had a drink, though I have seen him on most occasions behave as any gentleman should. It is in the family mostly on his father's side. Wild behaviour after alcohol.

> I need not mention how heartbroken we are. We will do all in our power to help him so whatever you recommend we will carry it out. Even to breaking up our home – and three of us living quietly.
>
> Marriage might be a solution, but he does not seem able to cope with too much worry.
>
> However you are the judge so will await your opinion.

The letter's tone was unmistakably desperate. There remained a great loyalty to her son, depicted as able ('very enthusiastic'), chivalrous ('on most occasions'), contrite ('I've nearly killed my darling mother') and open to help ('John asked me to see you') for a family problem ('mostly on his father's side').

But there was shock, too, at the extent of the episode ('He behaved so strangely'), a dawning awareness of prior episodes ('Betty told me'), and a preparedness to leave to Stephens the course of treatment ('you are the judge'), not excluding institutional care ('even to breaking up our home') – in catatonic Grace Kerr, now at Beechworth Asylum, there was a precedent.

Dr Stephens did not make so bold. Still seeking a physical explanation for Kerr's volatility, he now considered psychomotor epilepsy, but the results of an electroencephalogram at Royal Melbourne Hospital were inconclusive. Neurologist Reg Hooper wrote

Stephens that 'for the most part the record was well within normal limits and showed no paroxysmal disturbance of any kind'; the only 'rather suggestive' wave from the temporal lobe was 'not sufficiently diagnostic for our purpose'.

As with the aetiology of 'near nervous breakdown', this presented an interpretative challenge. Neurological research has now discounted association between electroencephalograms and aggressive behaviours. Under the rubric of today's *Diagnostic and Statistical Manual of Mental Disorders,* Kerr might now be a candidate for what has been called intermittent explosive disorder, a tendency to brief episodes of reactive violence disproportionate to their provocations. But for a definitive diagnosis, deeper evaluation of trauma and stressors would be necessary. And that, in 1949, Kerr was not about to receive – for at this point, his family abandoned Dr Stephens' ministrations. It's not clear in what they invested their hopes. In the five months preceding the death of Beth Williams, the recoverable history of John Bryan Kerr diminished almost to vanishing point.

***

To this stage in my research I had been doing what you do in piecing together a historical record – laying down fragments, making connections and drawing inferences. But hereabouts the story dissolved into a mess of bits from here and there. Kerr seemed to have spent a month or so with 2QN Deniliquin; he may have done some casual work at Myer or Tredways; he ended the year at the State Immigration Authority. But there was nothing to tell how long and in what order.

At some stage his engagement petered out. Betty Smith, as she told the police, moved out of the Meaghers' home into a house with two Tasmanian friends, then returned her ring. Kerr 'did not want me to go', but she 'could no longer go on' – by October, she was back in South Hobart, where she would marry another man three years later.

Rose would later describe her son as 'completely unnerved and incapacitated' by Betty's decision to end the relationship 'without the slightest consideration for his feelings'. But there was nothing else to tell of the effects, let alone directly. When people stop seeking help, as the Kerrs suddenly did with Dr Stephens, is it indicative of a problem ceasing or growing intractable? If previous behaviours are suggestive, do we assume that they are continuing when we're in no position to track them?

The past seldom surrenders secrets lightly or completely. For instance, an invitation survived for Kerr's regular lodge meeting on Saturday, 17 December, at the Masonic Hall, Prahran. Did he go? Did he not? What was he thinking? What was he *feeling?* If the Crown was right, he would commit murder ten days later. Maybe he was on a hair trigger. But maybe he was not.

One morning in Bourkey's office, the phone rang. The caller identified himself as eighty-five-year-old Wally Nash. He had heard that Bourkey knew John Bryan Kerr; that was a coincidence, because so had he. Next day I was in Nash's small living room in Werribee, hearing how the family had looked after Kerr in Warragul in 1946, and hosted him for Christmas in 1949.

Wally was thoroughly impressed with his mate John – 'a very handsome young man, always beautifully dressed, really smart'.

Violent? 'Not that I saw.' Arrogant? 'Not outgoing. But not aloof.'

The Nash family were pleased to see Kerr again, not least because of the evident rekindling of affections between him and Wally's sister Frances.

'They were in love,' Wally insisted. 'He doted on her.'

Wally had been a twenty-year-old country boy at the time. He might have misapprehended or misremembered; equally, there was no reason for him to distort or exaggerate.

As urgently as Kerr had tried to divorce himself from it, I had noted, his identity as a 'murderer' had tended to swamp all others. But on the morning of 27 December 1949, he was not yet a 'murderer' – simply, as Wally recalled, a twenty-four-year-old man on holiday. That day, Kerr rose late, enjoyed a country breakfast, talked to Margot, Frances and Patricia as they did the housework, then went to the Royal Hotel with Wally and his father, Peter, for a few beers and a punt. In mid-afternoon, they saw him off at the station. As the express pulled out, John Bryan Kerr gave them a wave.

5

'MURDER IS THEIR BUSINESS'

Bluey Adam was larger than life. Literally. Newspaper reports of his doings as Australia's longest serving Homicide cop almost always referred to him a 'strapping six-footer', 'six feet tall in his socks' or 'six feet tall and eighteen stone' – that last at the end of his career when he was almost as wide as high.

But when I accessed his police record, *Adam, Frederick John, Reg No.8409* was listed as merely five feet nine and three-quarter inches. His weight on joining the force as a constable in December 1928 had been eleven stone seven ounces – he could be said to have grown into his job. After twenty years' policework, he looked not unlike Hank Quinlan, the cigar-and-suspect-chomping cop played by Orson Welles in *A Touch of Evil,* and had a similar reputation for pursuing a collar.

Having brought John Bryan Kerr to the decisive night of his life, it was necessary to profile his pursuers: Adam and his partner, Cyril Currer. The case put their credibilities on the line too. Were they men who might have lied? As it happened, the former had already thrown down a sort of gauntlet. On his retirement in December 1966, Adam put his name to a series of feature articles in the *Sun,* 'The Bluey Adam Files', written in conjunction with tabloid doyen Tom Prior. He acknowledged his notoriety and defiantly repudiated it.

> Let's get one thing straight, right at the start: I'm not a sadist and I'm not a liar.
>
> I haven't tortured anyone to obtain confessions, and I haven't manufactured any confessions to obtain convictions.
>
> I haven't hit any person I've ever questioned as a policeman, and I haven't distorted or added lies to anything they have ever told me...
>
> Not ever? Over the years a lot of people have said you have...
>
> Of course they have. No matter what a man's attitude is when he's first questioned, when he's in court in a murder charge, he fights for his life with everything he's got.

Yet there was no mistaking how Adam reveled in being 'Victoria's most controversial policeman' in the *Sun,* marching at the head of a cavalcade of crime, from Freddie 'The Frog' Harrison and Norman 'The Chauffeur' Bradshaw to the Barwon River Murderer

Andrew Gordon Kilpatrick and the thirty-stone Sydney gunman 'Big Percy' Neville. On and on he went with tales of adroit detective work and gruelling late-night interrogation ... and *not once* did he mention the case in which his techniques had come in for their closest scrutiny, that of John Bryan Kerr. Most readers would have known it too.

There were other gaps in the stories of Kerr's pursuers – personal gaps. The personnel files of both Adam and *Currer, Cyril, Reg No.8369* listed them as 'Married' in the same impersonal official diction as their height, weight and religion: they were like certifications of personal steadiness rather than actual biographical details. But that implied descendants, and so it proved: Adam's granddaughters, who had fortunately not changed their surnames, and Currer's daughter, whose name popped up in a geneaology chatroom with a reference to the region she lived in, and who could then be plucked from the phone book. So did something of their stories begin to take shape. Adam and Currer, long dead and now all but forgotten, proved to have been men of their times, possessed of very human frailties indeed.

***

Bluey Adam's father, Charles, a British Army staff officer born in Bombay, had settled in Tasmania's wild north-west in 1893 and, as was popular, sunk a mine. 'Adam's Claim' yielded respectable amounts of gold in its twenty years; he also ran a store in a speck on the map called Moina, which served diggings at Bell Mount. There being no school nearby, his seven children by wife Charlotte had to be educated by a governess.

Born 20 December 1906 in Bell Mount, Frederick was a rangy, red-headed youth – thus the nickname. He had an outdoor upbringing, cutting timber, milking cows and mustering cattle, but his private education nourished a lively interest in literature, from Shakespeare and Shelley to Longfellow and Masefield. He revelled in reciting Adam Lindsay Gordon's 'The Sick Stockrider' to colleagues and friends; he later pinned Dorothy Parker's world-weary 'Resume' above his desk at Russell Street headquarters ('Guns aren't lawful/Nooses give/Gas smells awful/You might as well live').

By eighteen he was an ironworker in Melbourne; by twenty he was married; by twenty-two he was a probationary constable; after a year, he passed the retention exam. Somebody, perhaps wife Gladys, began clipping newspapers when his name appeared: chasing shopbreakers, separating pub brawlers, pinching hecklers at a United Australia Party rally, apprehending mother and daughter thieves who had robbed a Chinese grocer (who being a heathen swore his evidence 'by a lighted match'). When commendations came his way, Adam was listed for detective training. And from World War II sprang the case that made his name.

At 7a.m. on 3 May 1942, forty-year-old Ivy McLeod was found strangled in a shop doorway on Beaconsfield Parade next to the Bleak House Hotel. A score of detectives led by Detective Sergeant Sid McGuffie was deployed in the manhunt, but the perpetrator would strike lethally twice more, choking thirty-one-year-old Pauline Thompson and forty-one-year-old Gladys Hosking, before the arrest of Private Eddie Leonski of the 52nd Signal Battalion at Camp Pell in Royal Park, with the help of the identification of an Australian sentry, Private Noel Seymour, and the testimony of an American tentmate, Private Anthony Gallo.

Adam would always revel in the honour of being the first policeman to penetrate Leonski's initial denials. A day after the American's arrest, Adam took down an eerie first-person account of Hosking's murder:

> On Monday night, 18th May 1942, I was drinking beer in the Parkville Hotel. When the pub closed I went to the home of a friend with him and I lay on the bed for about 30 mins. Then I got up and went out. I walked up the street. On the corner I met a girl. It was a small girl. She had a dark coat. She was carrying an umbrella. It was raining and I asked her to let me walk along with her. She said 'Alright.' We walked along the street. We came to her house. I asked her to walk with me and show me the way to the camp. She said 'Alright'. We came along and soon came to a very dark part of the street. She stopped and said

> 'That's the camp over there.' She had a lovely voice. I wanted that voice. She was leaving to go to her house and I did not want her to go. I grabbed her by the throat. I choked her. I choked her. She didn't even make a sound. She was so soft. I thought 'What have I done? I will have to get her away from here.' I then got her to a fence. I pushed her underneath. I got over and pulled her by the armpits underneath it. I carried her a short distance and fell in the mud. She made funny noises, a sort of gurgling sound. I thought I must stop that sound, so I tried to pull her dress over her face. I became frightened and started to run away. Then I met a soldier [Seymour]. He asked me where I was going. I told him Royal Park. He said: 'Where do you live' I said: 'Area 1, near the zoo.' He said: 'Go this way.' I walked a long time and after a while I came to my latrine and walked in and some soldier [Gallo] asked me, 'Where have you been?' I told him I had fallen in the mud. I then went to my tent. I took my muddy clothes off and got into the bed. The next morning I awoke and saw the muddy clothes. It thought to myself, 'My God where have I been? What have I done?' I then got up and washed my muddy clothes.

It was Leonski's first step, via civil investigation and military tribunal, to the gallows at Pentridge. Although Leonski's defence counsel thought him so suggestible he would have signed nearly anything, his confessions were never seriously questioned.

On the contrary, the ebullient American struck up a strange rapport with his police captors; at their last parting, Leonski sang out: 'So long, Bluey!' And in time, especially after McGuffie's retirement in 1948, Adam became something like the keeper of Leonski lore at Russell Street, so much so that when ABC journalist Ivan Chapman began twenty years' research on his book *Leonski: The Brownout Strangler,* it was Adam who was his principal point of contact.

Interested in how an earlier author had gone about work comparable to mine, I retraced some of Chapman's steps in his papers at the Mitchell Library. There were, moreover, marked parallels between the murders of 1942 and 1949: solitary women strangled and beaten in the early hours of the morning for no apparent reason, clothes torn open but not sexually assaulted. And – or was I just imagining it? – those confessions even seemed to echo one another in their dreamlike, dissociated tone. (Leonski: 'We came along and soon came to a very dark part of the street ... She had a lovely voice. I wanted that voice.' Kerr: 'It was dark there. I was in the navy, I like the sound of the sea.' Leonski: 'I choked her ... She made funny noises, a sort of gurgling sound.' Kerr: 'I strangled her. She groaned while I was choking her.')

For that matter, Ivy McLeod's body was found not much more than a block from where Beth Williams' would turn up seven years later – in fact, it was with a trip to Beaconsfield Parade that Adam began escorting Chapman round the Leonski murder sites in September 1963. Except that Chapman, I sensed from his notes, found Adam, whom he described in his book as 'a man who claimed to know just about everything and everyone connected with the Leonski case', a rather unhelpful informant. In an *aide memoire* in his papers, for example, Chapman recalled how Adam persistently discouraged him from trying to find Noel Seymour, who ultimately proved a generous and forthcoming informant, perhaps because the watchful camp guard did not quite fit the story of detective derring-do.

> He said first that Seymour was now living away from Melbourne; then, that he'd heard Seymour had died; then (after I found out Seymour was a wharf-labourer) that the wharfies are a tough lot and would tear me to bits and that my appearance would probably touch off a nationwide dock strike. How wrong 'Bluey' Adam was!

Then there was the widespread rumour that the police had had Leonski in their grasp and let him slip, which if Adam did not originate he certainly spread. Of one version, contained in Alan Dower's 1965 book *Crime Chemist,* he was the indirect narrator – that on 17 May, after the murder of Thompson, Adam and three colleagues repaired for a cleansing ale to the Royal Park Hotel in Queensberry Street, and there encountered Leonski in one of his favoured recreations: drinking stout freely laced with condiments, spouting garrulously, grinning wildly. At that stage, the police had only fragmentary eyewitness descriptions, including from a constable on a beat in Parkville who had seen a baby-faced American serviceman in the vicinity of an attempted strangling.

Adam, wrote Dower, was at once suspicious:

> 'Cheeky peanut. Wonder if he knows we're police? Grinning right at us. Rubbishing us. Got strong hands too. Worth a check right now.'

The four detectives huddled in conference at the bar. They agreed that a constable at a nearby station was the one man who could settle the point.

Alas, when fetched, Dower reported, the constable shook his head. Leonski slipped away to kill again the following evening.

When Adam related the story directly to Tom Prior a year later, it had evolved further. In this version, an anonymous caller to Camp Pell after the murder of McLeod had left the message: 'About the dame who was murdered the other night: look for a guy who walks on his hands.' And while Adam and his comrades were breasting the bar of the Royal Park Hotel, it was *this* party piece in which Leonski engaged.

> There was an American soldier there making quite an exhibition of himself, mixing whisky and beer and aspirins and tomato sauce and drinking it down by the bucket.
>
> He was young and good-looking – 'baby faced' in fact – and then he started walking around the bar on his hands. I said: 'If this is not our bloke, I'll walk to Bourke. Let's pick him up...'
>
> I was itching to ask him a few questions. He was drunk enough to do a little boasting. But I was a low man on the totem pole in those days and I was overruled.

When the killer struck again, Adam said he knew what to do:

> I ran, I didn't walk, to the army camp, looking for an American who had been seen with mud on his uniform ... Sure enough it was our boy from the Royal Park Hotel. Private First Class Eddie Leonski confessed the lot, gave us all the gory details.

And this, Adam continued, was for him a formative experience:

> There's no point in any policeman being wise after the event and blaming himself for the crimes others commit. But the Leonski case taught me something I've never forgotten: to back my own

> judgement and to hell with what other people think.

Two variations – and Adam, it seemed, was the only policeman to remember either.

For in *Leonski: The Brownout Strangler,* Chapman tactfully dismissed the story of the encounter as 'a tale circulating after the war that Private Edward Leonski had attracted police attention in the pub one night' and 'that the potential strength of his fingers had been noted by a detective'. He quoted McGuffie and his colleague William Mooney, later Detective Inspector, as discounting that Leonski was 'even remotely seen as a suspect' until just before his arrest. Reading between the lines, then, Chapman sensed an inclination in Adam to improve on the truth.

There was danger in being too fastidious here. After all, telling shaggy dog tales to journalists was hardly the same as spinning lies around a suspect. But for Adam the Leonski case was clearly foundational – not just a rip-roaring tale, but a vindication of the instinct he would apply to pursuing the murderer of Beth Williams.

***

What was the Victoria Police Force like in 1949? After a convulsive 1923 strike over miserable pay and dictatorial conditions, following which a third of the force had been dismissed, it had been rebuilt along conservative and paternalistic lines. Unmarried men who worked at Russell Street also lived there, the top six storeys of the building's new tower being effectively a cross between a barracks and a dormitory. The building had a gym, a library and a commissariat. Tucked in a block away was the Police Club, a social club whose proprietor was also a Justice of the Peace – useful for getting those late-night warrants signed. Nurses attended Thursday-night dances held in a little auditorium on Latrobe Street.

Policework was very much a working-class occupation, with wages to match. Adam's offsider Cyril Currer was a thoroughly typical example. His first job had been as a boot clicker in a Richmond leather factory, where he met his future wife, Myrtle Mollison, a skiver. They were engaged eighteen years, for there was not the money to do otherwise; they never had a phone connected in their weatherboard home in O'Hea Street, Coburg; they never replaced the family's crank-started Buick, although Currer was proud of owning it outright. One day the car spluttered to halt outside police headquarters so noisily that the heads of his Homicide colleagues appeared at the window.

'Where did you get old bomb?' they chorused.

'Mine's paid for,' Currer retorted. 'Is yours?'

Joining the force and becoming detectives at roughly the same time, Adam and Currer were often partnered: they received commendations for joint murder investigations in November 1944 and

November 1946. But perhaps the touchstone murder of Currer's career occurred, in Adam's absence on holiday, just before the arrest of John Bryan Kerr. The body of septuagenarian SP bookmaker George Kent was washed in blood when police entered his rented room in Dorrit Street, Carlton: he had evidently been tortured for some hours before his death. On him, nonetheless, was found a tobacco tin containing a scrap of paper inscribed with the name 'Valez': the alias of a prostitute, Jean Lee, whom Currer had booked the previous year. Armed with a file list of her known haunts, police arrested her, her lover Robert Clayton and his friend Norman Andrews within a day.

The case became part of the growing legend of the Homicide Squad as a *corps d'elite.* Its squad room, to the right on a mezzanine at the top of a flight of steps from the headquarters' southern entrance, was noted for its unmarked door, in deference to sensitive visitors, and spartan interior of six shared desks, three phones, two cupboards and a tea urn, lit by bare bulbs dangling from the ceiling – Alan Dower likened it to a cave of plotting commandos.

At the time John Bryan Kerr was arrested, the unit's record was 131 homicides for 129 convictions: the only killers never found were of two crime figures, Leslie 'Scotland Yard' Walkerden in September 1945 and James 'Mark Foy' Coates in July 1947, protected by the *omertã* of the underworld. The self-same day Kerr was charged, *The Argus* published a long, glowing tribute ('Murders Are Their Business') to the department's successes:

> This team of experts is known as the Homicide Squad. They specialise in murders, and their remarkable achievement in solving major crimes has placed them right at the top of their class. Their successful detection of murders is unparalleled in any other State or in any country in the world.

Thanks to the 'fine teamwork of the squad', said reporter Robert Purnell, it usually took only hours for suspects to be apprehended for 'questioning'. To pre-empt any imputations of coercion in these interrogations, Purnell described Homicide detectives in terms more befitting of clergymen or counsellors:

> The suspect who expects to be bullied and shouted at during an interview finds that homicide detectives are very human individuals and full of sympathy and understanding. In a quiet, confidential manner the suspect is asked to tabulate his actions in chronological order. He is always given the benefit of any doubt, but as a rule makes a full, clear statement in response to quiet, patient questioning.

Purnell's reference to bullying and shouting was an allusion to the phenomenon of the 'bricking' or 'verballing' of suspects by physical or mental intimidation – about which, even then, innuendo circulated. In June 1945, for example, Homicide had arrested mechanic Thomas Croft for the eleven-year-old murder of an assistant stationmaster at Carnegie. But in court, Croft proceeded to allege a variety of pressures and threats brought to bear at Russell Street: being blindfolded, handcuffed to a chair, threatened with defenestration, and menaced with a mysterious headclamp. The two detectives involved: Bluey Adam and Cyril Currer. Three perplexed juries failed to reach a verdict.

Another of the detectives at Washington Street the night of Kerr's arrest, James McElwaine, had a year earlier been accused of beating up a burglary suspect, who further alleged he had been asked to sign documents he was told were 'duplicates' but which proved to be confessions.

Yet Homicide detectives hardly need to lift a hand in order to intimidate, such was the extent of their powers. Interviews were not recorded, either mechanically or stenographically, affording tremendous discretion to the note-taker. Police Standing Orders officially required that suspects be 'given immediate and ample facilities to communicate with a legal practitioner'; in practice, lawyers were made decidedly unwelcome. Once the door closed on an interrogation, it was every man for himself – and woman too.

If ever a case disproved the truism about honour among thieves, it was *The King v. Clayton, Lee and Andrews.* The perpetrators hastened to betray one another. Clayton first signed a statement that he had been at Dorrit Street but left when his confederates indicated their intention of extracting money from George Kent by violence. Lee responded bitterly – 'I love Bobby. But if he wants it that way he can have it' – with a statement containing extensive admissions. Then, wavering again, she refused to sign it. Meanwhile, having at first denied being with the other two, Andrews responded to Clayton's statement by saying that he *held* Kent while *they* tortured him.

The cumulative impression at the trial was of desperation on the part of the suspects and of coercion by the police. Justice Gavan Duffy's decision to admit the statements at the trio's trial became a ground of appeal when they were found guilty: Maurice Ashkanasy KC argued that, in line with English practice, judges should reject confessions obtained in circumstances not absolutely voluntary. In a majority ruling, Justices Jack Barry and Tom Smith agreed, quashing the conviction on the basis that 'the needs of law enforcement are likely to be best met if the courts insist upon observance of standards of fairness which commend themselves to the average sense of the community from which juries are drawn'.

Henry Winneke KC, the patrician senior counsel to the Solicitor-General, determined that such liberal wooliness could not go unchallenged, and coaxed the Crown into an appeal that would reassert the police's powers. The full bench of the High Court heard four days of complex legal wrangling over section 141 of the *1941 Evidence Act:* 'No confession which is tendered in evidence shall be rejected on the ground that a promise or threat has been held out to a person confessing, unless the judge is of the opinion that the inducement was really calculated to cause an untrue admission of guilt to be made'.

Ashkanasy argued for justice to be seen to be done: 'The view has been informally expressed that the attitude to confessions in Victoria by the jury has given judges considerable concern ... in the long run, if the obtaining of confessions is rigorously covered by rules, the result may well be beneficial to the administration of justice in Victoria'.

Chief Justice Sir John Latham was content with justice simply being done: 'A threat is very often the best way of getting at the truth. It is used with good effect on little boys and on those with the mentality of little boys'. And when the High Court upheld Winneke's appeal on grounds that the trio had exercised their 'free choice to speak or refrain from speaking', the detectives, absolved of 'any undue persistence or importunity', resumed business as usual.

***

Not that Homicide was pure prestige and power. The bare bones appearance of its squad room was not an affectation – there was no money for more than a happy few. On becoming inspector in May 1949, Bill Donelly had begun pestering superiors for additional resources – the squad's in-house forensics expert, Fred Hobley, for example, had to travel to Sydney once a week to use the NSW Police microscope. But the dour Scots Chief Commissioner Alexander Duncan had the purse strings in a virtual sheepshank. And when the squad boasted such a clearance rate, it was difficult to argue how more money might enhance performance.

There existed, too, none of the workplace protections or support mechanisms that those in stressful occupations can rely on today; detectives ate poorly, smoked and drank robustly, and drove on relentlessly, until the job was done and not before, without overtime or bonuses. The week Beth Williams met her fate was unprecedented in Homicide's history, involving no fewer than five murder charges – it would be unusual even now, when there are sixty homicides a year in Victoria, and seldom more than two a week.

By the time her body was found, detectives were already pursuing the Pearson and Stewart murders. Soon after, twenty-six-year-old Maisie Oakley was found on a council tip in West Melbourne, battered with a plank and nearly decapitated by a safety razor. Nearby, Currer found a scrap of paper on which was written 'Oscar Skyers', which proved the name of a Jamaican seaman, then aboard a ship that had just docked in Newcastle, where Currer flew and arrested him the next day.

Then forty-eight-year-old Myrtle Dabscheck was found dead in her armchair in a Hawthorn flat, where Currer smelled in her mouth the faint scent of bitter almonds: her boarder, retired sea captain Walter Cannon, was closely questioned at Russell Street until he admitted his guilt.

In such circumstances, family lives had to be sacrificed, sometimes irrevocably. Adam's already had been. Gladys and son Max remained in the family home in Appleby Crescent, where alcohol and tobacco were forbidden; Adam lived in an East Melbourne boarding hostel, Victoria House, where they were more or less compulsory. The couple never divorced, apparently so as not to jeopardise Gladys's entitlement to a police pension. But Adam became a cop who mingled business and pleasure, and was not in that respect unusual.

In July 1946, for instance, Adam was posted to Geelong when two bodies were pulled from the Barwon. Two tearaway girls in their twenties, clients of the same sly grog merchants, were called in for questioning, one of whom embarked on an affair with Adam lasting the duration of the investigation, causing the other to reflect how it was 'all too easy for police officers to use their position of influence to impress the impressionable and get what they wanted – including women'. That other was Peggy Berman, destined for notoriety as an entrepreneur of illegal abortion. A quarter century later, *her* affair with a policeman, Adam's colleague Jack Ford, would be a *cause célèbre,* ravaging Homicide. In the meantime, Adam's wants were served by a handsome, well-dressed mistress, June.

For Valerie Currer, then four years old, the Christmas–New Year week of 1949 was one of those periods when her father vanished. Growing up, she became accustomed to the sounds of squad cars arriving late at night, meaning Daddy would be gone in the morning, then the clump of boots in the hallway as Daddy walked up and down learning his 'hefosens' (evidence).

She shared with me letters from her parents' courting days. Cyril from Sydney, December 1922: 'I picked up a pair of jazz garters and I will bring them home. They are some style so don't wear them work or if you do you would have to come up in the lift.' Cyril from Russell Street, March 1929: 'By jove darling it is lonely on my duty calls around all the lanes and alleys. I bet you don't miss me darling like I miss you dearest.'

In hindsight, Valerie also wondered how her parents had ever married. He liked a bet with the local SP bookmaker; she strongly disapproved. He sponsored a Catholic family emigrating from Malta; she bristled with hostility towards Archbishop Mannix. He enjoined her to vote for Robert Menzies; privately, she always voted Labor.

And around Valerie's own birth, a family fog swirled. Unbeknownst to her for many years, she became a

Currer at eight weeks of age, at the Department of Social Welfare in Flinders Street, from which Myrtle brought her back in her swaddlings on the number 19 tram. She grew up adoring her father, growingly aware of his weighty responsibilities. Some weekends she would enjoy the privilege of accompanying him into Russell Street. The detectives called her 'Baby'; she called them all 'Uncle', including 'Uncle Bluey'.

Then, on Friday, 13 December 1955, her father did not come home, having suffered a catastrophic stroke at Moonee Ponds CIB. Twenty-seven years' hard living, including the Capstans he smoked even between mouthfuls at dinner, had caught up with him. He spent two years in hospital. Although he lived another seven, he never fully recovered his speech, and had to learn to write left-handed.

Homicide colleagues rallied to the Currers' assistance, organising a raffle that cleared the family's mortgage, and a working bee that refurbished their house. But it was in that time that Valerie began to piece her background together. It turned out that she had been neither adopted nor fostered nor anything at all. No paperwork existed. She had, as it was later put to her, 'slipped through the cracks'.

Not until Valerie was thirty-five was she able to locate her birth mother, a woman called Elizabeth Folks. At first their relations were cordial. She learned that Elizabeth had fallen pregnant aged twenty while working as a waitress in St Kilda, had given birth in a Salvation Army haven, had named her daughter Rhonda, then decided she had no choice but to give the child up – the day Myrtle had come in for collection, Elizabeth had been on the other side of a partition. About Valerie's paternity, however, Elizabeth remained reticent; then, as her mental health deteriorated with the onset of schizophrenia, the stories grew wilder and more contradictory. When at last Valerie was able to apply for a birth certificate, the 'Father's Name' space was teasingly blank.

In the meantime, Valerie had noticed similarities between Cyril and her own children, in physiognomy, physique and personality. It turned out when Myrtle died that members of her family had long nurtured the belief that Valerie was Cyril's own offspring, but refrained from saying anything out of politeness.

'The only difficulty I have with the thought is in coming to terms with the idea that Dad cheated on my Mum,' said Valerie. 'He just wasn't a "Bluey", I'm sure of that. But, then, I am old enough to realise that the most unlikely things do happen.'

Open secrets, agreed silences, lingering sensitivities: with their number one suspect, the detectives had more in common than they knew. Perhaps that was why Bluey Adam had shied from documenting his part in the pursuit of John Bryan Kerr: the sense that some stories are just best left alone.

6

THE BEST DEFENCE

At 9a.m. on Friday, 30 December 1949, Arthur and Grace Williams arrived at Our Lady of Mount Carmel Catholic Church in Middle Park for a requiem mass in memory of their daughter Beth. She was, for a brief instant, the most famous young woman in Melbourne. Her photo had appeared full length on the front of the previous morning's *Argus;* her parents, hatted and coated descending the gangway of a TAA DC-3 at Essendon Airport, had featured on the front of the afternoon's *Herald.* Reporters at the service kept a discreet distance, noting only the attendance of the Williams' three other children, and Martin Crosbie, who had discovered Beth's body.

Yet, even then, Beth Williams was fading from view in favour of the polished, presentable suspect and his family, around whom a vanguard of protectors were forming. At their head was Lee Murray, the first person the Kerrs had contacted, who set aside all other commitments and threw his energies into the rallying of a defence. Kerr had a barrister in thirty-seven-year-old Kevin Anderson, who had appeared at the bail hearing, one of few barristers still in town after Christmas and available for a brief.

The family also quickly retained as solicitor thirty-four-year-old John McDermott Jones.

Neither was experienced with murder, their legal careers interrupted by war service in naval and army intelligence respectively, and they did not appear a natural legal coupling – Anderson tall and courteous, Jones the Labor-voting, boxing-loving son of a family of pub-owners. But there existed a strong bond in their Roman Catholicism. Anderson, nicknamed 'Irish', once declined to act as best man at a Protestant wedding; Jones would never have been asked; between them they would sire thirteen daughters. One of Jones's wartime jobs, moreover, had been rifling the pockets of dead Japanese soldiers in New Guinea for documents of military significance – murder might almost have felt genteel by comparison.

Anderson and Jones were impressed with Kerr's account of the evening with Beth Williams and the subsequent evening with Detectives Adam and Currer. He was fluent, poised. His voice would be an attribute; his grooming too. Not every client testified effectively in their own defence; about Kerr, his lawyers felt no such misgivings. The 'confession' loomed large, but the Crown's failure to convict Thomas Croft, accused in the killing of the assistant stationmaster at Carnegie, had shown an intuition among jurors that not all confessions were equal.

On another interlocutor the following week, Kerr made an altogether different impression. As Pentridge's prison doctor, Raymond Tennyson Allan had seen them come and go, from Arnold Sodeman the child killer to Edward Cornelius the priest killer. As government medical officer for eleven years, he had espoused reliably reactionary attitudes to punishment, including a belief in the efficacy of flogging. As befitted a descendant of the Poet Laureate, he also allowed himself a certain licence in his responsibilities, mixing moral conclusions with medical ones. He left Prisoner 49194 with 'no doubt in my mind ... that he was guilty of the crime of murder':

> An unstable person subject to violent outbursts. Has a strong underlying sexual basis with perverted and sadistic traits. He is an egotist and full of an exaggerated sense of his own importance. Arrogant, defiant, cunning and untruthful when it suits him. I feel he has not been frank in discussing the crime or his sex life. A spoilt child who has lacked firm handling.

Here was a foretaste of a distinctive quality of *The King v. Kerr,* in which observers would review identical evidence and leave like encounters with entirely opposite impressions, mainly in response to the man himself.

Was he fluent or glib? Was he persuasive or histrionic? Was he smooth or oily? His vanguard were unshakeable: Lee Murray and Lynne Hollonds; sort-of sweethearts Frances Nash and June Clyne; family friends Lenna Gundersen and her brother John Amadio, the celebrated flautist; church friends William Murchison, who ran the Pocket Testament League of Australia, and Reverend Alex Stewart, Presbyterian chaplain-general of the Australian Army, who told Kerr, 'Simple truth must ultimately be victorious'.

As if in accord, Kerr began sounding a little like the boy who had once won a scripture prize at Scotch. He read the Bible. He borrowed from his mother *The Healing Knife,* George Sava's inspirational medical memoir, and *The Robe,* the bestselling biblical potboiler by Lloyd Douglas. Confident his circumstances were temporary, he accentuated the positives, in rather grandiose fashion.

'Being here has done me a great deal of good, mentally,' he wrote his parents in the first of many letters from Pentridge:

> It has made me see clearly what constitutes Life. Before, like all young people, possibly, I was apt to place values lightly. Now, with time to readjust my thoughts and outlook, the world has taken on a somewhat different appearance.
>
> This is indeed a great achievement, so my period here has been of great advantage to me. In that regard – it has allowed me to put my 'house in order.' What is in the future is, of course, unknown. But whatever the future holds, this understanding of life and my self, and what I wish to do with it, it cannot be refuted or obliterated.

On the eve of the inquest, he wrote in a similar vein.

> All life is planned, I believe, so why fear? Why not accept life at face value? If you do this, nothing can deeply affect you, because you become dependent on things of higher importance than material things. Then, naturally, follows happiness – not of an ethereal kind, but of reality.

D Division warders, used to more complaisant guests, took an almost instant dislike to Kerr. What kind of prisoner had his parents bring him two grey suits from Myer so he could see which fitted better across his shoulders? What kind of prisoner had his own barber come out to Pentridge to cut his hair? And when the inquest was finally held in the thirty-seat hearing room at the front of the City Morgue on 20 February, observers were struck by the insouciance of the figure at its centre, occasionally craning his neck to peep at maps and study photos but otherwise silent.

Truth thought him 'least of all concerned' as he 'lolled behind his solicitor'. His only words on the day, spoken when coroner James Burke SM committed him to stand trial having 'willfully, feloniously and with malice aforethought killed the said Elizabeth Maureen Williams', echoed variously: 'I am not guilty and have nothing to say'.

His supporters murmured assent. To reporters, Adam held up the end of his tie and yanked it tight.

***

The bar in Melbourne in 1950 was a small and collegial world, tightly bound by tradition and testosterone. At Selborne Chambers, where Anderson would host Jones and Murray, Room 30 still belonged to newly elected Prime Minister Robert Menzies, and a position as a reader had just been granted to the bar's only woman, Joan Rosanove, twenty-six years after her first application. Occupants all had open fireplaces, a sizeable minority still scorned telephones, and a musty odour from the building's cellar competed with the reek of cigarettes. These were days when 'learned friend' and 'brother judge' were genuine endearments, days when older lawyers might end the week having a singalong around the piano at the Savage Club in Bank Place, days when younger lawyers joined the Constitutional Club in Temple Court to take advantage of the 2/- cafeteria lunch, days when Rob Monahan KC was Melbourne's premier murder silk.

Nobody who knew Robert Vincent Monahan ever called him that. He was always Rob – jaunty and approachable but robust and precise. Of all the *dramatis personae* of *The King v. Kerr,* the coreligionist whom Anderson and Jones chose to lead them had the poorest background. The 1890s drought desiccated Monahan's west Victorian farming family. Achievement was young Rob's way out of ignominy. He excelled at St Patrick's in Ballarat, was among the first intake at Melbourne's Newman College in April 1918, and signed the bar roll five years later. In the village of

Melbourne legal affairs, his attributes soon stood out: ease with complexity, elegance of expression and an eidetic memory capable of retaining long numbers, exact pages and even whole conversations.

Funnily enough, he was correspondingly bad at remembering faces. In his first big trial in 1927, a banknote forgery case, he spent a week examining a bank manager in granular detail, then failed to recognise him outside the courtroom. But that case also evinced Monahan's self-possession under strain. His father dropped dead on the tram after watching the last hearing day, a Friday. Monahan organised for the return of the body to Echuca on the Saturday, its burial on the Sunday, then was back in time to address the jury on Monday.

An enthusiastic patron of the theatre and the races, Monahan made friends readily. In 1931, he was invited by Eugene Gorman KC to join a group of top-flight criminal barristers in Equity Chambers, their new purpose-built six-storey premises, and here obtained his first murder brief: defending a young labourer, Albert McKenzie, accused of murdering an old trapper, Daniel Robinson, in a hut at Tolmie, near Mansfield, in June 1934. The Crown case appeared overwhelming until Monahan had McKenzie demonstrate on the courtroom's coir matting floor how he had fought Robinson for possession of the shotgun which then went off accidentally – the jury settled for a manslaughter verdict. And Monahan found that murder rather suited him. The emotional man whose eyes would prickle at a sentimental song became in court a cool logician. The lover of the law could challenge an aspect of it he deplored: the death penalty.

Monahan was not a campaigner or a crusader. Capital punishment existed; he sought simply to save from it as many lives as possible. Once only in more than a hundred trials did he fail, and he never forgot it. In October 1938, Tommy Johnson, a forty-year-old with a history of sudden unaccountable episodes of violence from an extensive undiagnosed brain injury, was disturbed by hammering from overhead while reading the form guide in a doss house in Dunnolly. Johnson calmly took an axe, walked upstairs and killed seventy-three-year-old Robert Gray; he then killed sixty-year-old Charles Bunney, who happened to walk in on them. Johnson dragged the bodies into a room and locked the door, later readmitting himself in order to feed the doss-house cat that slept there. Then, growingly aware of having done something wrong, he thumbed a ride to Dandenong police station and confessed. Monahan took on the hopeless case with a vigorous insanity defence, Johnson making a poignant statement from the dock:

> I don't know what came over me. These men were my friends. I would never injure them in any way. It's just like a bad dream to me now, but it's coming back bit by bit. When I arrived in Dandenong, I had only confused ideas. Some things I said to the police must have been wrong. I had no intention nor idea of robbery. I'm sorry

> for the death of these two old chaps. I leave it in your hands. That is all.

The jury preferred to believe Tennyson Allan, who deemed Johnson abnormal but 'not an imbecile', and the death sentence was carried out despite the petitions of a ragtag group led by the Trades Hall Council. Though only five-and-a-half years old, Monahan's second son John could sense something amiss around the time. On the day Johnson was hanged, the Monahans were moving from Heidelberg to Kew, but the atmosphere was funereal: 'It was as if a pall had descended on the house'. His father would often repeat Johnson's last, uncomprehending words to his executioners, 'Just let me finish this fag.'

Because a barrister was then essentially obliged to accept any case that came his way, Monahan defended an astonishing variety of clients on murder charges: a cranky woolclasser who took a swing at a cook while drunk; a middle-class woman who had tried to help her WAAF sister obtain an abortion which then went wrong; a fifteen-year-old who shot an abusive father in defence of his mother; a seventeen-year-old who axed his dyspeptic mother after a day of rowing; an asbestos worker who mortally wounded his infant daughter and mother-in-law in a boarding house altercation but who Monahan got off on manslaughter; a vagrant woman who stifled a newborn infant but whose charge Monahan had knocked down to concealment of birth. Most notorious was Harold

Nugent, deemed by police 'a reckless and dangerous criminal who may resort to firearms if cornered', whom Monahan represented successfully on the charge of shooting a nineteen-year-old waitress, Pearl Oliver, as she fled a Fitzroy boarding house in July 1943. To Equity Chambers thereafter came a more or less constant stream of underworld malefactors seeking his services: Nugent's *confrère* Jack Twist, the story went, plonked a pistol on Monahan's desk in order to stress his sincerity.

Monahan never lost his versatility. He maintained a big workers' compensation practice. He represented Walter Lindrum in the billiards hero's divorce. He appeared alongside his friend Jack Barry KC at the fabled Pyjama Girl inquest, acting for Jeanette Routledge, who alleged that the girl found dead in a culvert in Albury in 1934 had been her daughter Philomena Morgan. Fourteen years later he appeared before the newly enrobed Justice Barry in the world famous 'Whose Baby?' case, representing a woman who claimed that her daughter had been switched with that of another woman shortly after their near-simultaneous births in Kyneton Hospital.

Yet murder remained Monahan's forte, his specialty the innovative defence. In November 1944, two young toughs hailed a Silver Top taxi with a vague plan to ambush the driver Eric Nicholls, then 'do him over' in the bush. Ron Eastwood, in the front seat, brandished a Colt.32; Roy Pugh, in the back seat with a girlfriend, told him to put it away. Eastwood and Pugh clashed; Pugh ended up with his head blown off.

As the cab slowed, the girl managed to open the door and get out. When found abandoned the next day in Doncaster, the vehicle contained the dead bodies of Pugh *and* Nicholls, the latter plugged with five bullets. On a double murder charge, Eastwood was strongly favoured to become the first man hanged in Victoria since Leonski. Monahan turned the attention on the Colt, leading intricate mechanical evidence from a gunsmith about the propensity of revolvers to discharge when knocked; in particular, he explained, certain handguns could continue firing automatically with the recoil acting as a trigger. In his summing up, he then presented Eastwood as *the victim* of a gun-crazy epoch:

> Just look calmly at the age in which we live. Compare it to the stone age, followed by the iron age, the machine age, up to the present age. Can anyone be blamed for describing this as the firearm age? Today's nations are leaping at one another's throats. When the war broke out the accused was fourteen. Think of your children during the process of this war. Why, you cannot buy a toy for them which has not something to do with killing and destruction. In Collingwood you may think that no one has grown up without a gun in their hand.

A judge once described a Monahan trial as beginning with twelve jurors and ending with thirteen, Monahan having somehow insinuated himself into their company. This must have been one of those augmented juries, for they returned a verdict of manslaughter.

Monahan's next client was a twenty-three-year-old labourer, Leo Cartledge, charged with murdering a black American seaman, Ray Combs, fished from the Yarra. Monahan constructed an elaborate four-stage narrative. Step one: Cartledge offered Combs hospitality in his home and was repaid with flirtatious and vulgar behaviour towards his wife. Step two: when Cartledge called Combs a 'dirty pig', the visitor 'became incensed and the inferiority complex of the negro race swayed up within him'. Step three: during a violent altercation, Combs fell onto glass on the floor from a broken beer bottle, and lapsed into unconsciousness. Step four: terrified that he had a dead body on his hands, Cartledge rolled Combs into the river near Fairfield.

This time, Monahan seized on postmortem evidence of salt in the left ventricle of Combs' heart, which implied that the victim had been alive when immersed; in a bravura cross-examination, Monahan outpathologised the pathologists. Cartledge even walked on a charge under the *Cemeteries Act* of disposing of a body without the coroner's knowledge.

The sides in *The King v. Kerr,* then, knew each other well – lately better than that. Through the second half of 1949, Monahan had been involved in an arbitration at Equity Chambers between two Jewish families, the Ravdells and the Gelbarts, related by marriage and estranged by business. When Monahan's client, the Ravdells, came out ahead, his wife began receiving anonymous telephone threats: 'Your husband has done me a terrible injustice', 'Your husband is not coming home tonight', 'You can tell your husband the game is on for young and old'.

Suspicion fell naturally on the Gelbarts, especially when the Ravdell patriarch Solomon was kidnapped, turning up several days later on a roadside. But nothing could be proven, not even when, on the evening of 28 October, a jam-tin bomb detonated in Monahan's front yard in Kew, shattering all the house's front windows. Describing the bombing as 'a terror campaign that is entirely foreign to anything hitherto experienced in Victorian crime history', Homicide chief Donelly assigned the investigation to his two best men – senior detectives Adam and Currer. Six months later, Monahan would be setting out to thwart them.

***

The King v. Kerr opened on 17 April 1950 in Court 4 of Melbourne's Supreme Court complex, less opulent than the ceremonial Court 1, but still with an ornate Victorian bench and canopy in dark polished cedar, soaring high ceilings and a balustrade cast-iron balcony in the public gallery. And it was on the gallery, *Truth* noted, that gazes were first trained, for it was packed to the rafters:

> The public gallery seats high above the court room were occupied long before the days' hearing and the overflow filled the area usually reserved for witnesses and waiting jurymen. Fashionably dressed men and women, mingling with thrill seekers and court habitués intently watched the unfolding drama with leading radio personalities and groups of law students were drawn to the scene in unusually large number.

Hundreds more outside blocked Lonsdale Street, hoping for a glimpse of John Bryan Kerr arriving in the police van. He lived up to his billing.

'Place John Bryan Kerr at the bar,' intoned Justice Norman O'Bryan's associate, and the defendant ascended to the dock from subterranean holding cells looking like a matinee idol: single-breasted navy blue suit, white shirt, dark tie, gleaming black shoes.

The defence was conspicuous: Monahan, Anderson and Jones were joined at the bar table by Lee Murray; behind them sat Donald and Rose Kerr with Reverend Alex Stewart and William Murchison.

The prosecution was stern: as he commenced his opening address, Henry Winneke, smart as paint in a traditional black jacket and striped trousers, gave the appearance of rather relishing it all. The son of a judge, forty-one-year-old Winneke KC OBE was a legal prodigy. The previous year, he had declined the job of running the new Australian Security Intelligence Organization on grounds he 'couldn't see myself getting round in a false beard', and accepted instead the new position of senior counsel to the attorney-general, rebuilding a Crown Law Department denuded of staff and dammed with cases – courts were sitting Saturdays in an effort to clear the residue of matters, some more than two years old.

Time was also of the essence in *The King v. Kerr,* Winneke now explained to the jury. The defendant and Beth Williams had been dropped off in Middle Park between 12.30a.m. and 1a.m. Kerr claimed to have been with her another hour; by 2a.m. at the very latest, they would hear, she was dead. The window of opportunity was too tight for anyone else to have squeezed through.

Monahan strove to open the window wider. With characteristic facility, he chipped away at Keith Bowden's certainty about the time. Hadn't the surgeon to the coroner first advised police that the murder was between 10p.m. and midnight? Mightn't he have revised his judgement to incorporate further information? Didn't his dogmatism about the 2a.m. deadline belie the differences medical science acknowledged between bodies after death? He threw textbook citations at Bowden about rates of abdominal heat loss and rigor mortis differing from the surgeon's expressed views, including from a volume he revealed Bowden to have edited – a little *coup de théâtre.*

More ambitiously still, but in the spirit of his 1945 defence of Leo Cartledge, he worked away at salt found in the fluid of the lung, floating the possibility that Crosbie and Constable Nelson had been right, and that drowning rather than asphyxia had been the final cause of death – an invitation to the jury to consider a manslaughter verdict.

O'Bryan could not be persuaded to admit the Kerr confession, on grounds Kerr had not adopted it as his own by signature, but Adam was permitted to refer to it to 'refresh his memory'. For all his rough edges, Adam in the witness box was stolid and imperturbable; the phlegmatic Currer likewise. Yet Monahan found weak points just the same. The police had to concede that the clothes they said Kerr had surrendered at Washington Street were actually those he wore to Russell Street, for which Adam blamed a hazy recollection. They had also to concede giving Jack Jones an incomplete copy of the confession, *sans* the postscript about Kerr's mooting an insanity plea, for which Adam blamed an overworked typist. A highly improbable confession in all respects, argued the defence counsel.

> Monahan: There are only 585 words in the statement and you took nearly one and a half hours to write it. That's about seven words a minute.
>
> Adam: Kerr was silent for minutes on end. Sometimes for seven and eight minutes.

Monahan: He was never helped along with questions during those awful silences?

Adam: No.

Monahan then asked the jury to consider the words themselves: would a well-spoken alumnus of Scotch College have perpetrated such solecisms as 'I always kiss women on their privates with whom I have been with' and 'there was bright lights there, I knew that I had had a neurasthenia'?

Monahan: What do you think a neurasthenia is, Mr Adam?

Adam: Some mental aberration.

Monahan: Is that so?

Adam: Yes.

A procession of witnesses shared their recollections: furtive Grinsted, callow Stevens, sultry Barbara Robertson, stiff Penno and Wood, awkward Stewart Patrick. The emotion of the occasion overcame brittle Pat Street ('wearing a powder-blue top coat and blue hat with feathers,' noted *The Herald).* She conceded that their landlady had warned about coming up the side lane late at night. She conceded that on coming back from her evening and finding the door of their room ajar that she had entertained the possibility of

Beth having returned and gone out. She was clearly haunted by her experience that Tuesday evening.

> Monahan: Were you tired when you got home?
>
> Street: I don't know. I can't think. I know I didn't sleep until 4a.m. I had nightmares at the time.
>
> Monahan: What was causing them?
>
> Street: I don't know but I think I might have an idea now.
>
> Monahan: What do you mean?
>
> Street: Well it seems that Beth was having quite a struggle at the time. I see some sort of mental telepathy...

Monahan worsened her nightmares. Drawing on Grinsted's evidence about the No Hopers Club where the girls had twice attended parties, Kerr's counsel began making an issue of the behaviours of Beth Williams – a girl running risks, including by implication the violence of a jealous lover, by attending dances alone and fraternising with sailors.

> Street: Did she?
>
> Monahan: You knew.
>
> Street: I did not.

Monahan: She was making a practice of going out with sailors.

'She was not,' said Street, bursting into tears. 'Have you got to rub it in all the time?'

A voice interjected, Patricia's mother: 'She has been under treatment ever since the trouble occurred'.

But when O'Bryan asked if she would like to stand down, she dried her eyes, straightened her back and replied, 'We might as well get it over with'.

John Kerr would have agreed. On the fourth morning, *The Argus* reported, the defendant exhibited his first signs of strain: 'His eyes blinked continually and his eyebrows twitched. He was pale and appeared tired.'

But he rose to the occasion. There was an expectant rustle when Monahan opened his defence after lunch, enjoining the jury to 'keep your minds open now and listen to John Bryan Kerr', and they assuredly did. Standing like a naval rating with feet apart and hands clasped behind his back, he gave evidence lucidly and quickly – sometimes too quickly for the shorthand writers. On the key questions he was clear.

Monahan: Did you kill Miss Elizabeth Maureen Williams?

Kerr: I did not, sir!

Monahan: Do you know anything of the circumstances of her death?

Kerr: No, sir!

Monahan: When you last saw her where was she?

Kerr: She left me at the corner of the lane and directed me to follow the tramline around until I got to South Melbourne Football Ground.

When Kerr slipped into his detailed and mellifluent account of the evening, Winneke was unimpressed: the performance was just a little *too* polished, *too* facile.

'As a radio person, do you have to remember scripts?' he asked pointedly during cross-examination. 'Have you a good memory?'

Kerr: I don't know, sir. I'm endeavouring to tell the truth.

Winneke: You've given a great account of your conversation with the police. Do you put this forward as accurate?

Kerr: Yes, I put it forward as accurate in most details. I would say the statements I have made are a substantially correct account of what took place.

Winneke: When you had the conversation with police, were you cautioned?

Kerr: No, those words were never used to me.

Winneke: Were any methods used which gave you fears of being hit?

Kerr: The only time I had any fear was when I told Detective Adam to call me 'Mr Kerr'.

Winneke: You were never in any physical fear?

Kerr: No.

Winneke: No effort was made to force you to sign any statement?

Kerr: I was never asked to sign any statement.

Winneke: How long was Mr Adam writing down your statement?

Kerr: I don't know but he wrote down about three quarters of a page.

Winneke: Is that all?

Kerr: That's all the writing he did in my presence.

The trial was now racing away. After the three-and-a-half days of Crown evidence, the defence was done in three hours, only the defendant testifying.

With a man's life at stake, it seemed almost too swift, too cursory. Word was getting around. This might be the last chance to see a 'murderer'. The public galleries were full an hour before Friday's proceedings, set aside for closing addresses. Counsel rose to the occasion. Monahan moved between dramatic moods. At times he was thunderous, passionate; at others he would lower his voice almost to a whisper, so that the sudden punch of his clenched fist would echo round the courtroom.

Monahan inveighed against the police for exploring no alternative explanations, for closing their minds the instant they knew of Kerr: 'They say, "That is enough. We have got him." And that is their mental approach from then on'.

Then he worked his way through the shifts and contradictions of all the witnesses – times, conversations, departures from remarks at the inquest including differing views of what Beth Williams had been wearing. From the courtroom at one stage came a wail from Pat Street, 'What was I supposed to say? What was wrong about it?'

Her mother shushed her and the crier shushed the galleries, 'Silence in the court'.

About the vigour of his approach, Monahan remained unabashed. 'I make no apologies to anyone I hit in this case. I will fight for this man, and I will fight this case as hard as it can be fought.'

Winneke implicitly chided Monahan for his characterisation of Beth Williams: 'Kerr himself says she was a decent kind of girl. I ask you to disregard any insinuations which have been made against her in this courtroom'. Nor, he continued, should Monahan's critique of the investigation stand unchallenged: 'The police force is not on trial today. It is the man sitting in the dock – John Bryan Kerr.'

Winneke was once likened to a movie star with an 'on-set' persona, a cross between Ronald Colman and Gregory Peck. His hawkish features tightened, his 'Oxford' accent grew more pronounced, his wit more acerbic. Now he assailed the defence's alternative explanation of death, 'Do you think it was the gentle lapping of the bayside waves that broke the girl's throat?' Once the jury was satisfied Williams was killed, he said, the defence broke down, because only Kerr had had the opportunity.

Saturday morning there was a transport strike in Melbourne; Saturday afternoon was round one of the football season. Yet taxis were dropping spectators outside the Supreme Court from 7.30a.m., well-dressed women and teenage girls conspicuous among them, while reporters abounded, despite there being no newspapers the following day. Focus was on the Kerr contingent, dressed as though for church, bearing homemade sandwiches for John, and cracking hardy.

'I'll stick with him to the end,' said Lee Murray proudly.

Justice O'Bryan was the kind of man the Kerrs might well have made a friend of under other circumstances. His home, Kinkora, was a block from Afton; bombed, gassed and wounded in World War I, he kept a photograph of an old Scotch Collegian, Sir John Monash, on his study mantelpiece; his son had rowed in the winning Head of the River crew the year before Kerr's calling of the race. His charge was studiously even-handed but frank: it would be a matter for jurors of whom they preferred to believe.

> If you accept the evidence of Dr Bowden that she was killed somewhere about 2a.m., you have the accused in her company very shortly before her death. That evidence would quite probably raise in your minds a great deal of suspicion about the accused. But if there were not other evidence, that would not be sufficient to convict him of murder ... The proof has to come from the police evidence ... If you are not convinced that the police told you the true story the accused is entitled to be acquitted.

Monahan had only one complaint: he asked O'Bryan to remind jurors that although blood had been found under the victim's fingernail, his client bore not a scratch. The jury finally retired at 11.30a.m. Spectators milled about, roving the building's long, cold corridors. Men read newspapers; elderly woman knitted and darned; John Kerr in his holding cell apparently requested chocolate, but settled for cigarettes instead. Football scores wafted in. Near where Kerr had walked that fateful December night, Murray's Collingwood were losing to South Melbourne;

at Arden Street, Kerr's Richmond were succumbing to North Melbourne.

Not until 5p.m. did the halls fill with shouts, as the jury returned. Their mien was weary: the foreman revealed they had been unable to reach a verdict, unanimity being necessary for both conviction and acquittal in capital crimes. O'Bryan asked if there was a likelihood of the deadlock breaking.

'I am quite sure that would be impossible,' the foreman replied.

Kerr gave a wan smile as O'Bryan remanded him for retrial, sending him back down the steps into the darkness.

***

Both sides could convince themselves they had had a good result. Monahan had prevented Kerr's conviction; Winneke had prevented Kerr's acquittal. They settled in for a war of attrition.

Pentridge's privations were taking a toll on Kerr. His fair complexion had turned sallow. He had lost 7 kilos. Soon after returning to D Division, he traded blows with another remand prisoner, a twenty-seven-year-old labourer, Edward Anderson, accused of bashing a wharfie to death. But his father described John to the press as 'standing up to it like a Briton', and in his correspondence the young man sounded almost beatific:

> I am preparing my mind and self for this second ordeal, through which it is inevitable that I must pass. Still, I find nothing as I search this life of which I should be afraid. My views on this subject are well known to you, so nothing further need be stated. Through every day I become more assured and conversant with the meaning of life, as I told you once before. At least this is one good thing that has arisen from this curious form of being. It's very true that if one searches hard enough, or tries hard enough, he can overcome almost insurmountable odds – not only overcome, but turn them to his advantage and experience.

In truth, his parents were probably finding it harder still. To visit their son, they had to walk through D Division beneath the scaffold – the same apparatus that had earlier done duty at the Old Melbourne Gaol, including an imported beam reputedly from the Tyburn Tree itself. At their fifteen-minute meetings, they were forbidden from discussing the case, and often drowned out by the din of prison life: the clank of heavy locks, the crash of cell doors, the clump of boots on pressed metal stairs and flagstone floors.

The Kerrs were sustained by the relentless positivity of Lee Murray, to whom Monahan had paid tribute during the first trial when the prosecution objected to his sitting with the defence. 'Your honour,' said Monahan, 'Mr Murray *is* the defence.' And Murray now received some potentially vital information, when he answered a caller, Albert Sievers – the waterside worker who had been in the vicinity of the crime scene at about 2.30a.m. on 29 December, and seen a man emerge, apparently loath to be recognised. Sievers explained to Murray how he had passed this on to the police, then heard no more.

Murray was exultant: it substantiated Monahan's argument that the police had lost interest in more than a one-dimensional investigation once they heard about Kerr. Both Sievers and his wife agreed to testify.

The defence also sensed where the prosecution would go next, from a brief exchange during Kerr's cross-examination that went unreported in the press but was replete with meaning.

> Winneke: Has there ever been an occasion when a policeman has come to your home?
>
> Kerr: No.
>
> Winneke: What about early in the war? Didn't a policeman come to your home and struggle with you?
>
> Kerr: Oh yes. I had got home and I was drunk, but I didn't struggle with the policeman.
>
> Winneke: Had you caused a great deal of breaking round the house?

Kerr: No, I had caused a good deal of disturbance to my father. The particular policeman was a friend of my father. He called the policeman because he thought he might be able to reason with me.

Winneke: Will you swear you didn't do damage to the house or disturb any furniture?

Kerr: Yes I will swear it. You are trying to make out that I am a lunatic and I object.

And that was what Winneke *was* inferring, sort of. His informant was Dr Henry Stephens, whom police had interviewed as early as 3 January in preparing to oppose a defence bail application. What the psychiatrist reported about Kerr's 'episodes of rage and confusion' arising on 'trivial provocation' struck Winneke as 'strong evidence of the authenticity' of the confession, and he had invited the doctor to testify. Stephens had demurred on grounds of professional privilege.

Winneke, by alluding to the 1944 incident to which Constable Tom Doig was called, had therefore offered just the briefest glimmer of their acquaintance. But after the first trial, Winneke received a call: Stephens was now prepared to step forward. Winneke had already resolved not to prosecute in the second trial, lest it appear he was pursuing a personal vendetta against Kerr. But he briefed his colleague Maurice Cussen on the emerging profile of their defendant. Police by now had also delved into Kerr's Tasmanian troubles, interviewing Winifred Metz, Betty Smith and Eric McRae; they had even located Studley Ruxton, now in Adelaide. The challenge for Cussen would be obtaining admission for evidence so obviously prejudicial, in that it went to the defendant's propensity to violent acts generally rather than his guilt of one violent act specifically.

Cussen gave a hint of what was to come in his opening address on 26 May: his reference to Kerr's 'perverted practices' alluded to the Smith statement, with its uncomfortable references to her fiancée being 'not like a normal person should be'. There was a shocked murmuring in the public galleries as Cussen spelled out the Crown's contention that Beth Williams had been 'strangled by Kerr in a fit of rage when she would not allow him to have some sort of perverted sexual relations with her'. How disappointing to miss such racy stuff for those women still queueing on the stairs for a seat, although they had the consolation of their picture in the afternoon's *Herald.* For the public's fascination with the trial showed no signs of abating. If anything, it was intensifying.

7

A CITY TRANSFIXED

No book was written or movie made about the murder of Beth Williams. It prompted no artwork the way Eddie Leonski's misdeeds inspired Albert Tucker, the Gun Alley case captivated Charles Blackman, or the Bogle–Chandler mystery engaged Gary Shead; it compelled no verse by Jordie Albiston or music by Ed Kuepper like the fate of Jean Lee. Yet there is no disputing its status as the crime of *a* moment, as Rob Monahan KC complained bitterly when the Crown foreshadowed its tougher approach in the second trial.

'There is not a tittle of truth in vicious, wicked and sinister rumours which are flying around Melbourne that this unhappy girl was the victim of violence brought about by sexual aberrations,' he told the jury. 'This trial has received the full blare of publicity. It has received more prominence than any other murder case in living memory!'

And living memory, I learned round and about my enquiries, had kept it curiously preserved ever since. Former premier John Cain, then a law student, could reel off the names of the counsel. Historian Michael Cannon, then a young general reporter on *The Age* whose well-to-do family lived the other side of Toorak

Road, recalled the pang of identification he felt looking at Kerr in the witness box: 'How did this fresh-faced good-looking young fellow with a good job and decent parents come to be involved in a murder?' Professor Geoffrey Blainey remembered that Beth Williams was buried in Werribee Cemetery, his wife Ann that a friend of hers at the time called Kerr was inevitably nicknamed 'John Bryan'. Radio personality Philip Brady, another Lee Murray disciple, still periodically tends the legend on his 3AW evening show by referring to his co-host Bruce Mansfield as actually John Bryan Kerr in disguise.

People at the time had not known what to think. Novelist Gerald Murnane, then a schoolboy, pored over the daily reports of the court fortunes of the 'radio announcer from Washington Street, Toorak' in his parents' copy of *The Argus.* 'One day I'd be sure he was guilty and the next be just as sure to the contrary.'

Two aspiring lawyers, Brian McCarthy and Bill Lennon, were sure they knew. One day they caught Kerr's eye in the dock, and he gave them an icy half-smile. That look! They agreed: he *had* to be a killer. But their friend Frank Hulls was so captivated by Rob Monahan that he made a promise, 'If I have a son, I will name him Rob'. Not Robert: Rob, just like the man himself. By the end of the century that offspring was Victoria's attorney-general.

Melburnians in 1950 liked to regard theirs as a law-abiding city, partly as a point of distinction from Sydney – *The Argus* ascribed the lower crime rate to the settlement of disputes 'by comparatively peaceful means, using fists, knuckle dusters and cordial bottles rather than the decisive and noisy firearm'. Yet for all the straightness of its lacing, Melbourne had always rejoiced in the devilment of crime. When the young law clerk Fergus Hume asked a local bookseller in the mid-1880s 'what style of books he sold most of', he was pointed to the works of the Frenchman Émile Gaboriau, creator of the hero detective Monsieur Lecoq. Hume's determination to write 'a book of the same class' turned into the first worldwide Australian literary hit, *The Mystery of a Hansom Cab,* with more than 100,000 copies sold in Australia, and more than a million internationally.

The Kerr trials sixty-four years later actually struck very similar chords to Hume's tale of family secrets and moonlit trysts. John Bryan Kerr had the smooth surface and social connections of Hume's accused murderer Brian Fitzgerald. Lee Murray reprised the role of Fitzgerald's public champion Felix Rolleston ('Gad, I wouldn't mind being a detective myself'); Rob Monahan emulated Fitzgerald's magnificent counsel Calton ('whose brilliant piece of oratory is still remembered and spoken of admiringly in the purlieus of Temple Court and Chancery Lane').

Part of Hume's success lay in his portrayal of the sensation around the mystery: descriptions of courtrooms thronged by 'fashionable Melbourne of both sexes', vigorous debates around Fitzgerald's 'popular character' and 'good looks', 'quotations' from the popular press. In *The Mystery of a Hansom Cab,* Hume had *The Herald* report Fitzgerald's arrest with a blaring three-decker headline:

HANSOM CAB TRAGEDY
Arrest of the Supposed Murderer
Startling Revelations in 'High life'

In the mystery of the handsome male, as it were, *The Herald* reported John Bryan Kerr's arrest in a quaintly similar three-decker:

'CERTAIN ADMISSIONS' IN BEACH CRIME, COURT TOLD
Radio Announcer Charged with Murder
'Went to Party'

The difference was that by 1950, murder had been democratised and commodified by Hume's heirs. The description of death by violence had become a consumer good, available in multiple formats and appealing to wide audiences. It was a vintage period for crime on the screen, especially with dark urban backdrops: *The Big Clock, The Naked City, Dark City, The Sleeping City, Night Has a Thousand Eyes, They Live By Night, Union Station.* Airwaves were crowded with 'The Adventures of Ellery Queen', 'Perry Mason Detects', 'Professor Burnside Investigates', suave Richard Rollison of 'Introducing the Toff' and slick

Larry Kent of 'I Hate Crime'; Lee Murray had himself had a go during World War II, producing 'Ginger, Detective', in which the ventriloquist's doll acted as assistant to crime-fighting Professor Pawnby.

In Melbourne, crime fiction was reviewed weekly by the respected A.R. McElwain in *The Herald* and 'Sweeney Todd' in *The Argus.* The vast bulk of titles were imported, chiefly from Britain: Agatha Christie, Margery Allingham, John Creasey, Dorothy L. Sayers, Ngaio Marsh (a thoroughly Anglicised New Zealander). But Australians and Australian settings were respectably represented by the likes of Arthur Upfield, Jon Cleary, Margot Neville and June Wright. The last, an Ashburton housewife who handwrote her work at the kitchen table, had launched her 1948 debut *Murder in the Telephone Exchange* at an almost unheard-of venture – a literary lunch, held at the Oriental Hotel. Then there was the world of Australian pulps, fostered by a wartime embargo on American titles and further encouraged by the end of paper rationing, their titles designed to arrest browsing eyeballs: *Death is a Habit, Sleep is Death, Wake Up and Die, The Dead Are Blind, The Lady's Eyes Were Green, Blackmarket Brains, Murder Makes Headlines, Stop Press: Murder!*

A taste for the thrills of crime, then, was now something that Premier Tom Hollway, who liked to 'go to bed with a good murder', could share with the notorious standover man Les Walkerden, who acquired his nickname 'Scotland Yard' from a penchant for the aforementioned pulp thrillers. *The King v. Kerr* paralleled *The Mystery of the Hansom Cab* in being the talk of 'Melbourne clubs and Toorak drawing rooms' – copies of Kerr's confession did indeed circulate in Melbourne clubs, and supportive petitions were signed in leafy suburbs and by church congregations. But the crowds on hearing days were not purely Hume's 'fashionable Melbourne'. Teenage girls were heavily represented within and without: when the second trial began, a crowd of more than a hundred stood in teeming rain for more than an hour outside the court to get a glimpse of Kerr leaving in the prison van manacled to another prisoner; nurses at St Vincent's Hospital ran a book on the trial's outcome. Well-dressed middle-class women were also conspicuous, although Rob Monahan's wife did her best not to be, affecting Garbo-esque reticence in scarf and dark glasses. *The Sun* described two elderly men who sat at the improvised press table reading detective novels, while *Truth* profiled a murder purist – sixty-two-year-old Fairfield Hospital Superintendent Sam Baxter, who purported to have attended every Melbourne murder trial since Gun Alley.

> 'It isn't just curiosity. I like to see the way a case is presented – particularly the cross-examination.'
>
> With real life cases his interests ends. We asked him whether because he was so interested in murder, he ever read mystery fiction.
>
> 'Thrillers?' said Mr Baxter. 'Lot of rubbish!'

These would have been happy days for Mr Baxter too. While Orwell had famously decreed 'the British murder' to be an institution in decline in 1946, it was actually growing more macabrely diverse: 1947 had seen Thomas Ley convicted of the Chalkpit Murder; 1948 had been the year of the child killer Peter Griffiths and 1949 the year of John Haigh the Acid Bath Murderer; already in 1950, Britain had hurried the hapless innocent Timothy Evans to the gallows for the grisly crimes perpetrated at 10 Rillington Place.

The publishers Penguin, newly established in Australia, had just brought the long-running *Famous Trials* series to a paperback audience: scandalous Madeleine Smith, benighted Oscar Slater, sleazy Sidney Fox, Brown and Kennedy of the Gutteridge Murder, Steinie Morrison of the Clapham Common Mystery, the depraved doctors Crippen, Palmer and Ruxton. At the cinema *Rope, Madeleine, Call Northside 777, The Good-Time Girl, He Walked By Night* and *The Street With No Name* were all inspired by real-life homicides; on radio, true crimes were dramatised on Edgar Lustgarten's 'Prisoner at the Bar' and Clive Brook's 'Secrets of Scotland Yard'. And now, in their midst, Mr Baxter and his fellow enthusiasts had a murder of their very own, complete with blonde victim and debonair defendant – for what could have been more exquisitely local than a fatal night unfolding from beneath the clocks at Flinders Street station, with all their romantic allure, to climax on a beach at the height of summer, site of innocent merriment? Thus *The Argus's* illustration of the reported discovery of the body, the headline 'Peaceful Day After Tragic Night' hovering over two children frolicking on Albert Park Beach: 'These children building sandcastles knew nothing of the grim struggle for life which Miss Elizabeth Maureen Williams made before she was murdered on Albert Park Beach on Tuesday night.'

The usually prim Melbourne newspapers of 1950 took ever more chances with *The King v. Kerr.* In their first reports of Kerr's arrest, for example, he was referred to, pedantically, as a 'clerk' – he quickly became a 'radio announcer', which made for a racier combination with 'attractive blonde'. And perhaps partly to justify their own interest, the newspapers' stock pictorial cliché became that of a crowd ('Onlookers gather outside the court yesterday'; 'Large crowds again attended the Kerr trial at the Criminal Court'). So lavish became the coverage, in fact, that the defence before the second trial sought a *nolle prosequi* on the grounds that, formally, it would be impossible to find jury members who had not already prejudged the case, and rather more cheekily, that confidence in the police might be undermined by 'further underlining in the press [of] the circumstances surrounding the committing to writing by the members of the Homicide Squad of the alleged verbal confession of the prisoner'.

More remarkably still, Henry Winneke did not dismiss this application out of hand: on the contrary, he told Attorney-General Trevor Oldham, it called for 'serious consideration', because the Kerr trial 'for some reason which I find it difficult to understand' was generating interest 'to a degree unprecedented in recent times'. And if a conviction was not obtained, he mused very frankly, 'other factors' like confidence in the police *would* come into calculations, 'where in the case like the present the vital issue was whether four senior members of the CIB were to be disbelieved in their testimony that the accused had confessed his guilt to them'.

In the end, Winneke told Oldham that the request for *nolle prosequi* should be refused – but only just, because he was 'unable to say that it is an unreasonable request, and I fully conceive that other minds might well reach a different conclusion'.

And how Winneke must have cringed when coverage of the second trial began in the normally staid *Argus* with a page where portraits of the leading characters were laid out like a cast list in a theatrical program:

> He found the body ... [Martin Crosbie]
> He tried to revive her ... [Constable Nelson]
> He conducted investigation ... [Bluey Adam]
> He leads the defence ... [Rob Monahan]
> He leads the prosecution ... [Maurice Cussen]

That same day, Justice Barry had to order that a photograph taken of the jury going to lunch not be published. But he could not prevent coverage by *The Sun* of the jury's off-duty weekend ('In the afternoon they drank beer and listened to sport ... In the evening most listened to the wrestling broadcast from West Melbourne stadium') and even the witnesses' fashion (Patricia Street 'attractively dressed in red suit, black hat with a long black feather, ankle strap black shoes and nylon stockings, black gloves and a dark handbag'; Barbara Robertson 'smartly dressed in a grey costume and white beret'). Privately, in fact, Barry came to hate the trial – the stakes, the strategems, the prurience, the voyeurism. And the trial was not completely happy with him either.

***

John Vincent Barry was Victoria's foremost liberal jurist, a foundation member of the Australian Council for Civil Liberties, an executive member of the Australian Labor Party. Like his close friend and erstwhile Equity Chambers co-tenant Monahan, forty-six-year-old Barry was from humble Irish Catholic roots, the son of a house painter. Unlike Monahan, he steadily abandoned his Catholicism, which became a source of mild tension between them. One day, ran an oft-repeated story, Monahan lit a candle in St Francis's Church for a friend who was unwell.

'While I was there I lit one for you,' Monahan reported to Barry afterwards. 'If you don't like it you can bloody well go and blow it out yourself.'

One area of agreement between 'JV' and 'RV', as they referred to one another, was in their attitudes to the death penalty – in Barry's case because of an early brush with it. As a young articled clerk he crossed paths with Angus Murray, the charming and articulate 'gentleman bank robber' hanged at the Old Melbourne Gaol in April 1924. That and reading Wilde's *De Profundis* aroused in Barry an interest in more progressive strands of criminology and penology. When Keith Murdoch editorialised vehemently in *The Herald* of the state's 'moral right to hang' Arnold Sodeman twelve years later, Barry led an abolitionist campaign in the paper's letters column: 'We have plumbed the depths of the sea, penetrated the mysteries of the stratosphere, split the atom, but the only solution of the problem of human delinquency is to strangle the offender'.

Earnest enough about his writing to join the Australian Journalists' Association, Barry was then elected chairman of its ethics committee – and, as he would show during the second trial, he was not above acting in that role informally. Yet for all his progressive credentials, Barry on the bench could be irascible, and the frictions of *The King v. Kerr* wore his patience thin.

Much of the second trial reran the first. Monahan worked his way minutely through the forensic evidence with Keith Bowden, and the confessional evidence with Bluey Adam, scoring from the latter a cute point. In Kerr's account of his questioning, Adam had thrown out a challenge by an alleged 'Mr Peterson' – what an 'amazing fluke' that this was just hours after his questioning a seaman of that name.

> Monahan: You were the one who picked up the seaman Stevens and another man?
>
> Adam: Yes.
>
> Monahan: What was the other man's name?
>
> Adam: I can't recall.
>
> Monahan: Was it Peterson?
>
> Adam: I think that is what Stevens said his name was.
>
> Monahan: You had a discussion with Peterson about the situation Stevens was in?
>
> Adam: Yes.
>
> Monahan: You agree with what Kerr said about Peterson?
>
> Adam: No, Kerr did not say that.

But the press of the crowds grew ever more intense. Police were called to form arrivals too late for a seat into a double row snaking into the street, with admission possible only if someone else left. In thirty years' experience, Barry's associate Jim Edwards never saw the like of these queues, reminiscent of those for a hit theatre show – and for a goodly proportion of those attending, in a pre-television age accustomed to leaving home for entertainment, the case doubtless served a similar purpose.

The size of the galleries seemed to deepen Barry's determination to limit counsel's scope. Just weeks earlier, in the prosecution of a Croydon woodcutter pleading guilty to three offences of homosexuality, Barry had compelled testimony from a reluctant psychiatrist, Dr Ainslie Meares: 'Very often the expert finds it difficult to explain his learning. But that does not exonerate a doctor from trying to help justice'.

Now he ruled against Cussen calling Dr Henry Stephens on grounds the psychiatrist's evidence 'would tend to distract the jury from the true issue, namely whether the accused actually committed the evidence for which the accused is standing'. This reduced Cussen's cross-examination to a mix of lunges and evasions.

Cussen: Do you not get into great rages at times?

Kerr: No, sir.

Cussen: You have told us you don't get into rages or grow quarrelsome. Don't go berserk?

Kerr: No.

Cussen: You were in the Air Force at Tocumwal in 1944. Were you ever sentenced there to 144 days on a number of charges?

Kerr: Yes, sir. But there should be something added to that.

Cussen: I will read the charges. Striking an officer?

Kerr: I can't remember.

Barry: Is that one of the charges?

Kerr: I can't remember back that far. I can remember a number of charges. I got discharged medically unfit. I only got fined £5 when the court martial realised there was more to it.

The 'more to it' had been Kerr's own admission that he had suffered from 'attacks before in civilian life when everything antagonizes me'. But Cussen, either poorly briefed or apprehensive about being pulled up, continued hastening cursorily through Kerr's violent episodes.

Cussen: Were you ever employed at Colac radio station?

Kerr: Yes, sir.

Cussen: Were you dismissed from there?

Kerr: No, sir. I was working there temporarily.

Cussen: Were you convicted at the Colac Court for assault, for smacking a man and knocking him out? The local publican?

Kerr: I was fined 10/-, I think, for offensive behaviour.

Cussen: I suggest you were convicted for assault before the local justices.

Kerr: Yes, but this requires an explanation.

Cussen: Well, while you were awaiting trial at Pentridge did you assault another man charged in the remand yard?

Kerr: No, sir.

Cussen: Did you assault a man in the remand yard?

Kerr: No, sir. I was assaulted.

Monahan tidied up easily afterwards. Kerr's explanations that he had been involved in a trifling altercation in Colac, an old-fashioned 'free for all' while drunk in Tocumwal and a skirmish with an aggressive prisoner at Pentridge rang true. And when Cussen repeated Winneke's caustic comment from the first trial about his seemingly uncanny memory, Kerr had the perfect retort, 'You don't have to learn the truth'.

At other times, ironically, Barry impressed the defence as clearly convinced that Kerr was a killer. The judge let their new tactic of positing an alternative murderer proceed so far and no further.

It was always a gamble. Monahan first cast sly sideways glances at the male threesome whom Grinsted had seen Beth Williams greet at 'between the half hour and twenty-five to eight' immediately before her attention turned to John Bryan Kerr. Who were they? Did they matter? Was it significant that James Stevens had, with Fossberg and Peterson, formed a party of three converging on Flinders Street station that evening? Could these trios be three in the same? Could Stevens have been jilted, as it were, by Beth Williams then gone to Page Street to exact revenge? These were questions that Monahan, bound to concentrate on rebutting the Crown case, was not free to ask outright, but which he urgently wished the jury to ask themselves.

The *Citos* three were actually not quite in accord: Stevens timed their arrival at the station at 7.40p.m., between Fossberg, who put it at 7.35p.m., and Peterson at 7.45p.m. Nor had the police precisely ascertained their activities after midnight, beyond mutual corroborations of returning to Elsternwick. So Monahan again called Stevens, who had to be retrieved from Sydney, where the *Citos* had paused en route to Japan.

Monahan's questions were subtle but pointed, and Stevens felt the pressure. He had just described what he said was his last sight of Beth Williams, accepting her telephone number the night before her death, when he fainted in the witness box and struck his head heavily – he was carried semi-conscious from the room. Yet when Monahan foreshadowed the evidence of Arthur and Betty Sievers, which would have placed an unidentified suspect nearby the murder scene, Barry said he would not let them appear.

Kerr's KC protested vehemently, 'If Your Honour does not allow me to call these witnesses, this trial will miscarry. This trial will *miscarry.*'

Anderson thought that Barry 'appeared startled' by Monahan's heavy emphasis, but 'it was evident that he considered the accused guilty', and the judge remained unmoved.

Thwarted in one direction, Monahan pursued another, intensifying his scrutiny of Beth Williams. What sort of girl was she *really?* Might the kind of girl prepared to frequent the disreputable Trocadero on her own *also* have been the kind of girl prepared to go *without underwear?*

Again, these were not questions Monahan could ask openly: he pursued his ends, through Stewart Patrick and Patricia Street, by indirection. The former admitted misgivings about the Trocadero; the latter conceded that, every now and again, her friend would return from a night out and go to the beach in a cooler dress *without a slip.* In discussing Beth's outfit of 29 December, Monahan slid in an inference regarding underclothing.

> Monahan: Now about Miss Williams' clothing. She would have been wearing briefs for certain?
>
> Street: She certainly would have.
>
> Monahan: Would you have known her to go to the pictures without stockings on?
>
> Street: No, I would not imagine that she would.

Whether Monahan actually *knew* something or merely wished jurors to *think* he did, his insinuations expanded until onlookers would have been pardoned for imagining the victim was on trial rather than the defendant. The Trocadero and the No Hopers Club, Monahan hinted to Pat Street, were not Beth Williams' only favoured nightspots, were they? She was a girl apt to 'pick up' sailors, was she not?

Pat played the ingenue. 'Pick up'? What was that?

> Monahan: You know that on the night before her death, she 'picked up' with a sailor at the Trocadero?
>
> Street: Is that what a 'pick up' is?

Monahan: Don't you know?

Street: I haven't a clue.

Monahan: When did you begin going to the No Hopers Club?

Street: About eight months ago.

Monahan: Miss Williams was in the habit of going to dances without you, say, at HMAS *Lonsdale* [the RAN base at Port Melbourne]...

Street: Where's that?

Monahan: Do you mean to say you don't know? Weren't you often to be found in the company of sailors?

Street: No, I wouldn't say that.

The Olympic Inn? The George Inn? The Oxford Hotel? Barbeta's? A Little Bit of Sweden?

'I don't know where they are,' Street protested. 'I have never been to any of them with Miss Williams and sailors.'

But the aim was clear: here was a girl on the loose after breaking up with her 'steady friend' Major Adams.

Barry now fumed. When *The Argus* published exchanges from the examination without qualification, he sent the reporters a stern rebuke via Jim Edwards that they had done the victim a 'grave injustice', and he expected fairer in future. In his charge to the (all-male) jury, he then came chivalrously to Beth Williams' defence.

> You heard Mr Monahan's attack upon this dead girl. It is trite to say she is not here to repel that attack. Do you think that the attack was justified? What impression do you get from a witness of whom you may not think much – Grinsted? Do you get the impression that she was accosting three men, or do you get the impression that she went up and spoke to three men she knew? Grinsted does not say anything to suggest that she was plying the trade of a prostitute at that stage. There does not seem to be any justification for thinking so. Williams was a nineteen-year-old girl [sic] as far as we know who had suffered a disappointment in love. I suppose that at that stage disappointment seemed far more grievous than it would at a later stage of her life. She did go out to the Trocadero. Is it any evidence of immorality that a girl goes unaccompanied to the Trocadero? Well, gentlemen, you have been about the dance halls of Melbourne – perhaps with regard to some of you, as long ago as before the war, but I think you will realize that even back as far as the 1920s girls did go around without chaperones and without escorts. This is an inevitable product of the economic independence

> of the female. Do you think there is any real justification for forming any view adverse to the moral character of Elizabeth Maureen Williams?

But did the well-meaning Barry overcompensate? After all, it was perfectly possible that Beth Williams *had* gone to the beach for sex. She shared a bed in a rented room in a house that forbade male visitors. The Mills Street bathing sheds had much to recommend them as the place for a nighttime 'pash'.

And so irked was Barry, it seemed to the defence, that in the rest of his charge he went out of his way to deprecate their case. Certainly the prosecution were delighted: Cyril Currer told Jim Edwards that Barry's remarks were 'the sort of thing that makes a man proud to be a policeman'. Barry's cunning, Kevin Anderson felt, was that the written record would not necessarily convey the judge's tendentiousness to an appeal court: 'He [Barry] read from the transcript so rapidly as to be almost unintelligible. As uttered and heard, it seemed a meaningless jumble of words, but, on paper, it would seem that he had put to the jury the whole of the evidence of the accused'. By the time Barry was finished, Monahan was fighting mad:

> As a preface to asking your Honor to mention certain other matters to the jury, I would like to point out that your Honour, from [page] 620, read in a monotone to a tired and uncomfortable jury the evidence for the defence. Your Honour scarcely complied with the formalities required.

Barry visibly bridled. 'If you speak to me like that I will ask you to resume your seat,' he retorted. 'When you are in a better position you may make your submissions.'

It wasn't 'JV' and 'RV' now. When Monahan pressed on, Barry almost shouted, 'You are insulting, Mr Monahan. Resume your seat at once.'

Monahan sat down, then literally bounced straight up to renew his objections. But Barry, while consenting to elaborate some aspects of the defence, would not substantially redirect.

When the jury retired at 7.15p.m. on Tuesday, 6 June, the verdict seemed too close to call, the scenario growingly macabre. The audience in the public gallery, many of whom had brought their own sandwiches, stayed put. With word spreading in the city that a verdict was imminent, others also began arriving, until the corridors were as busy as a crowded saloon. At around 10p.m., the building was then mobbed by theatregoers whose shows had just finished, and rumours that Kerr was about to be taken here or there sparked stampedes first one way then another.

At last, at 11.15p.m., Barry recalled the jury and told them to resume their deliberations the following morning. But no sooner had the chamber emptied than it was immediately refilled by the waiting hordes. Bobbysoxers milled about, souveniring scraps of paper from the bar and press tables, clustering round the judge's chair and the dock. Police had to shoo them out. 'Even experienced police and court officials were staggered,' reported *Truth.* 'Nothing like it had ever been experienced in Victorian criminal cases ... It was a shameful sight.'

It was also a media sensation, dominating the next morning's newspapers. The headline in *The Argus,* normally the acme of restraint, ran the full extent of its broadsheet front page and four decks deep.

TENSE FOUR HOURS AS CROWDED COURT WAITS
JURY IS STILL OUT IN KERR TRIAL
ALL-NIGHT RETIREMENT
'Come back with clear mind' – Judge

This last advice came too late. Shortly after noon on Wednesday, Barry recalled another weary lot of jurors. The doleful foreman admitted that a verdict had been beyond them. It was now up to the attorney-general whether they returned a third time. John Kerr cast his father a searching look, Donald Kerr his son a bitter smile. This time police stood guard at the entrances.

***

'My God!' complained Donald Kerr to *Truth* after the second trial. 'They're turning the boy's murder trial into a vaudeville show!'

It certainly had the quality of gripping drama, and it was the Kerrs themselves who made it more than a mere whodunit. Terence Rattigan's powerful play *The*

Winslow Boy had been a hit when broadcast on Lux Radio Theatre two years earlier, and Anthony Asquith's screen adaptation was still playing in Australian cinemas a year after its release. Inspired by the celebrated Archer–Shee case of 1910, in which a respectable family staked its entire reputation and fortune on defending its son from the false accusation of stealing a postal note from another boy at the Royal Naval College, the play pitted a family's unconditional love against an unfeeling establishment. The Kerrs were now the real-life equivalents of Arthur and Catherine Winslow, perhaps even more committed, as they had neither the resources of the Winslows nor the possibility of compensation.

Donald earned about £350 a year as a temporary clerk, compared to legal expenses after two trials of £1200. His family did not own Afton; they did not even own a car. As he told *Truth:* 'These two trials have taken every penny I have in the world. If there's another trial I will be flat broke.'

Rose confessed to *The Argus* that she had been forced to return to nursing, aged sixty-six, under her maiden name, presumably because a married woman could not be seen working. Indeed, on the final night of the second trial, she had been attending to an ailing private patient until 5.15a.m.

> There was no one I could get at such short notice to carry on and although it seemed then that the jury's decision meant life or death for my boy,

> and I should be with them at all times, I was persuaded that I'd do more practical and material good by helping my patient through a night which also could have been life or death.

They suffered petty cruelties too. Shortly after the second trial's end, a caller purporting to be Monahan rang Afton to tell Rose that her son had been discharged. Rose delightedly spread the news to neighbours, and was in the middle of preparing a homecoming feast when she learned from her husband that she had been the victim of a hoax.

As in *The Winslow Boy,* the Kerrs' public faith in their son was underpinned by his stoicism under questioning. The play's most stirring scene, which brought sustained cheering from audiences at the Lyric on opening night in May 1946, is Arthur Winslow's initial visit to the advocate Sir Robert Morton, who subjects the accused boy Ronnie to an examination of escalating fury: 'I suggest that by continuing to deny your guilt you are causing great hardship to your own family ... I suggest that the time has come for you to undo some of the misery you have caused by confessing now that you are a forger, a liar and a thief!'

Studying with appreciation Ronnie's tears of stubbornness ('I didn't do it'), the barrister casually accepts the brief ('The boy is plainly innocent'). If Rob Monahan did not go to quite the same extent, his faith in his client had a like basis. He would tell his sons that John Bryan Kerr was unique among defendants in that his story remained unshakeable – he never shifted ground, added detail or forgot steps. And that retort to Cussen was unimprovable: *'You don't have to learn the truth.'*

Kerr's resilience was matched only by Lee Murray's industry. The older man had now virtually abandoned his radio work, such was his obsession with the case. When not on the bar table, he was organising the fighting fund for Kerr's defence, circulating petitions proclaiming Kerr's innocence or answering mail from supporters. The family filled a 'cabin trunk' with sympathetic correspondence from round the world, especially when Attorney-General Trevor Oldham confirmed that there would be a third trial.

Now one donor pressed £100 on Donald Kerr; another pledged a fare for John, when inevitably he was freed, to a British-mandated territory of his choice, where he could start his life again, spared the public gaze. A doorknock in Toorak and South Yarra raised £27; other sums came from collections at Toorak Presbyterian, Albert Park naval barracks and among 'many well-known radio personalities' (according to *The Argus).*

Donald Kerr was buoyed. 'We'll win next time,' he told *The Herald.*

Yet for all the importance of public opinion, this was not what would determine *The King v. Kerr.* And to some, Kerr's flawless demeanour had become a source of downright antagonism.

***

On 17 June 1950, *Truth* sounded a very different note, clearing its throat and booming the voice of law and order under the front-page headline 'THIS IS A CHALLENGE TO YOU, THE CITIZEN'. If the public wanted the protection of a police force worth the name, *Truth* lectured, it was time to stand behind them, rather than conspire in their steady undermining.

> One morning you may find your son has been bashed to death and robbed, or your daughter has been ravished and left lying in a ditch.
>
> Either will have died a brutal death. There will be a distorted face and a broken body, the memory of which will haunt you as long as you live. There will be instant anguish, permanent grief and searching of your own conscience.
>
> But what will follow? A police constable with a notebook will arrive (when he can be spared) and take your names and addresses, and the name, age and other particulars about the dead person. There will be an inquest. After that there will be just nothing.

> There will be just nothing because there will not be a Homicide Squad in the police department – not the efficient one there is at present, anyhow...
>
> Why won't they be there? Because Mr and Mrs Melbourne and your relatives and co-citizens in Victoria ... you appoint your police and your detectives and pay them not very well – and you don't stand behind them...
>
> Police and detectives are disheartened and disgusted. As public servants they resent the constant imputation that they are of low character, ready to go to any length to get a conviction. As private individuals they are tired of constant vilification, which lowers them in the estimation of their fellows and neighbours.

The tirade read as though fresh from the Chief Commissioner's blotter. And although no individual cases or examples were cited, the imprint of the Kerr trial was unmistakeable, in the references to Homicide, ravished daughters, broken bodies and readiness 'to go to any length to get a conviction', not to mention the accompanying photograph of Court 4.

The response from the defence was rapid. Within two days, Jack Jones had applied to the attorney-general for another *nolle* on grounds the media was now intractable.

> It must have come to your notice that both trials have aroused extraordinary public interest. This is, no doubt, in great part to the fact that the daily newspapers inspired by a desire to outdo each other in sensational reporting, have treated the case in a manner which has scarcely any parallel in Victorian journalism. The space devoted to the trial was out of all proportion to its interest or importance; trivial incidents were magnified and actual occurrences completely distorted.
>
> The difficulty has not been lessened by a highly sensational article which has appeared in the *Truth* newspaper on the 17th inst ... In no particular paragraph is there any direct reference to the trial of Kerr but the text of a considerable part of the article may well and I consider should be regarded as an attack by inference and innuendo upon Kerr's defence. I feel that you will agree that the publication of this ill-timed and ill-advised article make a fair trial of Kerr almost an impossibility.

Again Oldham forwarded the application for comment to Winneke, to find that his note had changed too.

A third trial, Winneke recommended, should proceed regardless: this time there were no studious qualifications, no 'hesitation', or 'embarrassment', or admissions that 'other minds might reach a different conclusion'. It was 'impossible to conclude that a jury cannot be empanelled which, properly instructed, will deny the accused receives a fair and impartial trial'. The Crown were digging in. The bench had just the man for the job.

8

COLD CHARLIE, FROSTY FRANK

In February 2003, Barry Beach retired after twenty-five years on Victoria's Supreme Court bench. Since then, I was warned, he had suffered four strokes. Arriving at the Kew retirement home where he now lives, I was not hopeful. Hours later, we were still going.

As a young articled clerk, Beach had watched John Bryan Kerr in court intently.

'He was a good-looking, highly polished and articulate young man,' Beach recalled. 'You looked at him and thought: how on earth did you end up here?'

Yet Beach's overpowering recollection was not of the defendant, but of the judge at the third trial. Judges often earn nicknames. His own, he learned, thanks to a tendency to custodial sentences, had been 'Behind Bars' Beach.

'You know what they called Sir Charles Lowe?' he asked. *'Cold Charlie.'*

1950 found Lowe at the peak of his powers, not only acting Chief Justice but Chancellor of the University of Melbourne. And where Barry had cordially detested

The King v. Kerr, Lowe gave the appearance of coveting it. On 24 July, he heard counsel on preliminaries in the matter, in particular that Monahan wished an adjournment so James Stevens, then on board the tanker *James Stove* in the Persian Gulf, would have time to return. His Honour agreed, and in normal circumstances would have adjourned the case until the next sittings of the Supreme Court for a brother judge to handle. But behind the scenes, Lowe persuaded colleagues to leave the matter with him. It was the first in a number of subtly unorthodox manoeuvres stamping his wintry authority on proceedings.

Sixty-nine-year-old Lowe had made his way by hurling himself at difficult tasks – partly in reverence of his father, a Warrnambool storekeeper who lost his sight shortly before Charles's birth, yet provided for a family of eight. Lowe funded his own way into the law through tutoring and borrowing, then supplemented his early bar income by writing a commercial law textbook and running a general education course for fire-brigade cadets. He learned shorthand so he could work part-time for *Argus Law Reports;* he learned Braille in order to better communicate with his father; he learned Latin, Greek and French for fun. Each morning, he would skip to fifty and throw Indian clubs for ten minutes. Each evening he would play a few frames of billiards, then work, standing up, until midnight, refreshed only by a 10p.m. cup of cocoa.

In twenty-three years on the bench, Lowe had became known as a master of procedure, seen to advantage during Royal Commissions into the bombing of Darwin, into Eddie Ward's allegations of a 'Brisbane Line', and into the Communist Party in Victoria. He liked his justice unencumbered. Of medical evidence, for instance, he was dismissive, regarding it as 'a legal stratagem devised for the purpose of obtaining acquittal': Lowe was the judge who, to Monahan's lasting sorrow, had expedited the execution of Tommy Johnson despite his obvious mental deficiencies. Prime Minister Robert Menzies had paid him the famous tribute that 'no judge could be as wise as Sir Charles Lowe appeared'. Eugene Gorman KC had qualified it with a jibe. 'Sir Charles Lowe has a mind as sharp as a knife,' an acquaintance once said excitedly. 'And as narrow,' replied Gorman.

Lowe's judgements were renowned for being as impregnable as Verdun – seldom appealed, almost never with success. His first action when *The King v. Kerr* at last commenced on 28 August 1950 was a classic. Of the jury pool, he asked a question. Were there any among them 'not willing to find a verdict according to the evidence' – that is, any disquieted that murder brought with it a mandatory death sentence?

Young Barry Beach had never seen such a step taken before, but it *was* within Lowe's remit – the full court later upheld Lowe's action as 'not only not improper but desirable'. It was also effective: Beach remembered several men identifying themselves and being excused, any one of whom might have stood in the way of a guilty verdict.

The courtroom was again thronged: twin queues were backed up at the doors of the downstairs gallery and a conga line of teenage girls formed up the spiral staircase to the balcony. A heavy police guard ensured against a repeat of chaos at the second trial's conclusion. A hearty contingent of reporters kept pace with the cut and thrust, the faces and fashions (Kerr was 'hair sleeked-down, debonair', Pat Street 'dressed smartly in a canary-yellow hat, green belted overcoat, a straw handbag with a green top'). And the taste for sensation was satisfied immediately. The first witness was a constable called to testify that workmen removing tramway huts from near Albert Park Beach had discovered a pair of women's underwear.

Were they bloomers? Were they pants? Were they pantettes? The garments were passed round. Learned counsel debated. Jurymen peered. Onlookers watched. The underwear added nothing to the case, offering no useful forensic material and there was not even proof they belonged to Beth Williams. Yet for the next fortnight they would sit folded on a table in court – a motif of detection, a symbol of violated womanhood.

'I am *not* guilty,' said John Bryan Kerr when asked how he pleaded, newspapers noting the ringing quality in his voice. But they noted, too, his deteriorating shape. He still came fastidiously dressed and groomed, but appeared jaded and etiolated from 240 sunless days of D-Division fare and minimal exercise. Having attended closely to the evidence in the first two trials, he now occupied the dock pensively, and he could hardly have failed to perceive proceedings tilting against him.

It was not in overt ways that Justice Lowe steered the trial, but to the defence it felt like a policy of pinpricks. Lowe called the police by name, Kerr 'the prisoner'. He was solicitous of prosecution witnesses, skeptical of defence witnesses. For example, Monahan came intending a final reckoning on the forensic evidence, reinforced by the expert views of Professor Pansy Wright, dean of medicine at Melbourne University. The prosecution countered, bolstering Keith Bowden's views with those of Dr Edgar King, a pathologist at Royal Melbourne Hospital.

Lowe left no doubt whose evidence he preferred. When Wright introduced himself as university dean, the judge subtly ran him down, 'The position of dean is merely an administrative post, is it not?'

When King testified, Lowe softly built him up, 'And Doctor, are you not also the professor of pathology at University of Melbourne?'

King replied modestly, 'I have been informed of my appointment but I have not yet taken it up.'

Nothing inaccurate nor really objectionable – but, to the jury, perhaps a helpful hint.

Was the hint justified? For all the detail and complexity of the forensic evidence in *The King v. Kerr,* argued for hundreds of pages in all three trials, it condensed to a single issue: how precise could medical science be about time of death? Actually, as Bowden was prepared to admit, his preliminary estimates had been quite mistaken.

> Bowden: The initial opinion I gave was that the death could have occurred as far back at 10p.m.
>
> Monahan: Did you express the opinion that the other limit was midnight?
>
> Bowden: I have no recollection of that.
>
> Monahan: Are you clear about that, Doctor?
>
> Bowden: I have no recollection of that. I might have said that in conversation.
>
> Monahan: You might have said it...
>
> Bowden: It is possible I might have said that initially.

If the defence could deepen that doubt, they might weaken the underpinning of the Crown's circumstantial case, and also open the possibility of an alternative killer. Wright, who had modelled the heat loss logarithmically, challenged Bowden's view that a dead body could not cool any faster than 3 degrees

Fahrenheit an hour – it was 'too dogmatic a statement'.

> The general theory is that the rate of heat loss of an inanimate body is proportional to the difference between the temperature of the body and the temperature of the surroundings of the body. That, of course, would be accelerated if it is subjected to wind, if it is subjected to water, immersed in water, water being poured over it, anything of that sort ... I don't think anybody would say that it is absolutely certain that the girl was not alive at 2.30a.m.

But Bowden, while agreeing that his method was 'not scientific', did.

> Monahan: This girl may well have been alive after 2a.m.
>
> Bowden: I don't think she was.
>
> Monahan: But she may well have been alive.
>
> Bowden: I don't say that it is impossible that she may have been alive after 2a.m. That is not my opinion *from my experience.* [My italics]

Was this an area, I wondered, where the passage of years might have been advantageous? Had medical science advanced in such a way that there might now be greater clarity around when Beth Williams died?

It turned out that the opposite was true. As Professor David Ranson explained to me one morning at the Victorian Institute of Forensic Medicine, time of death is an area where doubt has multiplied as its complexity has been better grasped.

> What I often say about time of death is that you're very seldom establishing an actual time. You're trying to corroborate other information, like when someone was last seen alive, when a noise was heard ... You're saying: is something else possible? Mrs Bloggs heard a scream at 2a.m. Is it possible? That's about it. The best you will ever get is within five or six hours, even then you can't be sure, and you have confidence limits – you might end up with a time plus or minus ten hours.

The modern pathologist has better tools than of yore: rather than having to work off old-fashioned nomograms with multiple axes, Ranson had a time of death app on his iPhone. But even the app requires reliable data about the surrounding microclimate, and the information in the instance of Beth Williams could hardly have been less so: a partly exposed body, in the night, on a beach, washed by an encroaching tide as dawn approached, then driven around in an ambulance for an hour before its depositing at the City Morgue.

Overlooking us as we talked was a photograph of Keith Bowden – actually a most remarkable man, author in his spare time of a number of Australian history books, including the first biography of George Bass. But his certitude in this case, thought Professor Ranson, had been misleading. He had ignored Beth Williams' clothing and body mass. He had been too adamant about the upper limit on heat loss per hour, too restricted in his readings – his three readings had been from the abdomen, and in a dead body there can be a wide variety of temperatures. He also seemed to have modified his view to suit the Crown. 'A pathologist is not there to support one side or other,' said Professor Ranson disapprovingly. 'You're there to give disinterested advice to the court.'

Yet Bowden was the essence of restraint when compared with Lowe. In case they had missed his earlier hints, the judge's summing up of the forensic evidence accused Monahan of 'fallacious criticism' of Bowden, and more or less dismissed Wright.

Why? *Experience:* Bowden and King had done hundreds of post-mortems, Wright had only done scores, and back more than a decade. Lowe put it in appealingly everyday terms:

> You say the sun will rise tomorrow. Why will it? Because all your experience of the past has led you to find that the sun has risen and ... you think that will continue. You say that the female kangaroo is a pouched animal. Why? Because all the specimens you have seen have been pouched.

Against good old-fashioned empiricism, what price airy-fairy logarithms?

'Now gentlemen, I do not want for a moment to impugn the authority of Professor Wright in his own special subject,' said Lowe, commencing to do just that:

> He is the Professor of Physiology, that is the branch of medicine which deals with the phenomena of normal living life, and he told you that his experience of pathology, which deals with morbid conditions, goes back to some years ago when he was senior lecturer of pathology in the university, and then in that capacity he did some – not many, I think thirty to forty according to the evidence – post-mortem exams. Now had he expressed the opinion upon that experience, I think there might have been some weight attached to it, although you might easily say that his experience was a good deal less than that of the other doctors. But Professor Wright was not brought here on this question of loss of temperature to show from his own observations. Not at all. He merely did what he told the learned Prosecutor for the King could have been done by anyone with a sufficient knowledge of mathematics. He went to a book and he took a rate from it and he drew a graph and we have been told a lot about graphs and logarithms and what not. The graph, gentlemen, is simply a picture, a pictorial representation of what happens.

> The logarithm is a ready reckoner; you might put it as a rapid method of getting figures which you require to plot out your graph. But what seems to me to destroy the efficacy of Professor Wright's evidence on this point is his deducing from these graphs times applicable to this case.

Graphs and logarithms and what not: an aspersion as damning as it was misleading. But Lowe was to damage the defence still more deeply, by a means so subtle it might almost have been a trap.

***

'Cold Charlie' was not alone in making a tundra of Court 4; he was complemented by the new prosecutor, 'Frosty Frank' Nelson. Like his boss Henry Winneke and his quarry John Kerr, Nelson was an old Scotch boy, even if his progress had been a harder scrabble. Originally a solicitor, he had gone to the bar only after being laid off in the Depression by Mallesons. He took up Selborne Chambers quarters with his friend Max Bradshaw so they could split the one-shilling cost of a fire.

Out of court, Nelson could be warm and clubbable, a staunch Freemason, keen debater and amateur actor. In cross-examination, his mouth grew grim, his tone severe and his questioning icily clinical. As Cussen's junior during the second trial, he had watched Kerr closely – the slickness, the fluency. The way to ruffling this, he sensed, was Dr Stephens, and he flagged in his opening address the prosecution's intention to call 'a member of the medical profession, who specialises in the treatment of the mind'. The Crown had tried and failed in this course once already, but Nelson felt that Lowe would accept testimony from the psychiatrist as 'corroborative' of the 'alleged admission made by the accused'.

Lowe *was* operating on a broader gauge than had Barry. Unlike his brother judge, he allowed the defence to call Albert and Gladys Sievers. With Stevens, Monahan adumbrated his alternative scenario by allowing the seamen to deny it.

> Monahan: This girl was seen speaking to three young men under the clocks on the night that she was supposed to have met you. Were you one of them?
>
> Stevens: No sir.
>
> Monahan: It wouldn't be that you could not get rid of your friends and had to cancel the arrangements with her?
>
> Stevens: No.

In finishing, Monahan had then asked a string of apparently innocuous questions about his wardrobe. Did Stevens wear hats/fawn trousers/a raincoat? Did he part his hair on the left? Their significance became clear when Sievers and his wife gave evidence of their

2.30a.m. beach encounter with a furtive figure answering that description.

Nelson jumped to his feet and objected: 'It is quite obvious that what my friend intends, either explicitly to suggest or implant in the minds of the jury by inference, is that Stevens was the man who was seen coming up from the beach at 2.30 in the morning.'

Lowe sided with Monahan in allowing the evidence, but then used it as the basis for allowing Nelson to question Dr Stephens: if the defence could impugn the young seaman's character, then Kerr himself was fair game. This had probably always been a risk. Many years later, said Barry Beach, Monahan had privately rued pursuing James Stevens so hard, and in doing so opening the defence's flank; he simply had not been aware how damaging the psychiatrist would prove.

Nelson did not get everything he wanted. He also proposed to 'qualify Stephens as a psychiatrist' and ask if Kerr's psychological profile fitted with the confession. Now it was Monahan's turn to protest: such a step would be 'turning this from a trial by jury into a trial by psychiatrists'. Lowe duly advised the jury that the 'only legitimate purpose' of Stephens' evidence was in assessing 'the probability that what is alleged to be his [Kerr's] confession was actually made by him'.

But that was enough. As Stephens dispassionately listed Kerr's explosions of rage, it would have been all but impossible for jurors to ignore the imputation that the defendant had the potential for lethal violence. For Stephens had innocently misled Kerr at their first meeting. Seeing a psychiatrist in the late 1940s *was* still a stigma – to a lay audience, it implied a profound instability, a sick mind. Hearing the secrets of the consulting room, the galleries fell silent, and the jury leaned forward. After eight months of doubt, as former *Smith's Weekly* editor Harry Cox put it, here from a professional expert was what sounded like 'the first technical and impartial explanation of the strangely blind, insensate killing of the innocent girl'. Donnish, silver-haired Stephens peered out from front pages beneath headlines like 'Kerr's Doctor in Box' and 'Doctor: "Kerr Told Me He Had Outbursts of Rage"'.

As the first defence witness, Stephens' former patient followed him straight into the stand. He declined the offer of a seat in favour of his now-familiar 'at ease' stance, but looked weary, buffeted, conceding it when Nelson began his cross-examination with a question about evidence he had given at the inquest: 'That was a long, long time ago. I don't know whether my memory is getting worse, but I am very, very tired'.

Previously he had disposed of the confession calmly and fastidiously; now he wandered a little, not quite sure how he should depict himself. In recalling his exchanges with Barbara Robertson, he was drawn into agreeing he had 'not been averse to some amorous byplay', and 'may even have kissed her' had there been 'nothing else involved'.

> Kerr: Well sir, we were alone in the room, it had a bed in it, and she was putting make-up on her face and he [Penno] came in and evidently thought there had been some—
>
> Nelson: What was that?
>
> Kerr: He came into the room and evidently thought we had probably been making up, or something, there, and he said 'You had better get back inside', or something, or 'I don't like this sort of thing'.
>
> Nelson: By 'making up', you mean in some amorous fashion between you?
>
> Kerr: I think that is what he assumed.
>
> Nelson: Was that a fact?
>
> Kerr: Well, no sir, it was not. I did have my arm straight around Mrs Robertson when I was dancing with her and when I was in the room, but there was no amorous business going on...
>
> Nelson: Well, why did you go in there, for the purpose of some stimulating intellectual conversation?

Kerr: No sir, we were in there, we were talking and she gave me ... also wanted to give me her telephone number, which she did whilst we were in the room, sir.

When Nelson came to examining him about the confession, Kerr then became a prude.

Nelson: The next passage is 'I took her pants off'.

Kerr: Untrue. Very untrue.

Nelson: I suppose it is either untrue or not.

Kerr: I think it is a very disgusting thing for anyone to say.

Nelson: 'I wanted to kiss her on the privates'.

Kerr: That is the same.

Nelson: Untrue?

Kerr: Untrue.

Nelson: 'I don't think she wanted me to. She said: "John, John, John".'

Kerr: It is a lot of rubbish.

Nelson: 'I always kiss women on their privates with whom I have been with.' Never mind about the grammar.

> Kerr: A lot of rubbish.
>
> Nelson: 'I do it before and after sexual intercourse.'
>
> Kerr: That is just filth.

Taxed by Nelson about Stephens' damaging evidence, Kerr tried distinguishing between his 'outbursts' and homicidal instincts.

'I have had emotional outbursts when I have been provoked and I have been involved in fights,' he insisted. 'I certainly don't have any turns or anything without provocation ... No sir, that is a lot of rubbish.'

But about his court martial at Tocumwal he sounded evasive, insisting semantically he had only been 'charged'.

> Nelson: Do you know what a court martial is?
>
> Kerr: I was charged. I was not court martialled.
>
> Nelson: Do you know what a court martial is?
>
> Kerr: A court martial is where you are dishonourably discharged from the service. I was charged.

And about his brawl at Winifred Metz's house with Studley Ruxton, Harry Jones and Adrian Grayley he became almost petulant.

Nelson: Now, in the course of this argument were those three men holding you?

Kerr: Sir, they were not. I punched this chap [Ruxton]. And Jones remonstrated with him as well. Jones was going to punch him too because he had made advances to the girl I was at the party with. And that is when he said something about he wanted to make an appointment with her to take her out. And I said a few words to him. He said: 'I will do what I like.' I said: 'You won't do what you like here. You get out in the passage.' And I punched him. And I would punch him again under the circumstances.

Lastly he asked Lowe to be considered not volatile but virile.

Lowe: Put it in your own words. What do you say?

Kerr: When I have on these occasions been involved in fights and when I have been suffering from neurodermatitis, I have punched people, and they have punched me, under provocation, but I have no desire to hit or hurt anyone. I mean there is no desire, it is just the usual retaliation because I have been a victim of an attack or provocation.

Lowe: Well, in other words all that occurs is the perfectly natural and healthy reaction of any young man to some provocation which is being given to him by others. Is that what you say?

Kerr: Yes.

Lowe: Nothing abnormal about it. The sort of thing you would expect in any manly young chap today?

Kerr: Yes.

This might have passed for an argument in a saloon or a sports club, but on trial for murder it smacked of a casual impenitence – a man with a bad temper who blamed others for inciting it, without controls, without contrition, without conscience. It had, in short, been a disaster, compounded when Lowe in summing up negated what little the defence had gained by the admission of the Sievers' evidence, basically advising the jury to ignore what the couple had told them. He sided with the prosecution that the couple were quite possibly mistaken about the particular bathing shed they had been at, and had probably encountered a man who had 'gone behind the sheds for a natural purpose'. Cold Charlie could neuter even the act of taking a leak.

***

In Frank Nelson's papers, which were made available to me by his affable son Richard, I came across the notes for a lecture for law students headed 'Picking the Liar'. It explained the art of cross-examination as leading the witness to 'the limits of exaggeration' then 'bringing him up against the inconsistency', where one might 'see changes in his demeanour, discomfort or the changing of ground – the glibness with which he replies'.

It read very much as though Nelson was describing his experience of first unsettling Kerr then drawing him into evasion and self-justification. At the same time, Nelson added a caveat: 'But beware confusing nervousness with guilt; it is easy to confuse, easy to bully'.

So which had he done? Nailed a guilty man or confused an innocent?

All I had to go on was the transcript I continued reading at the Office of Public Prosecutions, which conveyed the changing temper of the court in Nelson's sarcastic sallies, in Kerr's elongating sentences, in the tone of Monahan's objections, almost plaintive, usually waved aside by Lowe.

> Monahan: My friend's question is quite unfair.
>
> Lowe: I don't think it is unfair.
>
> Monahan: Then I protest.
>
> Lowe: Your protest is completely unjustified, Mr Monahan.

There seemed at work, too, a tension inherent in cross-examination, that while a counsel must be meticulously prepared, a witness is required to be entirely spontaneous and unguarded.

'Are you afraid to admit you learned it off by heart?' demanded Nelson, as had both Winneke and Cussen.

'No, I am not afraid to admit anything,' Kerr retorted. 'And I have not learned my evidence off by heart.'

But Nelson was quick to detect anything that sounded factitious.

> Nelson: At no time were you lying on the sand?
>
> Kerr: We most certainly were not, sir.
>
> Nelson: The only part of you in contact with sand was the shoes you were wearing?
>
> Kerr: Yes sir, when I walked through the sand.
>
> Nelson: Well, explain how sand came to be under your thumbnail.
>
> Kerr: I can explain that. I showed the sand in my cuff to Detective Currer when I was at Russell Street before he took the dirt from my fingernails, and I said when I was telling Adam of the sand on my clothes and I saw this. I said: 'There is sand in my cuff, too, you can see that.' That proves I did go down on to the beach into the

spot, and I put my thumb in my trouser cuff. That is possibly how the few grains of sand got into my thumbnail.

Nelson: You had anticipated having to answer that question, hadn't you?

Kerr: Is that an honest answer?

Nelson: That is an honest answer.

Kerr: No sir.

Was this fair? Kerr had been on remand for more than eight months and undergone two previous trials. Was he *really* expected to answer questions with no forethought at all? Curiously, too, the evidence of Kerr's that sounded to Nelson least plausible was perhaps the most. For example, Nelson sought to debunk Kerr's claims to have been sick by ridiculing the idea of seeking out a convenience in which to do so: there were 'ample places available'.

Kerr: What do you mean by ample places? Do you mean the gutter or something?

Nelson: There were miles of beach, lanes and empty streets. You knew that, didn't you?

Kerr: I mean, I would not be sick in the street. And it would not matter if I was in the desert I

> would not be sick if I could go somewhere and be sick.
>
> Nelson: I take it that it was a matter of your own feeling of delicacy that you wanted to find a lavatory to be sick in rather than be sick in the street or on the beach?
>
> Kerr: Yes, sir, I asked her.

While it might have sounded like undue delicacy to Nelson, from someone of Kerr's pernickety sensibilities it actually had a believable ring.

But, then, Kerr was not quite consistent either. He presented as a young man of impeccable background and breeding, yet had hardly behaved as one. He had invited on a date a young woman waiting for another man. He had then ignored her in favour of flirting with another young woman. And he had not, by his own admission, *dropped her home.* Working-class James Stevens had deposited Beth Williams at her front gate. So had middle-class Norman Sharpe. But upper-class John Bryan Kerr had casually left her to walk up a dark lane on her own, and expressed no regret that the apparent sequel had been her death. Looked at this way, the gesture capped a night subtly inflected by class distinction, accentuated by the accidental circumstances of the initial encounter. This was not a couple who would otherwise ever have met. This was not a date that commenced a journey to marriage. It was a date about ... what? Sex? Youth?

Freedom? Perhaps it was in contemplating these questions that the jury's sentiment began shifting.

Whatever the case, Kerr's trouble now was that he was on the defensive: assailed from so many angles, he had too much to convincingly deny. His counsel, meanwhile, was almost as embattled. Another barrister, Tom Doyle, had joined Monahan to share examination duties. But to law student Brian McCarthy, who had attended all three instalments of *The King v. Kerr,* the change in atmosphere was palpable: 'Monahan had been brilliant at the first trial. By the third, he had run out of tricks'. He and his mate Bill Lennon had made a point of befriending Court 4's tipstaff – always good for tidbits of gossip and banter. The tippy told them that the juries in the first two trials voted ten–two then eight–four in Kerr's favour. That slight trend was now bordering on the inexorable.

***

Someone was lying. Someone had always been lying. As Justice Lowe began his charge on 8 September, he put the proposition as baldly as that: 'Well, gentlemen, these two stories, the story told by Adam and the story told by the prisoner are not reconcilable by any process whatsoever. They are in the flattest contradiction to each other'.

That being so, the question for the jury to answer was: who did they trust?

> You have got to make up your minds whether you think four police witnesses, three Senior Detectives and one Detective Inspector are so wicked and so abandoned as to invent an untrue statement for the purpose of attempting to convict a man of murder ... If the police themselves have invented that statement I cannot think of any comment which is strong enough to express the feeling of horror which every decent man would have against the men who would invent a statement of that sort; not only ought they not to be in the police force, they ought to be hounded out of civilised society.

Lowe clearly did not think that would be necessary. The jury did not even need to be concerned that the Crown had established no motive for the crime.

> In every crime it is satisfactory for the jury to be told there was some motive for the commission of the crime. But I ought to tell you that the presence of motive is not essential to the Crown case. One does not easily penetrate the workings of the human mind. Crimes have been committed in which it has been exceedingly difficult to find a motive. But in this case that observation need not bother you either, because if the document which is tendered as recording the confession made by the prisoner is accepted by you, then you will have a complete motive for what was done, a refusal by the girl to submit to the man's

> desire; he wanted to 'perv' her, according to the statement, and she refused. That expression has never been explained to you but you must interpret it as best you can, and it seems to suggest that he attempted some form of sexual perversion on her.

Kerr watched impassively from the dock. He had maintained sartorial standards throughout: the tip of a white handkerchief still protruded from the breast pocket on his blue suit; his dark hair remained smoothly swept back; almost eerily motionless, his only mannerism was a constant blinking of his eyes.

Otherwise, it felt like the end of a long road. The bar table was thickly strewn with papers, textbooks and leaves from 10,000 pages of transcript; Beth Williams' clothes, red jacket prominent, now lay on the floor of the witness box; the winter dimness was relieved only by occasional shafts of sunlight from overhead windows. On retiring, the jury was twice recalled in response to remonstrations from Monahan, then at last went into seclusion at 4p.m.

Wanting no repeat of the scenes at the end of the second trial, Lowe ordered the galleries cleared. But, again, the crowd did not disperse. Instead, more than 1000 people either milled about the stone-flagged corridors or spilled into Lonsdale Street. Reporters identified among them many lawyers, several stage actors and a well-known jockey in riding gear and jodhpurs. As evening approached, women in fur coats mingled in the vestibule with working men eating fish and chips. Jack Jones visited the underground holding cell, where he found Kerr picking at a meal ordered from a nearby hotel, and returned to quote his ruminations to reporters:

> Are all those people still upstairs waiting to hear my fate? I searched their faces in the public gallery today and I feel that their hands were as cold and clammy as mine. I'm very tired after the long ordeals I have faced but I still have faith in British justice. I will have faith in British justice until I die.

Would that be sooner or later? In the aftermath of Lowe's damning charge, an unfavourable verdict had seemed almost inevitable. But rumour had it afterwards that one juror remained unconvinced, and the longer the jury remained out of sight the better Kerr's chances seemed to be: in the event of another deadlock, the Crown would almost certainly agree to a *nolle.*

Seized by optimism, Rose Kerr left to ready Afton in case her son was freed; Donald remained with Lee Murray. When the Monahans returned from their usual Friday-night dinner at Menzies Hotel, eight-year-old Diana remained with her mother in the family's green Buick in the laneway between the court buildings – it was the first time she had been allowed to stay up late.

Minutes after clocks struck ten, rumour swept the building. Jurors were returning, and Kerr was being fetched – to a largely empty courtroom, the door still barred to the public. Kerr was seen to inhale and give a long blink.

Lowe asked the jury had they reached a verdict.

'Yes, we have,' the foreman answered. 'Guilty, with a strong recommendation of mercy.'

'What is the ground for mercy?' asked the judge.

'If it pleases your honour,' replied the foreman, 'the grounds for mercy were that Kerr was not responsible for his actions at the time.'

'And so say all of you?' asked Lowe.

When there were murmurs of assent, he turned to Kerr, and asked the prescribed question, 'Have you anything to say why the sentence of death should not be passed upon you?'

Kerr looked straight back. 'I am not guilty, and have nothing else to say,' he replied.

Formalities commenced. Lowe placed the black cap, a square of black cloth, atop his wig. 'You have been found guilty, and the recommendation for mercy will be forwarded to the proper authorities,' he intoned. 'My only duty is to pass on to you the sentence of this Court and that sentence is that you be taken from this place to where you will be hanged by the neck until you are dead. And may God have mercy upon your soul.'

As the last words were spoken, Kerr drew a handkerchief from his left sleeve to wipe his face, then scanned the room for his father. Donald Kerr was one of those who had been excluded from the court. The first he knew of the verdict was when a figure rushed from the courtroom into the corridor and announced, 'It's guilty'.

Colour draining, Kerr's father clutched the man.

'It can't be!' he cried. 'No! No! I want to see John!'

The crowd, hushed to silence, parted as Kerr's father pushed into the court shouting in a high-pitched voice, 'It's a frame up!'

He was restrained by court officials while Lowe made a few concluding remarks, including that he had previously advised the jury of the permissibility of their verdict. At 10.25p.m. the court dissolved for the last time.

Scenes outside were predictably chaotic. In the hope of seeing the handcuffed Kerr make his final departure, crowds converged on the exit to which the prison van had drawn up. Women were weeping, men shouting encouragement. Kerr paused briefly, lit up by camera flashes as though by bolts of lightning. As the van commenced to roll along a police guard, the jury were being ushered out a secret exit on William Street, dispersing into anonymity without trace.

Almost without trace anyway. One morning at the Supreme Court Prothonotary's Office, I was rummaging around the bottom of the file for *The King v. Kerr* and lit on a faintly pencilled note:

> To His Honor
> Mr Justice Lowe
>
> Is it permissible for a decision of Guilty with a strong recommendation for mercy on grounds that he was not wholly responsible for his actions at the time.

Underneath, barely legible, in the hand of Cold Charlie: '– Yes – Charles J. Lowe'.

It would prove the difference between a man's life and death.

9

THE MAXIMUM PENALTY

'Kerr is going to hang because of bastards like you.'

The speaker, John Thomas Tickle, was drunk but unambiguous when he gave Constable F.T. Russell his unsolicited view of *The King v. Kerr* on Royal Parade in Parkville the day after the verdict. Russell decided to arrest him for disorderly conduct. Tickle kicked him in the leg and pulled him over before being restrained, and having his various oaths about John Bryan Kerr recorded for later airing in a Carlton Petty Sessions. He was bound over to keep the peace.

'John Kerr is innocent. Everyone knows that.'

Dorothy Ponton was enjoying a hot dog in St Kilda a few weeks later after watching Oakleigh beat Port Melbourne in the VFA Grand Final when she gave her opinion of the Kerr verdict. 'He'll be hung by Detective Adam's lies. Detective Adam told his lies to hang John Kerr. Stevens the seaman is the murderer.'

St Kilda Petty Sessions would hear that she was warned by Senior Detective John McPartland, 'If you don't want a bed in a cell tonight you'd better go home.'

She was unrepentant. 'Everyone knows John Kerr is not guilty. Stevens killed Beth Williams. It's all police lies. The police are mugs. They all tell lies.' She was fined 10/-.

Not everyone was so outspoken, but the shock at John Bryan Kerr's conviction was wide. When news came through to a party at Warrnambool attended by Rob Monahan's son John, guests could soon speak of little else. His father was even then back at Equity Chambers with Kevin Anderson and Tom Doyle poring over textbooks for possible grounds of appeal.

'When I saw him yesterday,' Rose Kerr told reporters a couple of days after the verdict, 'he was still cheerful and a good omen was that the sun shone into the room where I sat talking to him.'

But omens were about as much as the Kerrs had left. The law was strict. 'Whosoever is convicted of wilful murder shall suffer death as a felon,' stated the *Crimes Act* even after a revision the previous year had finally done away with capital sentences for such crimes as 'setting fire to a ship with intent to murder' and 'setting fire to a house with persons inside'. And in its recent judgement in *The King v. Lee* the High Court had shown reluctance to second-guess trial judges on matters like admissability of evidence – the full bench of Victoria's Supreme Court would take their lead a month later, confirming that Justice Lowe had simply used the full extent of his reinforced powers.

That left the Privy Council, the longest of shots given that it had for the previous decade restricted itself to interventions where there had been an 'infringement of the essential principles of justice' such as a conviction in the absence of an accused or the exclusion of relevant witnesses – and no such grounds for complaint existed here. Nonetheless, the Kerrs committed to seeking leave to appeal there, appointing Gregory Gowans, another well-regarded Catholic silk, to represent them.

Kerr's own mood, meanwhile, fluctuated. Sometimes, he felt morose, like 'a sheep waiting in the abbatoirs'; at other times, he felt angry, deserted by everything and everyone. His letters home, hitherto calm to the point of detachment, were now edged with a grandiloquent acrimony, as if he had been abandoned by the entire Empire.

> At times I feel very bitter and disappointed in life. Perhaps I should qualify that remark. What I really mean is that I don't feel bitter or disappointed for my own sake, but rather for the world as a whole.
>
> It seems tragic, when one comes to think of it, that so many people, in the future, who had such faith in the system of democracy and British justice, like myself, are to be doomed to disappointment...

> Remember how I, as a child, like millions of others, was so proud of being British and a member of a Commonwealth of Nations which I thought was so far superior to any other – a land in which I believed that right was might, and truth the only code – a land in which we were so proud of our system of justice and fair play? Now, perhaps, you can see why, although perhaps I have been too much of an idealist, this last blow is so bewildering.

The case might be over, but Kerr remained obsessed with its details, expressing none of the contrition his gaolers now expected of him. Visited by the deputy inspector general of prisons, James Sinclair, he cut a rather unsympathetic figure.

> During the interview, Kerr did not answer questions directly, but rather made long statements, apparently repeating sections of the evidence he had given in court ... He maintains his innocence of the crime of which he has been convicted and was very bitter about the police who gave evidence against him, particularly Adam. His manner was theatrical, and even boastful, when asked about his relations with women. He appeared to be under strain during the interview as the muscles of his face twitched repeatedly.

Soon after came news no less distressing for being half-expected: in London on 7 December 1950, four lords needed only minutes to advise Gowans that leave to appeal to the Privy Council would 'not be granted'; the Crown representative was not even required to speak. One lifeline alone remained: the royal prerogative of mercy.

***

Section 560 of the *Crimes Act* didn't sound overly merciful. It entitled the King's representative, the governor, to extend clemency, and also to 'direct if he thinks proper that any offender so pardoned shall be kept to hard labour in irons', placed in 'solitary confinement' or submitted to 'further whippings'. The governor basically acted on the recommendation of Cabinet, with whom he met as what was called the executive council.

On the face of it, Kerr's chances looked good: the council had commuted twenty death sentences since Eddie Leonski had strolled amiably to the gallows in 1942. But just before the Kerr verdict, the political terrain had changed, with the collapse of the coalition between the Liberal and Country parties, and the displacement as premier of the Liberal Party's Tom Hollway by the Country Party's Jock McDonald, whose minority government ruled with the acquiescence of Labor's John Cain senior. Whom the state spared now hinged on the advice to a retired officer of the Royal Marines, Governor Dallas Brooks, of five dairy farmers, three wheat farmers, two orchardists and a grazier.

And as callous murders are apt to, the fate of the SP bookmaker George Kent had touched a populist nerve. Every day John Kerr walked the screened-off portion of the remand yard set aside for the condemned prisoners with Norman Andrews and Robert Clayton, who with their confederate Jean Lee had excited as little sympathy as he had much. Each night, Kerr would later claim, he and Andrews played chess by calling out moves to each other from their respective cells. Dressed in their identical prison greys, undergoing a like ordeal of dwindling appeal options and bureaucratic assessments, it didn't require a great stretch to imagine their sharing a common fate at the gallows in D Division under which they walked daily.

At least it gave Kerr's supporters the names of individuals to entreat. Petitions to the governor, which did 'humbly pray' that in the case of John Bryan Kerr he 'may be pleased to give full effect to the jury's strong recommendation of mercy', now flowed in from all over the map: 3000 signatures mainly from suburbs of Melbourne, but also from country Victoria, Albury, Hobart and Perth. Some wrote their occupations, revealing impressive concentrations of archdeacons, reverends and vicars, and of doctors, nurses and chemists, not to mention an ecclesiastical outfitter and a theatre usher.

Other family friends wrote directly to Cabinet members. William Murchison, for example, brightly assured water supply minister R.K. Brose that John

Kerr was a changed man. He had had a bit of a shock; henceforward, he would be a model citizen:

> I am thankful to now place on record a most gratifying report viz that John has become a completely changed character who fully realises the folly of his youthful indiscretions, and is determined to lead a new life in accord with his early aspirations and family connections ... He has certainly learned a fearful lesson during his terrible year of mental agony and remorse ... which have caused so much suffering.

Rose Kerr wrote plaintively to each Cabinet member, arguing her son's innocence. 'As his Mother, and with the training of a nurse', Rose told Attorney-General Tom Mitchell, she possessed insights 'obscure even to our most worthy judges'. John was simply too warm-blooded to have killed so callously, even in 'a sudden outburst of passion': 'I am quite certain owing to an exceptionally intense nature he would be the last to come home and calmly sleep, and then act in such a perfectly normal and natural way if he were guilty of such a shocking crime against a girl with whom he was on friendly terms of acquaintanceship'. As for that 'confession', it could simply not have been from her pedantically well-spoken son:

> My impression was that such a statement would be literally word for word what was actually said by the accused. When I read the statement, however, and before hearing my son's

> contradiction, it was perfectly clear to me that the wording and phraseology to a considerable extent was totally different to his scrupulously correct manner of expression. This is a point on which he was almost fanatical, causing hard arguments with some of his best friends. He had been well trained, and took pride in being strictly correct in his expression, which explains his most unusually successful career and experience.

Her son, Rose Kerr admitted, had had a problem with drinking, for which she reproached herself: 'I now deeply regret that I failed in my duty as a mother to warn and check him against this bad habit'. But he was a reformed character – you had only to study his deportment in court to see that. Rose Kerr was wasting her ink, and probably knew it: Mitchell was perhaps the most ardent proponent of the death penalty in McDonald's cabinet, and would resist its repeal right to the end, some quarter-century hence. But what else could a mother do when they planned to hang her only son?

When Kerr met Tennyson Allan, the government medical officer who had taken an instant dislike to him in January, he was subdued, while still protesting his innocence.

> Kerr didn't take kindly to prison, being rather arrogant and quarrelsome, and apparently felt he was the wronged one by being detained there. This attitude was more marked after being found

> not guilty [sic] at first. I am informed by officers that this attitude has changed considerably since being found guilty, and his final appeal having failed.
>
> When I saw him today I found him greatly humbled and not nearly so sure of himself, but I was disappointed seeing that untruths can't help him now, that he would not admit any guilt concerning the girl's death, even though I pointed out to him that the truth might now help in the study of criminal psychology.

Allan had just filed his report for the executive council on Andrews, Clayton and Lee, dismissing them as 'inherently criminal and antisocial, with little or no regard for others' and 'abandoned to a life of crime'. He was hardly more charitable to Kerr, whom he believed 'subject to abnormally intense sexual urges often with perversions and a sadistic tendency', and 'guilty of a foul crime against humanity'. But having consigned three individuals to oblivion that week, he refrained from adding a fourth.

> We are all born into this world whether we would or no [sic] and have no say in the qualities, good or bad, with which we may be endowed, or the environment in which we will be brought up. Kerr is one of the unfortunates born into the world with inherent mental defects and instability of his cerebro-nervous system. Good training may do a

> lot but not all to overcome these defects, and they often find themselves at the mercy of their primitive instincts and impulses.
>
> In my opinion drink on top of Kerr's inherent defects robbed him of responsibility and normal control when he committed the crime. It was a crime of impulse – an uncontrollable impulse – and not a premeditated calculated crime. At present and perhaps for some years Kerr would not be a safe person in the community, but in my experience I feel he might be capable of reaching a stage of stability over the years in the regular life of a prison, where he can be encouraged to apply himself to some useful aim and the best encouraged in him.

It is just possible that *this* is what saved Kerr – the distinction observers could draw between gradations of murder. Sacrificing Andrews, Clayton and Lee while sparing Kerr enabled the government to look stern *and* benevolent, resolved to punish brutality *but* able to pardon impetuosity.

'What do you think they'll do with me?' asked Kerr of Kevin Anderson one day, as they conversed through the bars of the condemned cell.

'I don't think they'll hang you,' Anderson replied. 'There are all sorts of extenuating circumstances. Yours is not the sort of case in which they usually carry out the death penalty.'

Kerr, Anderson recalled, became 'indignant'.

'I don't agree at all,' he said. 'My case attracted very considerable notice. They might well decide to hang me as an example to others.'

Anderson demurred. 'Look, don't flatter yourself,' he said. 'Yours was a very ordinary case, a tawdry case where a girl was strangled on a beach. It was only the fact that you personally attracted attention that the case even got into the papers and you had the misfortune to be accused and found guilty. If they wanted to make an example of someone convicted of murder they've plenty of others more notorious than you to use as an example.'

Anderson turned to a nearby warder. 'Isn't that so?' the barrister asked.

The warder nodded – one of them would be Kerr's chess-playing mate Andrews. The latter view was quickly confirmed. On the evening of 11 December, the executive council, on the recommendation of Cabinet, determined that the sentences on Andrews, Clayton and Lee would be 'carried into execution' four weeks hence.

There was an outcry – or, more accurately, *outcries,* from separate groups such as the Howard League for Penal Reform, the Labor Women's Organising Committee and the Women's Temperance Union of Victoria, because the Labor Party, while nominally against the death penalty, was compromised by its political alliance with McDonald. Where there arose a certain public squeamishness, it was at the prospect of hanging a woman – the first in Australia since the benighted baby farmer Frances Knorr in 1894.

But as Jack Barry noted privately, George Kent's killers were generally regarded as 'worthless people from Sydney, with no friends, not even a parliamentary representative', and 'none of the protest bodies could find any political significance in their fate'.

Later to be so influential in the debate around capital punishment, newspapers remained at this time rather above the fray. *The Sun* and *The Age* mildly sided with McDonald, *The Herald* mildly favoured mercy, *The Argus* noted most mildly that 'the people are not as stirred as they would be if this had been a crime of passion, or one committed in sudden ill temper'. Few would have missed the last allusion to John Bryan Kerr and the extenuations Anderson had described.

Cabinet met at last to discuss the Kerr verdict at 3.30p.m. on 18 December, with Sir Charles Lowe in attendance. No record was kept of their discussion, and only one note of the deliberations of the executive council which began an hour later: a bare minute, preserved in a heavy calf-bound folder at the Public Records Office.

Death Sentences
John Bryan Wallace Kerr

> Upon the advice of the executive council, His Excellency directs that the sentence of death passed on John Bryan Wallace Kerr, who was tried at the sittings of the Supreme Court on the 28th August 1950, and convicted of murder, be commuted to one of imprisonment for twenty (20) years with the benefit of regulations relating to the remission of sentences.
>
> The council then adjourns.

The council was not quite finished for the day. Six members returned at 6.45p.m. with a second item, agreeing to defer the executions of Andrews, Clayton and Lee until after an appeal now planned to the Privy Council – an appeal foredoomed, over which the Lords would deliberate barely three minutes.

And with that exercise of state power, the paths of the convicted murderers diverged. Andrews and Clayton continued on their terminal journey, at the end of which they would be reunited with Lee, alone through this time in Pentridge's women's section; they would be hanged on 15 February 1951. Kerr left D Division for A Division round the corner, and for a remarkably resilient corner of the public mind.

***

For a start, there was The Curse. Kerr might have escaped the death penalty; others involved in *The King v. Kerr,* it would be said, were less fortunate.

The first victim chalked up to it was testy Tennyson Allan. In the week Kerr's sentence was commuted, the fifty-eight-year-old government medical officer keeled over at his Caulfield home with a heart attack and died. In the week after, a heart attack carried off eighty-eight-year-old John McKenzie, Kerr's grandfather, after a long senility.

In the first week of the new year, twenty-one-year-old James Stevens borrowed a motorcycle from his friend Bill Wilding, had an hour and half of 'just yarning' over 'half a dozen drinks' with another friend, Russ Harris, in Elsternwick, then fancied some dim sims in St Kilda. The time was around midnight; the conditions were drizzly.

'Remember it's Bill's bike you're riding,' said Harris.

'I'll be right,' replied Stevens. 'Don't worry about me.'

As he negotiated a slight bend in Regent Street, Stevens lost control of the machine and hit a power pole, causing a shower of sparks as the lines parted. Harris insisted that Stevens had not been 'showing signs of drink', but his blood alcohol reading was 0.214, 'well under the influence of liquor', thought pathologist Keith Bowden.

'The front of the face was pushed in and the forehead was pushed backwards and inwards,' read Bowden's report to the coroner. 'All the bones from the maxilla upwards on the right of the face were fractured. The right eyeball was ruptured.' Did he recognise the young casualty as a fellow survivor of cross-examination by Rob Monahan? *The Argus* did. For a final time, Stevens featured on its front page: 'CRASH KILLS KERR TRIAL WITNESS'.

Saddest of all was Stewart Patrick, the guileless son of Beth Williams' gentlewoman friend Madeleine. Thirty-five, a military clerk who still lived at home, he had been Beth's consort at various barracks social events, and nursed an unrequited devotion to her, only to find himself one morning identifying her body at the City Morgue. In the death notice he placed for her in *The Argus,* he described Beth as his 'dearest friend'. There was a momentary sensation at the third Kerr trial when Monahan challenged Bill Donelly, who was unaware of it, over the discovery of a wallet in a private garden in Dorcas Street containing a photograph of Beth Williams. But when it proved to be Stewart Patrick's, and it turned out he also kept a photo of her above his bed, no further enquiries were deemed necessary – they were viewed as the mementos of grief.

On Monday morning, 26 February 1951, Patrick came in from the shed in the backyard of the Patricks' Harold Street home and sat on his bed. Madeleine's visiting friend Lillian Seaton went to ask if he wanted breakfast.

'I don't want anything,' he replied. 'I have just taken poison.'

When she laughed, he insisted he had, and explained that he'd heard 'some young fellows' behind the pavilion at the South Melbourne Cricket Ground plotting to tar and feather him because he was 'still in the army'.

Hurriedly consulting a first-aid book, Madeleine and Lillian administered soap suds to induce vomiting; a doctor came at their summons with coramine and magnesia. But Patrick had swallowed two fluid ounces of a bath cleaner, spirit of salts, which was basically concentrated hydrochloric acid. He died that evening in Prince Henry's.

None of Patrick's family or friends could make sense of his death. In two weeks' time he had been due to holiday in Tasmania. 'At no time have I ever heard my brother make any mention of taking his life,' stated his brother Graeme, 'and he had no worry what-so-ever.'

One worry, corrected the investigating detective, Henry Crisfield: Beth Williams, whom Patrick discussed 'very frequently with mutual friends' and regularly referred to 'in correspondence with mutual friends of himself and the girl'. He theorised before the coroner that Patrick's death was a sequel to Stevens', that 'the deceased was very attached to her and it seems the death did affect him. Her death seemed to prey on his mind and this was accentuated by the undue publicity revived in the press following the recent death of another witness in the Kerr case'.

Right or not, a pattern was building, and a 'curse' was in the making. One possible addition was missed: a month after Patrick's death, Harold Thom, the publican who'd incurred Kerr's ire in Colac in August 1945, suffered a lethal stroke. But a decade hence, when Alan Dower from *Truth* retold the story of 'THE NIGHT THEY CAUGHT KERR', it had become a full-fledged legend, originating at the guilty verdict.

> Kerr swayed on his feet and rubbed his hands dazedly across his eyes as he was led to the prison van that took him to the condemned cell while his appeal was lodged.
>
> And here, it is said, he shouted the words still called The Curse of Kerr.
>
> 'Curse them all,' he allegedly shouted. 'At least I will die with a clear conscience!'
>
> Kerr did not die.
>
> But others did.

To the list, Dower added not only two jurymen who'd fallen gravely ill after the trial but recovered, but Frances Nash, 'a girl of simple, clean beauty' who would visit Kerr as regularly as her chronic nephritis permitted until she died in West Gippsland Hospital in February 1953. What Dower excluded were all those left untouched, and even who did well by their involvement.

In the circles of the law and law enforcement, the tensions arising from *The King v. Kerr* soon dissipated. Collegiality was restored. Recognition was offered. Under the headline 'Prosecutor in Kerr Trial Gets New Post' in February 1951, *The Argus* reported Frank Nelson's promotion to Crown counsel. Among his perquisites was an 'extremely comfortable yet ornate' swivel chair, left behind by the High Court when it quit Melbourne for Canberra; he also rose within his beloved Freemasons, eventually to Pro Grand Master, the highest executive rank.

In due course, Nelson would join Rob Monahan and Kevin Anderson on the Supreme Court bench, which Henry Winneke led as chief justice after eighty-two-year-old Sir Charles Lowe's retirement. '*De mortuis nihil nisi bonum; de vivi nil,*' said Cold Charlie in a typically austere farewell speech. 'Of the dead say nothing derogatory; of the living say nothing.' In the longer term, Monahan, Anderson and Winneke would also all be knighted. The last would succeed Brooks' successor as governor.

First Currer, then Adam, were promoted in the year after Kerr's conviction. 'For a judge, presiding at a murder trial is a heavy and exacting task,' wrote Jack Barry in a congratulatory note to Currer, 'and it is great help to have complete confidence in the chief police witness as I have always in you in the cases in which you have given evidence before me.'

Adam went on growing, in bulk as well as legend, an institution of sorts: man hunter, man's man, man about town. In the mid-1950s, when he was his father's associate, Brian Monahan knew that whenever a policeman booked him for speeding in his Austin Healy, Bluey was the man to see.

'Did you get his number?' Adam would growl. 'It'll cost you two bottles of beer.'

At a grand dinner held in Adam's honour in August 1962 when he was promoted to the sinecure of Detective Station Officer, tributes were lavish. The highpoint of festivities at the Mayfair Hotel was an epic poem, 'Sir Blue', specially written for the occasion by Justice Jack Starke – a long and flavoursome work, evocative of a cosiness between the police and the legal profession that would now be thought untoward.

> He had brandished high 'Excalibur' to cleave a path to fame,
>
> Amongst murderers and varlets who have trembled at his name,
>
> And in his courtly jousting he has parried many a blow
>
> (Some have been above the belt, a few a little low)

> But when the storm was at its highest, he was not a man to shrink,
>
> As many a lawyer will tell you, who in his armour found no chink,
>
> And so was born a reputation and with the years it grew,
>
> 'Til we dubbed him 'Knight of Policeman' and christened him 'Sir Blue'.

What about the curse, Kerr was asked after leaving gaol. It was a nonsense, he answered – he had said nothing of the sort. If anyone was cursed in the whole affair, Kerr thought bitterly, it was him.

***

I had now been forward and back, side to side, and over and over through what seemed as much as remained of *The King v. Kerr* – the ragged records, the copious coverage, the remaining eyewitness testimonies. I had found a sister of Pat Street. I had located friends of Barbara Robertson. Both women were dead, like Betty Smith and the man she finally married, Bill Humphreys; like Lee Murray; like Bill Donelly.

Some byways were sad; some were bizarre; some were both. June Clyne, I learned, had become a celebrated stage actress. I collected her reviews. I found photographs of her in the Performing Arts Museum. I listened to a recording of her voice at the National Film and Sound Archives – polished, round, flattening on certain vowels. She had died in Whittington Hospital, Islington, in July 1967, aged forty-one, overwhelmed by multiple cancers, leaving behind a slim volume of posthumously published poetry. Her cat, star of a pet-food campaign, had then become the object of a custody battle between the pet-food company and a man purporting to have married Clyne on a tugboat in the North Sea. At one stage in what became a torrid legal feud, the man had abducted the cat and requested political asylum for it at the Soviet Embassy. In a kind of research frenzy, I found a Facebook profile that fitted the man, and sent him a message. Perhaps fortunately, as there was clearly sufficient material here for another book, there came no reply.[2]

For every success, there had also been a failure to rue. For example, I had employed a genealogist to help me locate relatives of Beth Williams. Her family had lived in Werribee for a while, where their house still stood. Her mother had died in 1963, her father six years later. It was just possible a sibling survived, but none of the list of possibilities through which I dutifully worked checked out.

---

2 Should anyone aspire to writing the definitive masterwork on Arthur the Cat, I recommend 'Friends Call Him Arthur' in Australian Women's Weekly, 24 December 1969.

'Hello, I'm a journalist from Melbourne...': every time I commenced a phone call like this it sounded slightly more ridiculous. If I found them, what then? What could I possibly ask? What could they possibly say? Was this defensible curiosity or pointless completism? I'm bound to say that when I ticked off the last name to no avail, I felt twinges of both shame and relief.

Otherwise, I had a touch of what Wilkie Collins in *The Moonstone* dubbed 'the detective fever', so tightly in the story's grip that I saw it everywhere. I plotted routes in old street directories; I explored the intact streetscapes of Albert Park and Middle Park, timing the distances taken at normal walking pace; my iPhoto album bulged with crime scene photos and Crown Law Department files.

I never passed beneath or even glimpsed the clocks at Flinders Street Station without considering the singularity of the initial encounter – Beth Williams catching a glimpse of John Kerr as he rounded the corner with Swanston Street and, bored, singing out. The clocks: they were not just scenery in this story; they were part of the swirl of influences. Where could Beth Williams have felt safer? Where could Beth Williams have felt more open to the suggestion of a handsome interlocutor? Where else could John Bryan Kerr's path have crossed with the typist daughter of a shearer?

What I did *not* have was a view. I had begun my enquiries possessed of the journalist's classic arrogance, confident that an assiduous and disinterested appraisal of the facts would lead me to a conclusive sense of what had happened. I had achieved *some* clarity. I had a fair grasp of the pressure points of *The King v. Kerr.* By modern standards, the case was a mess. The unsigned confession was all but impossible to believe in as a verbatim transcript, as purported by the police. Our scepticism has hardened towards such documents. In a 2004 High Court judgement in *The Queen v. Kelly,* Justice Michael McHugh gave a scathing historical assessment of the old 'unsigned typewritten record of interview where the accused allegedly confessed freely and in great detail to a police officer but refused to sign'.

> There are good grounds for supposing that over the years many of these 'records of interview' tendered in evidence have been fabricated. This is so even though an objective fact or facts often seemed to point to them being an accurate record of a real interview. Frequently the details of the offence were interwoven with or linked to some fact or facts, unconnected with the offence, that the accused admitted was true and which the police officer claimed had not been known to him until the accused confessed ... Many records of interview, if they were fabricated, were works of art, worthy of an award-winning scriptwriter.

The forensic and the psychiatric evidence had dated badly. Dr Bowden appeared to have been too dogmatic about the time of death, Dr Stephens too convinced of the inference he drew from Kerr's electroencephalogram – the latter's testimony, too, was arguably so prejudicial it should not have been admitted.

Today the prosecution case might well have fallen at the first hurdle. It is now standard practice for a defence to subpoena records of an investigation to ensure that police have eliminated all 'alternative hypotheses consistent with innocence'. But once Kerr loomed into view in 1949, Homicide, caught up in the stress and strain of a week of five murders, dropped every other line of enquiry. No effort was made to pin down the alibis of the three sailors after midnight; nobody troubled to question Albert and Betty Sievers, or respond to Percival Richie's detailed description of his Page Street voyeur.

And yet ... and yet ... the case had to be understood by the lights of justice in 1950, when instinct was a policeman's first and best tool, long before the protections which would have placed a lawyer at Kerr's side throughout, long before the DNA testing that would probably have dispelled the mystery with little further ado. The facts available to Adam and Currer when they entered that interrogation room fitted Kerr's guilt: he had the means and opportunity to kill, and the disinhibition of alcohol could have made of a motive of anything. It required no stretch of imagination, no leap of faith. It involved no vengeful stalking by a spurned suitor, no chance meeting with a roving killer. The facts that came to light subsequently would have reinforced their original belief: Kerr was a tinderbox of temper, with a history chequered with explosions of violence; Kerr was a sexual braggart, with habits outside contemporary parameters of normality. How Beth Williams might have provoked him would never be known, but it was hardly difficult to imagine. In a sense, then, the question of Kerr's guilt was a choice between competing heuristics: confirmation bias, the tendency to favour information supporting one's beliefs, and Occam's razor, the admonition that the solution involving the fewest assumptions is best.

So for a few weeks I hemmed and hawed, at the point where most true-crime tales conclude, with the incarceration of the guilty and the moving on of the survivors. You *can* change your mind in the course of research. True-crime's first great practitioner, William Roughead, commenced the writing of his 1914 classic *Trial of Mary Blandy* with the intention of proving the convicted parricide wrongfully executed in 1752, but on the basis of 'a more intimate knowledge of the facts upon which the adverse verdict rested' had ended up satisfying himself that she was 'no victim of judicial error'.

The modern cautionary tale is of Joe McGinniss, who in the course of investigations for his 1983 book *Fatal Vision* about Jeffrey MacDonald, an army surgeon convicted of murdering his pregnant wife and two children, came to believe in his guilt, inspiring journalist Janet Malcolm to her celebrated *j'accuse, The Journalist and the Murderer.* But much like those first two juries, I had not so much changed my mind as failed to satisfy it.

In that sense, the third jury became the most interesting of all, trending as it did so oppositely to the first and second on essentially the same evidence, with the addition only of the testimony of Dr Stephens, who seemed to provide a continuum of behaviour in which a murder could fit, and the prompting of Sir Charles Lowe that acquitting Kerr would be to accuse his accusers – decorated police officers – of bearing false witness. From the vantage of posterity, its verdict might be thought to reflect an era's trust in experts and institutions – nowadays, we are more at home with differing experts and frail institutions. There was also a third possibility, not lightly dismissed: that for all the irregularities of the investigation, the shortcomings of the evidence, the bent of the judge, and the general unfairness of the process, which wore the defendant and his counsel down over nine months, the jury had reached the right conclusion.

10

PRINCE OF PENTRIDGE

Perhaps because of white Australia's penal beginnings, the names of its gaols ring powerfully: Port Arthur, Long Bay, Fannie Bay, Boggo Road, Yatala. But none contains so solemn a portent as Pentridge, which actually perpetuates the original name of the Melbourne suburb, Coburg, in which it was situated. Closed almost twenty years it still exhibits paradoxical qualities. The profile of its battlements and turrets from Sydney Road lend it the outward bulk of a medieval castle. Yet within, one's impression is of smallness in every respect – in the yards, the divisions, the cells, the possibilities.

In this sense it was perfectly fit for purpose, total isolation having been the prison's originating precept when construction commenced in the 1850s. My hosts on a visit in June 2014, archaeologist Adam Ford and project manager Marty Ryan, were keenest of all on these early footings, the remains of Pentridge's panopticons connecting the prison to the genesis of penal practice, to Jeremy Bentham, Pentonville Prison in London and Eastern State Penitentiary in Philadelphia. I was trying to imagine the prison of almost a century later, in the time of John Bryan Kerr, but the continuities were strong, hardly surprising given that if gaols are about anything they are about continuity.

In the husk of the old A Division, it could have been the 1950s as easily as it could have been the 1920s or the 1980s. Time here would have marched much the same – virtually on the spot. On each cell wall at about the height of a bed was visible a musty halo of constant habitation combining damp, fat, dead skin, tobacco ash and general maleness – a kind of human radiation, like those outlines of victims vaporised at Hiroshima, except accreted over decades.

As of 1950, John Bryan Kerr's previously fortunate life contracted to the dimensions of nine feet by six feet for eighteen of every twenty-four hours, with light from one tiny barred window above head height. The day began officially with the opening of the division's 200 cell doors at 7a.m., allowing the escape of plumes of cigarette smoke.

Breakfast was the tasteless but filling prison hominy called burgoo, lunch usually stew. Distraction was offered by reading, and by cards, draughts or dumps (a prison game that involved throwing a piece of lead into a square drawn on the ground). Locking in was at 4p.m., with more burgoo for tea. Kerr found his stomach contracted after a while anyway, in line with his privileges, such as they had been.

In D Division, Kerr had been accustomed to fifteen-minute visits twice a week without supervision; in A Division, he could receive one twenty-minute visit every twenty-eight days with a warder constantly present. Letters were similarly restricted, and vigorously censored. When two hundred men shared a 25-metre by 10-metre exercise yard, there was then nowhere to hide.

'I felt for the first time in my life that I was utterly alone,' Kerr recalled. 'I didn't know anybody there ... I was the centre of quite a lot of idle curiosity. They wondered what sort of a chap this bird was. That didn't make me feel very comfortable.'

Facing him was two decades of isolation without privacy, interaction without society. The only consolation was that A Division, the first-offenders wing of Pentridge, was better than the alternatives. B Division housed the long-term hard core of the prison population, the 'professional' criminals; C accommodated the short-term bottom level, the passing drunks, derelicts and vagrants, in tiny, unsewered, candle-lit cells. The noticeboard in A, where censored pages from the newspapers were posted daily, featured the exhortation 'Think clean, talk clean, act clean – and Play the Game'. That officialdom sought to motivate prisoners by a dash of Henry Newbolt signified, if palely, slightly higher expectations of its occupants.

Yet at the time Kerr was gaoled, there was no 'game' – just work in the prison industries, which included a print shop, tailor's shop, bootery, and factories making wire netting and coir mats, intended originally to instil habits of diligence, but mainly now to stave off boredom. Hard labour prisoners still broke rocks, manually reducing bluestone pitchers to gravel. The only education was provided by a state school for juveniles.

For the painfully respectable Kerrs, the ordeal was perhaps as bad – *The Winslow Boy* gone wrong, in which devotion goes unrewarded. Some friends cut them; others tendered clumsy aid that felt like pity. Donald and Rose, dropping in their monthly tube of Ipana, cake of Palmolive, cigarette papers and four copies of *Collier's,* felt their son's mood flattening; Lee Murray brought copies of *Turf* until his young friend lost interest. How reading *The Old Scotch Collegian* and listening to the radio must have rankled: all those careers on the up and up, all those voices and personalities he knew so well.

'For myself, I have no feelings very much,' he wrote after he had been in prison about a year. 'Whatever comes I will accept it. It is useless in this world to seek further for understanding or belief. I am too tired to care anymore.'

When his old schoolfriend John Gundersen passed through Australia soon after, he found Kerr 'withdrawn and depressed': 'There was no animated profession of his innocence. I felt the energy had dissipated and that he had accepted his fate'. Yet the nature of that fate was about to undergo a remarkable change.

***

In June 1950, Mary Barry of the Labor Women's Organising Committee described Pentridge Prison, recently rocked by two fatal escape attempts, as 'not fit for a dog'. The inspector general of Prisons, Alec Whatmore, more or less agreed.

'Pentridge is not a modern gaol, and we would like to change it,' he said resignedly. 'But you can hardly expect a great deal of money and materials to be used at present on gaols, when there is a grave shortage of houses and hospitals.'

Yet Whatmore was not being disingenuous about his desire to improve Pentridge, overstuffed, understaffed, insecure and unhygienic as it was. And, in a fitful way, he would.

Whatmore, a former RAAF squadron leader, was a tough-minded autocrat, but he had not long returned from a world tour of penal practice in Europe and North America seized with reforming ideas, including for a Parole Board, a women's prison and youth training centres. Perhaps his most lateral proposal was to expose certain prisoners to civilising indulgences through education programs. In June 1953, Eric Shade, a former high school history teacher, offered the first in a planned range of classes in Pentridge's A Division – music appreciation. Symbolically, he used a room in which had previously been stored a whipping triangle, cat-o-nine-tails and leg irons. And if for no other reason than that it entitled them to be out of their cells after 4p.m., the fifteen volunteers who attended were engaged and compliant.

With that, a gym hour was offered, then classes in modern literature taken by *Age* critic Reg Kirby, in art appreciation by *Herald* critic Harry Driscoll, and a group play reading organised by the Council of Adult Education; the Council even brought a travelling production of John van Druten's comedy *Bell, Book and Candle* starring Jessica Noad, a former Miss Australia entrant. Divisional visiting hours were also liberalised to two hours per month on a Sunday afternoon using the neatly tended lawns out front of the bluestone building, rather than taking place through two wire screens. Relatives could bring as many cigarettes and as much confectionery as they wished, although these had to be consumed during the visit.

The next step was greater licence for individual prisoners, for which Kerr was first in line, when A Division inmates elected him president of a Prisoners' Advisory Council to liaise with authorities. He was permitted to undertake an International Correspondence Schools course in journalism and short-story writing, in the pursuit of which he was allowed a portable typewriter, fountain pen, a *Roget's Thesaurus* and daily copies of *The Argus* and *The Age.* He wrote for a prison newsletter, *Stockade,* and talked on a prison radio station, 3PD. And when Kerr then became involved in a revue and a concert, his letters home took on an improbable perkiness.

> Firstly, we need one good microphone for stage use – compere and vocalists. If possible we don't want the lend of one but would like it permanently. I think one of the radio stations could spare us this necessity. Then we need the lend of a guitar and bass fiddle for the concert. We need these three things urgently, and, if possible, permanently. Allans must have numerous musical Instruments, second, or third hand available. It doesn't matter how old they are. We can use them. Lastly, we want some quickfire comedy sketches, also some cross patter for before-the-curtain presentation, between the comic and the straight man.

With the revues, Kerr felt his performer's sap rising. 'It was good to be back in the old business again. As you are aware, it is the only thing I really feel alive in.' But the activity into which Kerr threw himself hardest was debating, a class of fifteen which began in October 1953, run at first by a local accountant, Ian McLaren.

Melbourne had at the time a vigorous debating scene. For more than twenty years clubs had been competing in a two-division competition: in 'A' for *The Age* and *Leader* Shield, in 'B' for the *The Herald* and *Weekly Times* Shield. Robert Menzies, B.A. Santamaria, Chester Wilmot, Frank McManus, Maurice Blackburn and Ralph Gibson were among those who had represented the Constitutional Club, which fielded multiple teams; it faced enthusiastic competition from, among others, the Christian Young Men's Society, the ES&A Bank, Essendon Jaycees, Balwyn Speakers, Ford Motor Company, the Young Labor and Young Liberal associations.

To test Pentridge's prowess, McLaren organised a friendly debate with Young Labor which the prison team won, leaving John Kerr extremely chuffed.

'We feel more than anything that such a victory will do more for the Education Scheme here when people become aware of these achievements,' he wrote his parents. 'We don't worry about the personal angle too much, although we are only human and derive pleasure from a good win, but we are happy, as I expressed before, to help the system that has given us so much.'

Had he mentioned that he was the highest score? 'Don't broadcast this latter part too much, as it may seem boastful to some on my part, but I only mention it to you as interest in me and also in our efforts here...'

Whatmore was moving fast – too fast for his deputy, James Sinclair, and for Pentridge's governor, James Edwards, both of whom quit in protest at this new 'kid glove treatment'. But he was not stopping. 'I'm in charge here,' he growled when one of his personnel choices was questioned. 'I can appoint a greengrocer from Moonee Ponds if I want to.' And six months after classes began, there were fifty a month, with attendance of more than 1000, and growing outside interest in the initiative.

'In the exercise yard, the talk has swung from crime gossip, to Gilbert and Sullivan,' wrote an appreciative Frank Colyer in *The Argus,* whose article featured testimony, doubtless rather idealised, from old lags. 'When I was outside I spent most of my time in the pub or the snooker room. I thought Shakespeare was the name of an hotel. Now I've learnt to like *Henry V.* When I get out I'll be able to take my wife to a play and enjoy it.'

The showcase, however, was to be a prison debating team, named Latrobe, competing in *The Age* and *Leader* Shield, coached by an eager young lawyer, twenty-five-year-old Brian Bourke.

Bourke, a publican's son from Wangaratta, had done a five-year articled clerkship at Brew and McGuinness, albeit at his own pace, because he would intersperse his filing and issuing of writs with detours to watch the action in Court 4. *The King v. Kerr* had been a favourite, on which he had dropped in at least once a day, developing a nodding acquaintance with the defendant. When next they met the well-cut suit had been replaced by prison greys – what warders used to call 'club colours' – but there was no mistaking John Bryan Kerr.

***

Bourke had debated for the Constitutional Club, CYMS and Young Labor with some coming men: the future Liberal senators Alan Missen and Ivor Greenwood, the future judges Barry Beach and Daryl Dawson. But while his new charges were neither coming nor going, they had a strange *esprit de corps.* Membership was by nomination and there was a waiting list to join. The club actually preferred members on longer sentences, on grounds they had the greater opportunity to improve.

Kerr was very clearly keenest, his enthusiasm carrying others along. Indeed, Bourke thought he had hardly met a man so sure of himself, so unbowed by circumstances. One day he was going through his usual checklist of dos and don'ts – how to stand, use their hands, maintain eye contact – when Kerr interrupted.

'Mr Bourke, would you stop please?' he asked, and turned to the prison official by the door. 'Warder, I think you're distracting people from this little talk we're having. Would you mind leaving the room, please?' To Bourke's astonishment, the warder complied.

There were no concessions to Latrobe in their participation. *The Age* and *Leader* Shield was a deadly earnest competition debating deadly serious propositions. At their first start, in June 1954, Latrobe, led by Kerr, met the number two team of the Constitutional Club, arguing the affirmative of the case

'That the present dominance of political parties is in the best interests of democratic government'. They won.

Latrobe was then asked to argue against such propositions as 'That SEATO is doomed' and 'That Formosa should be defended by Western Powers', and for other propositions including 'That the British Empire is founded on Greed' and 'That Fashion is Tyranny'. They won these too, only going down narrowly in the semifinal to the eventual Shield winner, the Young Labor Association. For Whatmore and Shade, Pentridge's debating club was an external quality certification of the education program. For Kerr, he admitted to his parents, it was mainly about winning.

> Whilst one does many things just for the sake of helping one's fellows, it's useless to pretend that we are partaking in a scheme of this nature just for love – to allege that would be hypocritical, and above all else we should try to rise above that very common human failing.
>
> Let us do things, by all means, but let us not try to deceive ourselves, or hoodwink others, into believing that our endeavours are always aimed at the improvement of mankind.
>
> To return to the debate ... Our opponents were the Young Labor Association, which had finished the season in first position. Their third speaker is a member of the Victorian debating team, and,

> as you know, I again defeated him on the night. I am now two-to-one up.
>
> I am glad the reports emphasised the general improvement of the team, and that my ability was so highly regarded. In fact, I was told that if I hadn't been here I would have been well in the running for the Victorian team. I don't make these remarks in a purely egotistical fashion, although, being only human, I like praise and flattery as well as the next man.

To Kerr, then, debating was his means of making a mark on the world. Much else in his life did he later slough off, seek to discard and to forget. When I looked through his effects, he seemed to have kept almost everything about his debating, carefully organised, neatly stored. In style, he tended to the florid. Arguing 'That the Moral Fibre of the People is Declining', he sounded like a cross between Elmer Gantry and B.A. Santamaria:

> When an animal dies in the desert, for one moment it can see nothing in the clear sky. Then suddenly from the mountain fastness and the rocky crags, great vultures of the skies come down to this glittering rottenness to devour it. Then corruption reigns, and these winged monsters appear, shrieking and croaking at their banquet of death! They are avengers as well as scavengers, they are a judgement in death...

> When a civilization begins to decay, morally and spiritually, that is when its moral fibre is weakening – other vultures appear and they are equally a judgement on corruption ... Such is the invasion of communism to be the scavenger of our decaying civilization. Communism was produced out of what was putrid, foul and rotten in the atheism and materialism of our civilization. It is the judgement of God upon our weakening moral fibre to do his will – to do that which is right, in line with the dictates of conscience.

In preparation, none could have been more meticulous. Latrobe debating club had many disadvantages, but two advantages. The first was that it always debated at home, and a bleak and freezing mess hall containing seventy or so convicted criminals in great coats could be an intimidating environment. The second was that Latrobe had extensive preparation time, of which Kerr made full use. Arguing against the prolongation of retail trading hours, he solicited information by mail from the Taxpayers' Association of Australia and the Shop Assistants and Warehouse Employees Federation of Australia. Arguing for the abolition of state governments, he rustled up copies of Geoffrey Sawer's *Federalism in Australia* and Frederic Eggleston's *The Education of a Victorian Liberal* from the Victorian Public Library. His notes were dense wodges of close typing with barely a misprint, which he reduced to bullet points on small cards, then memorised. And when Latrobe hosted the

Constitutional Club in the final of *The Age* and *Leader* Shield on the evening of 23 November 1955, John Bryan Kerr put himself back on the front page – albeit he was not allowed to be named.

In a freshly painted mess hall before seventy prisoners and fifty visitors, including Whatmore, Shade and reporters from *The Herald, Sun, Argus* and *Age,* Latrobe argued against the proposition 'That intolerance is more dangerous than ignorance' – by contending, rather cleverly, that intolerance arose from ignorance.

'Fellow prisoners went mad with delight when their team won,' reported *The Argus.* 'Five warders, who had stood silently at the rear of the hall during the one and a half hour debate, clapped and cheered. Minutes after the judges gave their decision the gaol's own paper, *Stockade,* triumphantly announced the victory in its stop press.' This was perhaps not surprising as Kerr had, in addition to his other duties, become editor of *Stockade.*

Nor was it surprising in view of contemporaneous events at Pentridge. Warders may have clapped and cheered in A Division that evening; elsewhere in the prison they were embattled by overcrowding, poor pay and crumbling infrastructure. It was three months since five inmates, including the infamous William John O'Meally, had escaped using smuggled firearms and human shields; it was three weeks since three teenage ruffians had attempted escape in a stolen car, which prison officers had riddled with bullets. Whatmore's regime was the subject of a government inquiry that would lead to the establishment of H Division, a maximum-security annex off A Division.

No wonder John Bryan Kerr became known privately as the 'Prince of Pentridge' – there could hardly have been a better advertisement for the morally therapeutic qualities of Shade's work. Personally, Whatmore had little time for Kerr ('intelligent but arrogant', 'regards himself as superior to staff and prisoners'); publicly, Kerr was useful, permitting self-congratulatory remarks in the departmental annual report ('No prisoner who has debated in the Latrobe team has ever been back to prison in Victoria. It is considered that a man's confidence gained as a debater is important').

The best was to come. When Latrobe began the 1956 debating season successfully, coach Bourke proposed a novel idea. The Debaters Association of Victoria was scheduled to host the Interstate Debate Series in the first week of October. Why not have John Bryan Kerr represent Victoria in the opening debate against Queensland? Whatmore and Shade agreed with alacrity; neither the association nor the visitors posed any objection; 3UZ agreed to broadcast; the organisers, with perhaps a touch of whimsicality, had Victoria debate the negative of 'That Luck Plays the Major Part in Shaping Man's Destiny'. The full Victorian squad attended, squeezing into Barry Beach's Ford

Zephyr for the drive to Coburg, pockets filled with cigarettes, which they knew prisoners appreciated.

Bourke, Missen and Kerr emerged triumphant – and, in Kerr's case, empassioned. *The Argus* was so captivated by the irony that it neglected to observe the usual protocols of anonymity in its report.

> Fifty prisoners and 60 visitors at Pentridge Gaol last night heard lifer [sic] John Bryan Kerr claim: 'A man's destiny is shaped only by himself.'
>
> Speaking emotionally, Kerr said: 'Life is not a gigantic wheel of fortune. Man is not subject to the cruel laws of chance. Man is the handiwork of God. He has the singular gift of free will. Luck is like a ship that passes in the night – it has no lasting effect. There is no doubt that man is the master of his fate and the captain of his soul.'
>
> The prisoners gave him the loudest and longest ovation of the night.

Did Kerr actually believe his message? Was this his taking responsibility for where he now found himself? It was, to be sure, only a debating topic. But debating for Kerr was not frivolous – it was his only remaining means of proving himself. It was difficult not to read into his 'speaking emotionally' a resolution not to remonstrate with the fates, or with God, to accept his lot, if not his guilt. The response from inmates to this improving message, assuming it was not fond imagining on *The Argus's* part, read just as poignantly. Yes, they had free will; yes, they could master their fate; yes, they could captain their soul. When they were released, anyway.

For his own part, Kerr was euphoric. The report in the special edition of *Stockade* run off in Pentridge's print shop that night was unsigned, but bore Kerr's signature exclamatory style.

> Tonight, history was made in the mess-room of A Division at Her Majesty's Gaol, Pentridge. The Victoran Debating Society conducted the first of its interstate debates in the mess room of this division at Pentridge. In itself this debate would make history. Certainly such an event has not previously been witnessed in Pentridge, nor in Victoria, nor in Australia, nor, probably, in the world. However there is another aspect of this debate which enhances our claim to the uniqueness of this occasion – for the Victorian team consists of two solicitors and an inmate of the division of this gaol. In such a short time Latrobe has produced a debater of such merit as to warrant a position in the Victorian team.
>
> The pages of history; the corridors of time; are crowded with figures who have overcome circumstance, chance, color and creed, and have left behind them an eternal beacon glowering with a matchless message; an incomparable vision; that emblazons human destiny with hope!

There was another reason to take Kerr at his word – because he said so. In March 1959, the Victorian Debating Society held another night at Pentridge: a singles competition, broadcast live on 3AW, hosted by Norman Banks. Kerr was the drawcard, pitted against a Stan Moore from the Jumbunna Debating Club, *again* on the topic 'That Luck Plays the Major Part in Shaping Man's Destiny', against which he *again* argued passionately. Afterwards, *The Herald* reported:

> At the conclusion of the debate, one of the Latrobe team – a convicted murderer – told the prisoners he had specially requested the topic because he felt strongly about it.
>
> He told them luck would govern their lives only if they let it.
>
> 'I think it depends on ourselves and what we do with our lives. That's not just a lot of hot air. I believe it.'

Which was another reason to dislike him.

***

With his fireproof confidence, air of superiority and featherbed of privilege, including a sought-after job in the prison store, John Bryan Kerr was widely disliked at Pentridge. It could hardly have been otherwise. The Shade reforms imbued him with a growing sense of mastery over his bordered world.

He was the presentable fellow who proposed the vote of thanks when visitors came to the gaol, as increasingly they did: from footballers like John Coleman and Ian McLean to actor Melvyn Douglas and director Stanley Kramer. He was the polished performer who interviewed athlete Herb Elliott and the writer Alan Marshall when they were guests. He was the local celebrity with a stream of well-to-do visitors, including the always resplendent Lee Murray, the flautist John Amadio, the actress June Clyne, and another pretty young girl whose name nobody knew but who appeared to be a sweetheart of sorts. He was the model prisoner who kept himself immaculate trim and his cell antiseptically clean. Ironically, it was not so much other prisoners he irritated so much as staff, used to more tractable types. An email I circulated among the Retired Prison Officers Association, a tight-knit and tribal community, brought forth a number of reminiscences, none flattering. A favourite story, cited by more than one respondent, involved Kerr's exchange with a senior warder, Jack Dihm, noted for his earthy ways and manual skills with metals, woods and motors.

'Look at those filthy hands,' Kerr observed. 'They're disgusting.'

Dihm grunted, 'Better dirt than blood.'

'He was neat, clean and good-looking,' remembered David Biles, then one of Shade's young education officers, on his way to becoming a leading criminologist. 'Also light-hearted, talkative, the ultimate extrovert.'

Biles and his colleagues were eager for prisoners to express themselves. Kerr, he recalled, needed no encouragement. 'He was a show-off, a drama queen, loved an admiring audience, probably had what you might call delusions of grandeur.'

Unknown to Kerr, Biles once made him the subject of an experiment. 'I was doing a double major in psychology at the time and there was an exercise you were encouraged to do to assess personality involving a half-hour conversation, broken into ten-minute blocks. The first you would offer the subject slight reinforcement, the second heavier reinforcement, the third no reinforcement.'

Biles still chuckled at the result. 'Kerr spoke unbroken through all three. It made no difference; nothing checked the flow of his words. Anything to show what a wonderful man he was.'

Yet looking round him, Kerr would have felt pretty secure in his superiority. A Division might have been a first-offenders area, but many of those first offences were vile in the extreme. There was Lionel Lee, who had coolly stalked then cold-bloodedly shot a former fiancée, Betty Leighton-Jones. There was Morris Brewer, who had strangled his fiancée Carmen Walters when she admitted she was not a virgin – he was being retained 'at the governor's pleasure' after Rob Monahan had succeeded in having the jury consent to a manslaughter verdict. There was teenager Michael Allen, who had beaten up a homosexual male nurse, stolen his belongings and rolled him into the Yarra to drown. There were thieves, embezzlers, bail-jumpers, illegal aliens.

And Kerr, as he never tired of repeating, was innocent, the victim of a trumped-up confession and gussied-up evidence. Disgruntlement with this attitude spilled over in September 1955 when former prisoner Maxwell Skinner, an habitual criminal making a noisy affair of going straight after release from B Division, collaborated in five articles about life inside with *The Argus's* colourful police reporter Geoff Clancy. There was no doubt, Skinner agreed, about whom the public were keenest to know.

> The main enquiry is about John Bryan Kerr, the radio announcer, who murdered Beth Williams at Albert Park beach and was sentenced to 15 years [sic] after three trials.
>
> Most crims and officials are convinced that Kerr was definitely guilty. He is unpopular in the gaol among the crims because he tried to 'bignote' himself.
>
> He tries to be one of the boys while he is alone in their company, but, if a senior warder or an official appears, he changes his manner and voice.

> Kerr works as a writer (clerk) in the gaol store and is head of the gaol debating team.

Kerr's supporters were incensed. Lee Murray quickly bobbed up in the *Argus* letters columns under the heading 'Guilty?' – a designation to which he took severest objection.

> What justification has Mr. Skinner for such a statement? How does he know that most of the men serving sentences at Pentridge and the officials who look after them are convinced that John Kerr is definitely guilty?
>
> Was he allowed to mix freely with all concerned in all divisions and discuss the question of guilt or innocence in the Kerr case? If not, how does he know the views of most of the men at Pentridge to the extent that he is justified in expressing, so glibly, views on their behalf and use the columns of a highly respected daily newspaper to do so?
>
> Has Mr. Skinner also the confidence of the officials at Pentridge to the extent that they would be willing to express their innermost thoughts to him?
>
> The truth is that time alone will supply the answer to the question, John Kerr guilty or innocent?
>
> –LEE MURRAY (Collins Place, Melbourne)

Nor did Murray stop there. He went straight to the top – to *Argus* editor Bob Nelson, who proved surprisingly sympathetic. The son of a well-sinker from Cloncurry proud to be a Labor man, Nelson had joined *The Argus* as night editor shortly before Kerr's arrest, sent by the paper's new owners, London's *Daily Mirror.* To an organ previously rather proper, he had brought some of the *Mirror's* peppery, populist tone, forbearing allegations in Federal Parliament by Labor renegade Stanley Keon that the 'Red Argus' had been infiltrated by communists.

Pentridge intrigued Nelson. The year before, he had personally edited, at great length, writings smuggled from the gaol by the multiple murderer James Robert Walker – 'a freak among crooks' in being 'a man of literary talent ... yet one who preferred cunning and sharp practice to honest effort in spite of his never-ending, gnawing instincts for good'. So when the fuming Murray demanded that everything Clancy wrote about Kerr in future be vetted by him beforehand, Nelson quickly put him at ease. It was probably at this meeting that Murray took *The Argus's* editor into his confidence – the Kerrs were planning a campaign to have their son's case reopened. Melbourne's oldest morning newspaper was about to become John Bryan Kerr's greatest champion.

11

MR X

Donald and Rose Kerr never abandoned hope of springing John from prison. Their plans to lobby for a retrial began even before the state spared his life, after a quite extraordinary approach from an unmarried forty-nine-year-old kitchen hand living on Beaconsfield Parade, James Roberts, who claimed to have seen Beth Williams murdered on Albert Park Beach. He contacted Lee Murray after reading in the newspaper that Kerr's Privy Council appeal had been refused, and two weeks later swore an eyewitness account of the night of 27–28 December 1949.

Roberts explained that as an asthma sufferer he was accustomed to seeking out the fresh air in summer, and liked to sit on the beachfront benches with his radio set and field glasses watching 'the loading of ships ... and any other item of interest which may occur on the foreshore connected with shipping or otherwise'. Roberts claimed that shortly after midnight he had observed a couple cross the road in the direction of the Mills Street bathing sheds, and 'moved nearer to them' so he could 'hear them talking'. The girl he recognised as a local; the man, wearing a hat and dark suit, 'had a very big chest and appeared to be very powerful'. They had then been joined by a second man, 'about 5ft 10in' with fair hair and black shoes. Neither fitted Kerr's description.

Roberts lost sight of the trio momentarily as he brushed off an importunate prostitute, but at 1.10a.m. heard a scream about fifty yards away.

> I immediately put on my glasses and then saw the man raise his arms above his shoulders and bring them down on the girl. Her hands were not moving nor were her legs. Prior to this, when I first looked through the glasses I immediately stooped down and crept along the footpath sheltered by the wall, and moved up approximately 30 yards towards St Kilda. I was then able to get a better view. When I stopped I heard groaning, the man still held the girl and I could see his elbows moving, putting on pressure. During the time that the man was putting on pressure, I could hear him grunting, at the same time as the girl was groaning. When this ceased I crept back to the old position close to the steps. Then I saw him get hold of her right leg, pull it up high and at the same time drag her by the one leg towards the water's edge, leaving her there with her feet about a couple of feet from the water.

'Upset and shaken', Roberts decided he had to 'get away', but as he walked towards Port Melbourne saw what he took to be the 'second man' approaching.

> I saw him coming and I jumped over the wall and hid behind the shelter seat. I had forgotten to turn my wireless off and when this man came near me he appeared to hear the wireless and instead of going towards Kerferd Road he hurried to the wall and jumped over. He stood there facing St Kilda, brushing his clothes and looked all around him very slowly as if making sure that he had not been seen. I turned my wireless off and crept over the beach, jumped the wall and crept up closer to him to within fifteen yards. The man was facing St Kilda, he then took out his cigarette case and lit a cigarette.

Roberts observed the two men – the killer and his apparent confederate on watch – for 'about ten minutes' before turning for his lodgings.

> I felt sick and walked up Kerferd Road. I passed a milk cart coming up Beaconsfield Parade and I went home. I could not sleep, I was crying. I was unable to eat the next day and felt sick. When I returned home on the same afternoon, I spoke to the man in the store on the corner of Kerferd and Montague Street and said I had a good idea that there was something suspicious going on the beach last night. He was busy serving and didn't take any notice of me.

What happened next to this intricate and revelatory account, however, rather dimmed its significance – nothing.

Murray did not press it on the authorities. On the contrary. His initiative was to hire a local private detective, Christopher Coe, to continue investigations in the Middle Park area. Coe was renowned as the first policeman awarded the King's Medal for Bravery, for taking four bullets while disarming a couple of burglars at Highett railway station in May 1932. It was Coe who actually advised his former colleagues of the existence of the Roberts statement.

But apparently after consultation with Rob Monahan, Murray kept it to himself. For one thing, the times were awry, tallying poorly with Kerr's own account of the evening; for another thing, Roberts himself invited scrutiny, as to why he had kept to himself for a year information so precious. *Asthma sufferer?* He better fitted the description of one of those peeping Toms for which Middle Park was known, and who did not make hugely credible eyewitnesses.

The story, nonetheless, was alive and well in the public mind, and other disclosures were forthcoming. Early in 1951, a young woman, Ruby Eastgate, was at a tram stop at the corner of Mills and Danks Streets when she began discussing the Kerr case with another traveller. This woman explained that her sister, Isobel Clark, had escaped an assailant in a dark lane near her home on Beaconsfield Parade two weeks before the murder of Beth Williams. Eastgate was a friend of Lynne Hollonds, Lee Murray's girlfriend, and the pair of them paid a visit on Mrs Clark, who confirmed the story: returning from her waitressing job at 11.30p.m., she had been ambushed from behind by a light-footed attacker, who placed his hands round her throat, but who took to his heels when she screamed.

To Murray, a third informant then came forward. Seventy-four-year-old Christopher Carson was a retired brewery employee who worked weekends as a street photographer – that is, he took photographs of passers-by with their consent, and sold them the negatives. Late on the afternoon of 27 December, he had met a young woman in a tartan skirt with 'biggish cheeks' and a 'small pointed chin' who spoke of hailing from Tasmania. She was in the company of a burly and swarthy man who 'I felt I did not want to argue with' and who 'seemed anxious to get away'. Carson had taken their photograph but brooded on the pairing: 'What is a decent young girl like this doing with a man of this type?' On seeing newspaper images of Beth Williams, he had become convinced that she was the decent girl in question. But who was the man? Not for another two years would there arise so much as a hint, when two death trails became curiously entwined.

***

In August 1953, widow Ellen Mary Degraves of 104 Mills Street, Middle Park, received a visit from two journalists, Jeff Utting of *Truth* in Melbourne and Reg Foster of *Truth* in Sydney. They were seeking information about a former lodger, a twenty-three-year-old Polish émigré Leszek Richard Kacprzak, previously a member of the Free Polish Forces, who had arrived in Melbourne in November 1949 after deserting a Norwegian freighter. Degraves confirmed that she had rented him a room at the back of her bungalow. He had worked briefly as a waiter at the Manchester Café in Collins Street, for several months after Christmas as a shark fisherman, then in June 1950 done a flit without paying his rent.

The reporters' interest was very particular. Thirty months after quitting Melbourne for Sydney, Kacprzak had attempted to strangle a woman, Edna Neilson, as she entered her home in working-class Waverton. At her screams he bolted, bursting into a rundown stone cottage round the corner occupied by a petrol pump attendant, John Bull.

'Hide me!' he demanded. 'I'm running from the police.'

They scuffled; Kacprzak again fled. Early the following morning, he forced his way into another nearby home, where he attempted to strangle another young woman, Olga Anderson, then menaced her and her mother with a bottle, demanding money. Three days later, in what seemed too eerily coincidental, the body of Bull's niece, twenty-one-year-old machinist Shirley Butler, was discovered on a vacant lot a hundred metres from Bull's cottage. She had been strangled and beaten, her clothes torn and her underwear removed, although there were no signs of sexual assault or robbery.

The Crown elected to pursue Kacprzak only for the attack on Anderson, and succeeded in having him sentenced to twelve years in Long Bay. In Butler's case, the media had to settle for a sensational inquest, strong on squalid detail. *(Sun Herald:* 'Sick at heart, she sought temporary pleasure in the bright lights of Sydney hotel lounges and "fun" parlors, the sordid darkness of slum parks and refuse-littered alleys. Men who accosted her found she was a willing participant in any drinking bout and that she kissed easily, eagerly – hungry for even spurious affection.')

The respective *Truths* wanted more, and in a sense found it – for they could now demonstrate that Kacprzak, while a lodger, had dwelt 150 metres from where Beth Williams lived and 300 metres from where she died. When Lee Murray cheerfully volunteered his information, a file took shape. Isobel Clark signed an affidavit about her experience, Christopher Carson swore that pictures of Kacprzak resembled his intimidating photographic subject, and Melbourne *Truth* editor Len Rigg condensed the material to a seven-page screed for Victoria's Attorney-General Bill Slater.

Slater was unmoved. Accused persons, he responded, could not exculpate themselves from charges 'by proving that some third person or persons have a known propensity or disposition to commit that type of crime' – the law just didn't work that way. *Truth* had proferred nothing 'capable of casting any doubt upon the validity or propriety of the verdict returned by the jury'. Murray attempted an end run, seeking an appointment with Premier John Cain senior to 'place the new evidence before him in detail'. Slater headed this off too.

'One cannot help being struck by the rather strange methods adopted to have this case reopened,' mused Winneke to the attorney-general. He had not seen anything yet.

***

The Crown Law Department kept a thick file of correspondence directly and indirectly received regarding *The King v. Kerr.* Some interlocutors were remarkably persistent, if not eccentric. Miss Ena Smith, a spinster nurse in her fifties who knew Rose Kerr, started firing off letters in October 1950 when Kerr's innocence was proved to her 'in a dream'; she also claimed to have encountered Beth Williams, and to have detected 'a bad girl's look about her'. In addition to local authorities, she wrote to the King, Prime Minister Menzies, Opposition Leader Ben Chifley and the head of Scotland Yard, and composed a tract about the crime she invited the attorney-general to read:

> I am sure you would be vastly amused. I hope the public will enjoy my story also – am thinking of becoming a short story writer. It will get quite a few readers. One must have a popular theme to keep this reading public as you know and having everything of interest in black and white should prove a huge success. I may add that young Mr Kerr is one of my heirs to a share in a 1000-acre property – not bad for him to have.[3]

Another regular writer was Leslie Brandon, who owned a plastics firm in Malvern, and who reproached himself bitterly, repeatedly and confusedly for having failed to run down a man he was convinced was the killer when he had had the chance.

> On the night (or the night before – I have never been able to remember which) that Beth Williams was murdered on Middle Park beach by John Bryan Kerr (now serving in Pentridge gaol) I was sitting in my car a few yards from the spot where her body was found. I was accompanied by a lady whose name I don't know.
>
> Suddenly my companion screamed and shouted there was a man peering through the glass. I turned to behold the man's face pressed against

---

3 If this was ever the case, Ena Smith changed her mind: on her death in 1963, her estate was divided simply among various friends, relatives and charities.

> the rear window. It was the face of a crazed maniac. Startled and terrified by his dreadful and hideous appearance I started my car and quickly drove away. Through the years I have become more and more certain in my own mind that this was the real murderer of the Girl. I now feel utterly sure of it.

The certainty became all-consuming; likewise the uncertainty about his mystery companion. Brandon's increasingly fevered communications finally petered out with a telegram admitting that he was 'collapsing under terrible strain'.

Most correspondents had no particular insights; they merely wanted to vouchsafe an opinion. All received polite but firm replies that the matter was now closed. But they were also indicative of an abiding discontent about the sentence on Kerr, of which Murray was resolved to take advantage. He wanted to reopen *The King v. Kerr* in the forum of the public in the hope of reopening it in the circles of the powerful.

That was where *The Argus* came in. Bob Nelson reused the style he had established with the paper's earlier series, of Maxwell Skinner's reminiscences and Robert Walker's writings, and 'The John Bryan Kerr Letters' were launched on 18 February 1956 with an open letter from Donald and Rose Kerr.

JOHN, our son, has been imprisoned at Pentridge for just over five years. He is serving a 20-year sentence for murder.

Ever since his arrest in late 1949 he has protested his complete innocence. Our belief in John has never wavered, and our greatest wish in life is to see his name cleared.

We live in Toorak, and were able to educate John at Scotch College, but we are not well-to-do folk. We do not own the home in which we have been living for the past 17 years.

Our legal costs for John's three trials, and the subsequent appeal to the State Full Court and the Privy Council in London totalled well over £2000, and we have never begrudged a penny of it.

During 1950, the year of the trials, we received more than 1000 letters of sympathy from strangers, and these strengthened our resolve to continue the fight indefinitely.

Monthly, since the beginning of 1950, we have been receiving letters from John, written in most cases midway between our visits to the gaol.

We believe these letters reflect John's true character – that of an intelligent, sensitive young

> man, devoted to his parents, relatives, and friends, chivalrous almost to 'old world' extent in his attitude to women – interested principally in artistic pursuits, but also in sport – philosophical in outlook – eager to find religious faith without becoming what he calls 'churchy'.
>
> THESE, WE ARE CONVINCED, ARE NOT THE LETTERS OF A MURDERER, AND WE BELIEVE IT WOULD ASSIST OUR CONTINUING CAMPAIGN TO PROVE JOHN'S INNOCENCE IF THEY COULD BE STUDIED BY THE PUBLIC AT LARGE.
>
> WE THEREFORE AUTHORISE *THE ARGUS* TO PUBLISH ALL 60 LETTERS, AND WE HOPE THAT, IN THEM, THE PUBLIC WILL FIND THE REAL JOHN BRYAN KERR WE KNOW SO WELL.

Nelson made still bolder by having *The Argus* present Kerr's predicament as an emblem of the barbarism of the death penalty, the subject of a four-year Royal Commission in the United Kingdom. The Liberal/Country coalition in office since May 1955 had shown progressive instincts elsewhere, initiating a parole and probation system in its *Penal Reform Bill.* But Premier Henry Bolte was not about to emulate the recent example of New South Wales and retire the noose: Gallup pollsters reckoned that still only about a quarter of Australians were outright abolitionists. All of which made Nelson's campaign about 'The Man They Might Have Hanged' more of a crusade – unprecedented, in fact, and predating by five years the strivings of the Anti-Hanging Committee to save Robert Peter Tait, and by a decade the anguish around Ronald Ryan.

> CONSIDER the Kerr case in the light of the Victorian Government's refusal to follow Britain's lead in abolition of the death penalty.
>
> Had the present L.C.P. Government been in power in December, 1950, John Bryan Kerr might have been hanged.
>
> Premier Bolte said on Friday: 'Capital punishment is the policy of the L.C.P., and will remain the policy of my Government.'
>
> Mr. Bolte offered no arguments in defence of the Government's stand BECAUSE THERE ARE NONE TO OFFER.
>
> Thirty-seven countries have abolished capital punishment WITHOUT ANY SUBSEQUENT INCREASE in the murder rate, or attempted-murder rate, per head of population.
>
> A great danger in death penalty systems is that innocent men and women may be executed...
>
> IT CAN ONLY BE A MATTER OF TIME BEFORE STATE MURDER – A BARBARIC SURVIVAL FROM

> THE DARK AGES – IS ABOLISHED FOREVER IN VICTORIA.

It was brave editing by Nelson, not only to hurl capital letters at capital punishment, but to commit to a series of such stupendous length. 'The John Kerr Letters' ran daily for a month and stretched beyond 50,000 words. It commenced also by profiling both Murray and gorgeous, pouting June Clyne, who professed her undying belief in Kerr's innocence in a front-page article reeling off her stage credits *(Larger Than Life, See How They Run, Is Your Honeymoon Really Necessary?, Time Out for Ginger)* as though they were criminological qualifications.

> I saw him at Pentridge at Christmas. His spirit was wonderful. I felt stimulated by his confidence and outlook.
>
> He told me: 'I could go mad thinking and brooding on the injustice that has been done to me. But I do believe that truth must prevail.'
>
> I've never doubted his innocence for one second. I'll stake my life on him.

Then, and only then, did *The Argus* begin divulging the substance of the pro-Kerr counternarrative.

'Is there a second man?' it asked on 25 February. Yes, there was 'sensational new evidence', it promised on 29 February. Yes, it revealed on 1 March, there was not merely a 'second man' but a 'second girl'.

The new case was bullet-pointed under the front-page headline 'JOHN KERR: VITAL FACTS', with Kacprzak referred to as 'Mr X', a 'man with homicidal tendencies'.

With that, the news moved into a reaction phase. On 2 March, Bolte was quoted tersely undertaking to respond; on 3 March, speaking 'by radio telephone' from 'the Waterloo Hotel, Wellington', Chief Secretary Arthur Rylah promised *The Argus:* 'I will meticulously examine new evidence on the Kerr case when I return to Melbourne'.

And readers' responses poured in, exquisitely divided, between the likes of Mr F.C. Petty of Olive Street, East Malvern...

> The letters *The Argus* has been public-spirited enough to publish show a young man of considerable courage, intelligence, and a fine regard for other people's feelings.
>
> If John Kerr is innocent – and his guilt was always in serious doubt – a set of unfortunate circumstances placed him in his present predicament; circumstances, possibly arising out of indiscretion on his part, but which should make every thinking man echo John Wesley's famous words: 'There but for the grace of God...'

...and the likes of S. Green of Elizabeth Street, City:

> As several readers have pointed out, Kerr's letters do not ring true. It is quite obvious he is not a 'brutal killer', but that is not the type of crime he was convicted of. He is fortunate in having influential friends. What about sparing a little sympathy for the victim's relatives?

Kerr had been dividing people all his life; now he did not even need to be there. People drew violently opposite conclusions merely from his words. *The Argus* enlivened the contention by running letters in pairs, one for and one against, the effect being of a chamber of simultaneous arguments.

Gwen Baxter of Princes Street, Campbell's Creek was moved: 'John Bryan Kerr's letters have been an inspiration to me. Society needs a lot of men like him, and may he soon be free again'. M. James of Brighton Road, Elwood was not: 'The tone of Kerr's letters suggests he is a most self-centred young man, and it is difficult to understand how anyone serving a life sentence can be so concerned about himself'.

B.G. of Hotham Street, East Melbourne thought Kerr deep: 'Only an innocent man could have written such beautiful letters'. P.R. of Birch Street, West Preston thought Kerr shallow: 'I have read them all and think they are the ravings of a selfish man with a warped sense of values'.

R.E. Mills of Mason Street, Hawthorn praised Kerr and the paper: 'I think *The Argus* a truly wonderful paper to take up the case of John Kerr ... His letters show a good upbringing, courage, and pride'. J.C. of Queens Road, City, did the opposite: 'The letters show Kerr to be vain, selfish and conceited ... I think you have lost much prestige in your handling of the issue'.

A reader lasting the distance might have wondered how their understanding of Kerr had *really* been improved. The letters, composed to buoy their addressees and bowdlerised by prison censors, hardly contained innermost thoughts. There was lots of name-dropping ('Mr. Harold Holt and his wife must have enjoyed their overseas sojourn recently'), favour-cadging ('I need the lend of a German naval cap and a dark navy naval officer's coat to match – one that will button across the front'), windy epiphanies ('The common people have ever been the "tools" and "serfs" of the small "upper crust" of society') and precocious fogeyism ('It was great fun to hear Mr. R.G. Menzies' last speech from Brisbane, although, apart from the humorous aspect, it was disgusting to hear so many young people behaving in such a manner').

The only teasing personal details were of the mysterious girl visitor of rumour, who always appeared as 'A______': she was described as the daughter of a grazier who clearly held a candle for Kerr after visiting him in prison, but who subsequently married and moved overseas. But if Kerr evinced any love interest, it was in Clyne. Readers learned that he kept her photo by his bed, and had sent her an orchid during the Melbourne season of *As Black as She's Painted* with a card: 'To my favorite blonde, darling June, from her sincere friend, John Bryan Kerr'.

The point of the campaign was less its diffuse content than, for the Kerrs, its scale, and, for *The Argus,* its exclusivity. Overall it probably lacked true urgency: Kerr *might* have hanged, but was in no danger now; Kerr *was* in gaol, but didn't seem to be suffering unduly. The abolitionist message was timely: an anti-hanging Private Members Bill was even then being passed in the House of Commons, doomed to founder in the Lords. But that initial editorial cry was gradually muffled by the din of the amateur sleuthing.

The cumulative effect was nonetheless powerful. Six months before television, newspapers enjoyed untrammelled influence. *The Argus* left the most innovative feature of its crusade till last. Page three of the 10 March edition carried a cut-out ballot paper allowing readers to vote 'Yes' or 'No' to a reopening of the case, to 'eliminate once and for all the suggestion that a young Victorian is paying the terrible price for a crime of which he is innocent' – social media *avant la lettre.* Readers had only three days to respond but more than 4000 ballots arrived, and the 'Voice of the People', as *The Argus* called it, ran ten to one in Kerr's favour.

The newspaper then responded indignantly when Bolte and Rylah resiled from their preliminary undertakings, and announced that Cabinet was against 'any special form of investigation'. *The Argus* proclaimed its firm belief 'that a fair case has been made for a new deal for young John Kerr – and will not consider the premier's "brush-off" the end of the case'. Nor did it.

***

The irony of Murray's investigations was that they had yielded much the same as the police six years earlier: a suggestive but nebulous case based mainly on circumstantial evidence. And where the police at least had the 'confession', disputed as it was, the Kerrs lacked anything to bring it all together. So they hired Frank Galbally.

The previous year, Melburnians had been enthralled by a legal drama that *The Herald* described as 'arousing more public interest than any Criminal Court trial since the Kerr case'. Geelong police constable James Broome stood accused of murdering his wife, Una, while she was preparing dinner; he claimed he had shot her accidentally while cleaning his rifle. The Homicide Squad presented a coruscating circumstantial case involving Broome's affair with a theatre usherette, and his wife's flirtations with a truck driver. Read in court, Broome's post-arrest *billets-doux* were pure *Peyton Place;* he also confided that two Homicide detectives were 'out to hang me if it is the last thing they do'. One of them was Bluey Adam.

Galbally, Broome's thirty-two-year-old defence counsel, turned the case topsy-turvy by holding the Homicide Squad's rough-and-ready methods up to scrutiny. He humiliated Adam in the witness stand by requiring him to decrypt two foolscap pages of untelligible scrawl purporting to be a comprehensive record of a four-hour interrogation. The jury acquitted in forty minutes.

With Monahan having now ascended to the bench, Galbally became overnight Melbourne's most sought-after defence lawyer, the police's least-liked advocate, and the Kerrs' next best hope. On 16 June 1956, another front page in *The Argus* divulged Galbally's involvement in a petition for mercy under section 610 of the *Crimes Act,* quoting Rose Kerr as being 'terribly excited'. Nelson printed another reverberating editorial.

GUILTY OR INNOCENT?
The great controversy over John Bryan Kerr rages on.
But everyone is agreed about one thing:
THE KERR CASE SHOULD BE RESOLVED.

> The great doubt produced in a large part of the public mind by publication of Mr. Lee Murray's new evidence in *The Argus* three months ago must be removed.
>
> *The Argus* has never questioned the method of conduct of Kerr's three trials, or the decision of

> the jury that convicted him in 1950 ON THE EVIDENCE THEN AVAILABLE.
>
> But the facts uncovered by Lee Murray since the final trial cannot lightly be dismissed.
>
> It COULD be coincidence that:
>
> • A homicidal migrant was living within 100 yards of Beth Williams' home at the time of the murder.
>
> • He left Victoria suddenly a fortnight after the murder.
>
> • He subsequently tried to strangle a girl in another State, inflicting identical injuries to those that killed Miss Williams.
>
> But the point is: DO THESE, AND THE MANY OTHER RELATED FACTS, CAST A REASONABLE DOUBT ON KERR'S GUILT?

The leader bore out what made the drifter and gaolbird Kacprzak, still unnamed, such an innately appealing killer: he had gone from being merely a 'man of homicidal tendencies' to a full-fledged 'homicidal migrant', one of those swarthy 'New Australian' outsiders increasingly conspicuous in Australia, with their mysterious foreign customs and accents.

Yet his links to the death of Beth Williams were tenuous at best – and Murray and Galbally knew it. On 29 June, Murray went to Sydney to meet Detective Sergeant Harold Crowley, Kacprzak's previous pursuer. He pressed Crowley to sign a ready-prepared statement agreeing strong similarities in the modus operandi of the murders of Shirley Butler and Beth Williams, and the attempted strangulation of Olga Anderson.

Crowley pointed out, quite reasonably, that there *were* differences. The attack on Anderson, for example, had been a break-in during which Kacprzak had demanded money and in which lethal force had not been applied; the description of Kacprzak as 'a thick set powerful man' characterised by 'a rough complexion with the appearance of never being clean shaved', meanwhile, applied to numberless men.

There were other problems too. How had Kacprzak known to find Beth Williams on the beach? Why had Kacprzak absconded *after* Kerr was charged, when he would have known himself to be safe? Yet it was almost as though the petition had achieved its own momentum, and that if it did not happen now, never would. So to link together new statutory declarations from Isobel Clark, Christopher Carson and Ellen Degraves, Murray and Galbally at last deployed the testimony of the furtive eyewitness James Roberts – a dangerous gambit, because its timing at least was at odds with Kerr's own testimony.

Now there was no turning back. 'JOHN KERR'S PETITION NOW WITH RYLAH', reported the banner on *The Argus's* front page of 2 July, Murray posing for a photograph with Donald Kerr.

The gambit failed. Rylah's appointed independent reviewer, Douglas Menzies QC, president of the Law Council of the Australia and cousin of the Prime Minister, made short work of the dossier, dismissing the circumstantial evidence as 'inadmissable even had Kacprzak been on trial', and the Roberts testimony as so 'inherently improbable' as 'to be treated with the greatest suspicion' given his 'failure to communicate with the Crown or other proper authorities over such a long period'.

Menzies' conclusions were echoed by Henry Winneke, now Solicitor-General, and Thomas Mornane, the new Crown solicitor. The trio accepted the open invitation to turn Roberts' words against Kerr. If the witness *did* see a murder taking place at this time, they concluded, it was 'strongly confirmatory of the petitioner's guilt', because Kerr *must* have been the killer.[4]

---

4 Elusive Kacprzak seems to have served until July 1961, according to his smudged and battered Correctives Services NSW Description Card, and not been heard of again: his deportation was certainly considered, although it is unclear whether it was carried out. Enigmatic Roberts seems to have fallen on still harder times. 'Speechless' and 'bed-ridden', he was admitted to Kew Asylum on 10 December 1965 with 'acute brain syndrome', arterial

The announcement on 6 September that the petition had been rejected surprised nobody, except perhaps *The Argus,* who devoted to the story one final editorial: 'There should have been an open judicial inquiry – for the sake of the public conscience. The Kerr case will now be argued forever – with thousands of Victorians steadfastly affirming the reasonable doubt of John Kerr's guilt'.

But even Kerr's unflagging newspaper supporter had other concerns by now: Suez, Hungary, the Olympics and a spicy new court case involving a Tasmanian philosophy professor, Sydney Sparkes Orr, and the undergraduate object of his affections, Suzanne Kemp. Then, early in the New Year, *The Argus* was itself sentenced to death, being suddenly closed by its faraway British owners – perhaps, were you a believer, the ultimate victim of the 'Curse of Kerr'.

The Kerrs refused to give in. Hopes of a retrial dashed, they channelled their efforts into obtaining a remission of their son's sentence. In April 1957, they filed a plea *ad misericordiam* seeking early release on grounds of John and his family's hardship. In May 1958, they had the member for Scoresby, Sir George Knox, petition Arthur Rylah for early release on grounds of Donald's ill health – he was suffering an inflammation of the heart muscle. In July 1959, Murray seized on a remark on television by the criminologist

---

hypertension, cerebral thrombosis, diabetes, mellitus and right hemiparesis, and died ten days later.

Norval Morris in regard to the unreliability of confessional evidence. Morris was referring to the controversial case of Max Stuart, an illiterate Arrernte man condemned to death in South Australia for the murder of a nine-year-old girl on the basis of a suspiciously fluent statement in his name. Surely, Murray wrote Rylah, it was time for a royal commission into the case of John Kerr, as the South Australian government was to hold into Max Stuart.

Their efforts received predictably short shrift, and Kerr had at last outworn his media welcome too. In his new job as crime guru at *Truth,* for example, Geoff Clancy did not forget having been so rudely shoved aside by Lee Murray, divulging in May 1958 that Kerr had been given two days' solitary confinement in Pentridge's newly opened H Division for talking back to a guard.

> KERR PUT IN 'HELL' CELLS!
>
> Murderer John Bryan Kerr was put in Pentridge Gaol's 'Hell' division this week for insolence to a warder.
>
> Kerr who was previously in the gaol's busiest section – A Division – is alleged to have severely abused the warder.
>
> Before Kerr's outburst, a warder had reprimanded him severely.

> Kerr is alleged to have replied to the warder in 'shocking' terms...
>
> Gaol officials say Kerr's outburst this week could jeopardise the good conduct award.
>
> They said that despite more-than-average encouragement, his conduct in the gaol had worsened in recent years.

Murderer John Bryan Kerr: how some readers would have relished that. Kerr spoiled to sue, sending Galbally a closely typed eleven-page tirade scored with underlinings, peppered with exclamations and reinforced with references stretching back to Magna Carta. 'If this is not defamation then I am at a complete loss to understand the law!' he fulminated. Galbally presumably decided *Truth* best left alone because no defamation action eventuated.

In official circles there was also ever less interest in even the mention of his name. In June 1959, a Melbourne University law student, Peter Coldbeck, foreshadowed in *Farrago* a plan to restage the third trial of *The King v. Kerr* as part of a university exhibition, where it would feature alongside exhibits of artificial kidneys, meteorological balloons and 'an electronic brain'. Coldbeck had debated Kerr at Pentridge and been fascinated by him: a man convicted of murder who presented as though he 'ran the gaol'.

This 'model trial of a famous criminal case', Coldbeck wrote, would be both a 'demonstration of lawyers' work' and 'interesting in itself', as Kerr remained 'very much in the news'.

That was the problem. When the student approached the Crown Law Department, Winneke refused him a copy of the transcript, forcing a groveling apology in *The Age* to those who had attended in expectation.

Kerr's day of court reckoning never came – except, in a way, for one extraordinary night at Pentridge.

A courtroom drama performed by prisoners: whoever conceived of the 'Pentridge Players' staging *The Caine Mutiny Court-Martial* in A Division in October 1960 had, at the very least, a droll sense of humour. But the play, an adaptation by Herman Wouk from his famous novel of naval justice, had much to recommend it. Several successful productions had been staged in Australia already, Melbourne's innovative Little Theatre putting it to air live on television station HSV-7 in January 1959. And now the Little Theatre's costumes were available to be borrowed, while the play itself involved an all-male cast and the minimum of props.

When undistinguished sailor, court-martial defendant and accused perjurer Kerr read the script, he must have recognised the defence counsel Lt Barney Greenwald as a role he was born to play. What about that exchange between probing Greenwald, appointed to defend youthful Lt Stephen Maryk, and blustering Captain Queeg?

> Greenwald: You are accusing Mister Maryk of perjury?
>
> Queeg: I'm not accusing him. He's accused of enough as it stands. You're likely to hear a lot of strange things from Mister Maryk about me, that's all.
>
> Greenwald: Isn't one of you obviously not telling the truth about that interview?
>
> Queeg: It appears so.
>
> Greenwald: Can you prove it isn't you?
>
> Queeg: Only by citing a clean record of over fourteen years as a naval officer, against the word of a man on trial for a mutinous act.

Isn't one of you not telling the truth about that interview? was essentially the same question as had been posed at Kerr's trial a decade earlier, entailing the same prosecution riposte – back then it had been the clean record of a police officer against the word of a man on trial for a murderous act.

What an opportunity – as Greenwald, Kerr could get the better of a supercilious psychiatrist, an overweening intellectual, an outraged prosecutor, a consternated judge and, best of all, a bombastic accuser ensnared in his own delusions and fabrications. No wonder he threw himself into the effort, snapping off lines replete with personal meaning: 'I hate this case, do you know? The more so because I want to win it so bad'.

Preparations, overseen by forty-four-year-old Hungarian *émigré* Gábor Baraker of the Little Theatre, took more than a year, disrupted by prison releases and transfers of several key actors. But when the production finally played to an A Division mess packed with prisoners and visitors, *Herald* drama critic Kenneth Joachim described it as a colourful triumph.

> The actors bowed low, blew kisses, bowed again – and again. I thought the audience would never stop cheering last night.
>
> When they did, they – Melbourne's top lecturers, debaters, TV personalities – invaded the stage to shake Lt Barney Greenwald by the hand, clap Captain Queeg on the back, cluster round Judge Advocate Challee...
>
> The astonishing thing was that but for stone walls, and warders watching over blue-jeaned prisoners who comprised a third of the audience, A Division Pentridge might well have been mistaken for the Princess Theatre, Spring Street.

The Herald thought the outstanding performance came from 'a man serving a long sentence for murder'; *The Sun* dispelled any ambiguity about the identity of same by referring to 'a former radio announcer' giving 'an almost perfect portrayal of defence counsel Lt Barney Greenwald'. A young law student in the audience, John Coldrey, later a Supreme Court judge, remembered Kerr 'clearly soaking up the adulation and looking for approval of his acting'; he also remembered losing his security pass in the excitement, and the jocular cry of the warder whom he told: 'Set another place for breakfast!'

The linocut program printed at Pentridge was admired. The actors formed a muscular chorus line for photographs, Kerr at their centre. Then reality intruded. Having mingled for fifteen minutes, the visitors were swept out and the cast gathered up, cell doors closing behind them.

Only in fiction would John Bryan Kerr ever beat the system.

12

'THE KERR LEGEND WILL NEVER DIE'

'Adelaide has had its Stuart case. Tasmania has had its Orr case,' began *The Bulletin's* widely read 'Batman' columnist in May 1962,

> But it may surprise you to know that in Melbourne we too can have our grand passions. Any day now John Bryan Kerr will step out of Pentridge Gaol a free man. Perhaps you have forgotten the name. We haven't forgotten here. Nothing like this case has ever stirred up such a swamp of local emotion.

The King v. Kerr was now something in which to induct a new generation. 'Batman', the inimitable Keith Dunstan, explained the fascination. Kerr had been 'a very engaging young man', from the 'right' address and the 'right' school, a radio announcer with 'the good looks of the playboy-actor' and 'an overpowering, volatile personality'. Nor had Kerr vanished on being sent to gaol: 'Go to any Victorian newspaper office and you will find that the file on John Bryan Kerr is almost as fat as the files on Mr Menzies and Mr Calwell'. Batman recalled the 'Kerr Special Editions' of

The Argus as an 'onslaught that went on for months' and foretold something similar.

> In recent years there have been stories that Kerr is fascinated by television. He has spent five years studying all he can about it, in the hope of becoming a TV announcer. Although Kerr, of course, has never seen a TV set. There has been a suggestion that one commercial TV station has a contract ready and that as soon as he comes out Kerr will personally tell his story onscreen. This is extremely hard to believe, but from what we have seen over the past 12 years Kerr is most unlikely to go into shy retirement. He is not a shy retiring man. He is certain to make some attempt to state his innocence.
>
> The arguments still continue as to whether he is innocent or guilty and there are some who feel he should never be released. Most times it is better to let prisoners depart from gaol as quietly as possible, but this one is different and it is impossible not to wait and watch with a good deal of fascination.

Kerr had actually applied for parole nearly fifteen months earlier, his sentence having already been reduced by remissions for the Coronation in 1953 and the Royal Visit in 1954. He had even been offered a job by Kenneth Wright, the successful car salesman who was the patron of the Victorian Debating Association.

At the time, however, the memory of the campaigns in his name had worked against him. The Parole Board was chaired by none other than Jack Barry, the uncomfortable judge at Kerr's unruly second trial: his voice would have been influential. Kerr, Barry and his fellow board members concluded, was 'a person of attractive personality and of quick intelligence' who had 'held the interest of the sensational press during his imprisonment'. As such, they deemed it unlikely he 'would be able to keep out of the limelight' while reporting to a parole officer. He was moved instead to Cooriemungle Prison Farm, the minimum-security camp in the Heytesbury Forest near Timboon, 250 kilometres from Melbourne, where prisoners nearing the end of their terms were often sent to reaccustom them to bigger spaces. The board would have felt confirmed in their view of his continued celebrity: no sooner had Kerr's move been foreshadowed than *The Herald* published a page of photographs of the facility under the headline: 'JOHN BRYAN KERR MAY FINISH GAOL TERM HERE'.

In the event, Kerr spent only four months at Cooriemungle before returning to Pentridge. But reality was dawning. Kerr was a thirty-sixp-year-old man who had spent more than a third of his life in prison. How would the outside world deal with him? His elderly parents, who had been compelled to give up Afton in favour of an apartment near Hoddle Bridge whose name 'Chadwick Mansions' belied its size, had their misgivings. While Kerr's application was being evaluated, they received a visit from a sympathetic and even-handed parole officer, F.G. Hyland. He liked them. Donald he found 'well-adjusted and socially mature', Rose 'a calm, intelligent woman'. And he detected just the vaguest hint that their public avowals of faith in their son had not been entirely unequivocal.

> In the past she has fought fiercely to have Kerr's case reopened but she now appears to have accepted the inevitable and is making practical plans for her son's rehabilitation when he is released. She agrees that he is a most difficult person to handle, but is confident that he will not do anything to further embarrass herself or her husband.
>
> Throughout his story of the offence, Kerr gave no signs that he was guilty and seemed to firmly believe that the girl had met another man after they had parted and returned to the beach with him. It could be that he has no actual recollection of the offence as he had been drinking very heavily. His mother subscribes to this point of view as alcohol had had an inordinate effect on Kerr on previous occasions in as much as he had no recollections of his behaviour when he sobered up.

His mother subscribes to this point of view: perhaps Hyland misheard or misconstrued Rose's remarks; perhaps it was a decade of wondering over the past, recent nights of worrying over the future. But this was not the same voice as had written to the attorney-general of her absolute certainty that her son's 'exceptionally intense nature' ruled out his having killed then calmly slept, whose 'scrupulously correct manner of expression' made such a stumbling, inarticulate confession possible. It was the construction of a mind trying to reconcile faith with doubt, love with life.

How, meanwhile, would Kerr cope with the outside world? He had lost so many years, missed so much. While he had been in gaol, Melbourne's population had grown almost a third. Its streets were now lined with parking meters, its buildings ablaze with neon, its skylines raked by television antennae. Kerr, nonetheless, felt ready. And having missed the 1950s, he was not about to miss the 1960s. Why, he already had a girlfriend.

***

One day early in 1962, the news tips phone rang in the ramshackle Latrobe Street office of *Truth.* On the line was an agitated man named Joseph Kelly with an extraordinary story. His wife Yolanda was having an affair with John Bryan Kerr.

Did he have proof? Well no, it was just a feeling. People rang *Truth* with all manner of crazy yarns, and this sounded like one of them. Kelly's East Bentleigh residence was on the way home for thirty-eight-year-old news reporter Owen McKenna so he promised to look in, but when he drove past the lights were off and the house apparently deserted. He returned to reporting the torrid affair between GTV-9 personality Hal Todd and ex-Miss Moomba Honi Freger, which, unconstrained by bluestone walls, had scandalously produced a love child.

But Joseph Kelly was onto something. His attractive, dark-haired thirty-three-year-old wife Yolanda *was* infatuated with Kerr. She was the daughter of a prominent British Maltese lawyer whom she idolised, the more so for his premature death, aged forty. Despite marrying Joseph aged seventeen and becoming a mother at eighteen, she retained a fascination with the law. She had followed the Kerr trials closely, then pored over the 'John Bryan Kerr Letters', finally writing to Rose Kerr to ask if she might pay a visit to Pentridge.

After a *coup de foudre* on the A Division lawn, a correspondence began of steadily escalating endearments. Rather like Margaret Chandler, destined for Professor Gilbert Bogle's doomed embrace on the banks of the Lane Cove River, Yolanda was an intelligent woman marooned in the suburbs with two children looking for adventure. Kerr was a giddying love object, with his star's aura, martyr's status and temporary unavailability.

That last was about to end. On the afternoon of Friday, 4 May 1962, Kerr was taken to the Pentridge front office and 'signed out'. His personal property and clothing were returned. He was given £140 – prison earnings of £300 reduced for dental and educational expenses – and moved for the weekend to a cell in C Division where on Sunday at 9.30p.m. he heard the lights-out bell for the last time.

He awoke on his release day to cheerful cries from other cells. 'Hey John! All releases are cancelled!' 'It's all right here, sleeping on the floor with a plate of burgoo and a bun for breakfast – why do you want to go out?' He had one final tin-shed shower, and dressed in the suit in which he had been convicted.

The system was determined to treat him as just another ex-con. On the recent releases list in the *Police Gazette* he was sandwiched between two housebreakers as 'Kerr John B., alias JOHN BRYAN KERR, 49194, IB NO H14833', among loiterers, drunks, and convictions for carnal knowledge and insufficient means.

But his special private release acknowledged a change in the mores. Kerr had gone to his imprisonment through great crowds; he left it through television and radio vans clustered outside the gaol. To confuse them, Kerr was put in one of two Black Marias, one of which turned left out the gate and the other right.

Kerr took his first free steps at Eric Shade's Treasury Place office.

It was actually a big day in crime. Also thickly attended by reporters that morning was an inquest into the death of the underworld hitman Norman Bradshaw. Kerr had known Bradshaw inside. It was Bradshaw who had marked out the courts and erected the backboards for basketball courts at Pentridge, on which Kerr had become an enthusiastic player. Now he was dead, and Kerr alive. His old and new lives already seemed to be diverging: as the coroner inquired into Bradshaw's death in a suspicious light plane accident, Kerr was keeping a 10.30a.m. appointment with a discreet hairdresser at a Little Collins Street salon.

He found the city recognisable; the people slightly less so. Fewer women wore gloves, fewer men hats. Hemlines were shorter, suits slimmer. He visited Henry Bucks for a fitting. By then it was time for the long-awaited reunion, for which had been booked the deluxe Molina's Restaurant at the top of Lonsdale Street, and where Kerr and his parents were joined by Brian Bourke.

It was a long lunch – or at least it seemed long to Bourke because Kerr was unbearably cocky, preening and pompous. It occurred to him that Kerr had been the master of his little prison domain; the world would not be shaped so readily. But at that moment, Kerr's thoughts were probably elsewhere. That evening he flew to Sydney, where he was planning to rendezvous with Yolanda Kelly.

***

John Bryan Kerr was a celebrity again. His name had a powerful ring; his presence too. One day, aspiring broadcaster Brian Smith arrived at Kelvin Hall to find Mr Murray in conversation with a handsome figure in a black-and-white houndstooth trenchcoat. An introduction was affected: 'This is John Bryan Kerr'.

Smith surveyed the visitor. He was immaculate. His perfectly parted hair gleamed. The word that leapt to mind was 'supercool'. Everything about him suggested one with all the money and all the time in the world.

The impression was misleading. Dunstan was right that there was curiosity about what he might do – a curiosity that would abate. Kerr went the obvious route. *Truth* had not always been kind to him, but they had always been interested, and for £500 he was prepared to appease them. Owen McKenna was appointed his amanuensis. Their first meeting was rather like that of Holly Martens and Harry Lime in *The Third Man.* McKenna was told to wait under a particular street-corner light in Toorak; his interviewee stepped out of the foggy night as if from nowhere. Like Smith, McKenna was struck at once by Kerr's attire: pepper-coloured raglan overcoat open at the top to give a glimpse of a crisp white collar and dark silk tie, shoes so shiny you could see your reflection in them. The pair walked the short distance to Chadwick Mansions, where Donald and Rose poured drinks and left them by an open fire. Now McKenna's attention was captured by the voice, rich and deep, and the hands, as smooth and scrubbed as a surgeon's, with a black onyx ring on his right hand. Could those hands, he could not help wondering, have fastened lethally around the neck of a twenty-year-old girl?

Kerr and McKenna would spend most of two weeks together, and so decided to get to know one another. There wasn't much common ground between them. They were both ex-RAAF, but McKenna's had been a dangerous war flying Kittyhawks and Vengeances round Morotai. They had worked in the media, but McKenna's pre-*Truth* career had been on the unglamorous *Catholic Young Men* and *Labor Call.* Fortunately, both liked a drink. They visited Lee and Lynne Murray in their Alexandra Avenue flat. They visited June Clyne before a Little Theatre show. They visited Albert Park Sports Centre where Kerr shot hoops for the photographer – a nod to Norman Bradshaw. As a further reminder of where Kerr had spent the twelve preceding years, they went for beers one night in a Port Melbourne hotel with a large and faintly menacing acquaintance.

'That was Swede Olsson,' Kerr said conspiratorially as they left. 'Swede says if I have a problem with anyone to let him know. He extends that protection to you too.'

Kerr had other errands to run. He had Brian Bourke line him up to see two people. One was Rob Monahan. Having found Kerr hard to take at first, Bourke was now genuinely moved: when Kerr arrived in chambers, Monahan rose in his judge's underrobes, walked round the desk and embraced his former client, tears in his eyes.

Kerr's reciprocal regard was equally clear. Lunch stretched into the afternoon, Monahan deprecating word from his associate they were due back in court. 'Damn it, they can wait,' the judge said.

If Bourke felt a little superfluous at an occasion so intimate, he felt downright unnecessary at the next meeting he organised, for Kerr wished to meet Bluey Adam at Russell Street police headquarters.

'I'm pleased,' said the detective on the phone. 'First time a bloke I ever had anything to do with convicting wanted to see me.'

'I'll leave it with you,' Bourke replied.

What passed between them? When Adam collaborated in his retirement testament 'The Bluey Adam Files' four-and-a-half years later, he seemed to allude to the meeting.

> I am on first name terms with several men who have served long terms for murder on my evidence and who have since been released from prison.

> I wouldn't say we're exactly buddies, but, as one of the most famous – or infamous – of them said to me one night in a hotel in Spring Street.
>
> 'There's no animosity on my part, Bluey. We both did what we had to do.'
>
> By that I presume he means branding me a liar and a perjurer in an attempt to win an acquittal.
>
> As far as I'm concerned he did his time and that's that. But he was guilty and I didn't lie.

Kerr's account was a mirror image, roles reversed. Later on the day of the meeting with Adam, he adjourned with McKenna and *Truth* colleague Brian Hansen to the paper's watering hole, the Sabloniere Hotel on Queen Street. Then, after a phone call to licensee Harry Hopman to clear the way, the trio kicked on to the nearby Amateur Sportsmen's Club. Hansen was transfixed by Kerr, who drank copiously, almost competitively, yet showed no signs of inebriation.

Drink emboldened Hansen to ask questions. He wanted to know: what had Bluey Adam said to him? Kerr explained that it had been the detective who had walked up to him and said 'No hard feelings'. For his own part, Kerr had simply accepted Adam's outstretched hand, there being no point in his antagonising the police so early in his liberty.

So the relations between Adam and Kerr ended as they had begun, with irreconcilable accounts of the same event, both self-serving, neither satisfactory. Adam's version sounded typically exaggerated, Kerr's as though there was something missing – for could he really have requested the meeting then gone through a ritual so muted?

Perhaps. If it's not clear what Kerr sought to accomplish in facing his former adversary, maybe that's because it was not clear *to him* – it merely had to be done. Even simply standing before Adam enabled Kerr to prove he was unbowed, unembittered, capable of self-control despite the sorest provocation. He later narrated another story of his early days out of gaol – apparently trivial, oddly expressive.

> Peak-hour passengers crowded the bus as I boarded the rear platform. Before I could move inside it drove off. Several people were in front of me. The conductor called out aggressively: 'Come on – move further inside or get off!'
>
> I continued moving down the bus off the platform. Coming towards me the conductor put his arm out to bar my way and grasped me tightly by the shoulder. More aggressively he shouted: 'You'll have to get off. Didn't you hear me?'
>
> 'You don't expect me to get off a moving bus, do you? I'm going inside as fast as I can.'

> I managed to move past his restraining arm.
>
> Belligerently he said: 'Don't try to be funny with me!'
>
> Controlling my anger, I looked around at him and said quietly but firmly: 'Good luck to you.' He let the matter drop.

Without further explication, Kerr let the story drop. But to him it was clearly an exchange of great weight. *Controlling my anger:* for Kerr this was more than a phrase, it was a life's challenge. Looking Adam in the eye and accepting his hand was a proof he could meet it.

That evening at the Amateur Sportsmen's Club, Hansen pressed on.

'We've been talking for hours and it's all about writing your story in *Truth,'* he said. 'Yet I haven't once heard you say you didn't do it or that you want the real killer found.'

'And you won't hear me say it,' Kerr replied evenly. 'My comments about the case are all on record. I do not need to keep repeating them.'

Kerr was as good as his word. To McKenna, he would say nothing of the fateful night. He confined himself to his Pentridge ordeal, although even then within agreed limits. He would discuss, for example, being a member of Eric Shade's Prisoners Advisory Council, his debating and acting. But he grew chilly and remote when questions neared the bone, concerned his reputation...

> McKenna: From what one hears you seem to have emerged as the Crown Prince of Pentridge.
>
> Kerr: I think the tone and temper of that question is in poor taste so I'll ignore it except to say that in all committees on which I served I was democratically elected by the prisoners to the positions.
>
> McKenna: But...
>
> Kerr: Never mind about that. As I was saying, the positions I held provided me with the privilege of taking a leading part in the organisation and development of various programmes.

...or the reputations of others:

> McKenna: Did you meet W.J. O'Meally?
>
> Kerr: Yes, I met Bill O'Meally during my term of imprisonment.
>
> McKenna: What sort of a chap is he?
>
> Kerr: Look, I'm not prepared now or ever to discuss the pros and cons of another prisoner. If you want to find out what sort of a chap Bill

O'Meally is, I think your best source is Bill O'Meally himself.

McKenna: Is there much gambling at Pentridge?

Kerr: Gambling? At Pentridge? (silence)

McKenna: I can see that on matters like that you are not prepared to make any comment.

Kerr: At last I see you are getting the message.

To McKenna, the message lay in what Kerr did rather than what he said.

Kerr was struggling with liberty, he thought, more than he let on. Sometimes it would be too much. Kerr would pale, start sweating, grow tetchy, whereupon McKenna would suggest they break off and have a beer. He had a host of characteristic, obsessional gestures. He was constantly brushing his clothing with his hands to remove invisible specks of dust; he was nervously aware of his onyx ring, which he would stretch his arm to admire, and furbish incessantly.

One habit set McKenna's teeth on edge – the way Kerr spoke to his parents, whom the journalist personally found polite and gracious, as though they were servants. McKenna arrived one morning to find Kerr in the last stages of dressing, and watched him wordlessly hand a clothes brush to his mother, then extend his arms to be attended to. More than fifty years later, Owen McKenna still shook his head at that.

Yes, here we were, so long after events, trying to make sense of them. Owen McKenna, ninety-one, was in a dark, two-room flat in an RSL retirement village; Brian Hansen, eighty-two, was living with his wife in Highett, deprived of his voice by motor neurone disease and restricted to communicating through an iPad app.

At mention of John Bryan Kerr, however, they came alive: his looks, his manner, his voice, his ... yes, his conviction. For both had thought long and hard about it, and drawn conclusions. Owen McKenna had awaited a protestation of innocence and been disappointed, suspecting that this pointed to Kerr's guilt. Brian Hansen saw instead an understandable desire to seal the past off, and supposed more positively that Kerr was simply too intelligent to have given the 'confession' claimed.

By the terms of journalism, McKenna's view had perhaps the greater force. On 26 May 1962, a full week ahead, *Truth* flagged its four-part series: 'ANOTHER BIG EXCLUSIVE COMING UP ... JOHN BRYAN KERR TELLS ... MY 12 YEARS IN GAOL'.

But the description forewarned of anti-climax:

> *Truth* makes journalistic history in Australia by presenting this plain, unvarnished picture of life behind bars as seen through the eyes of an

> intelligent man cut off from the outside world. Kerr and *Truth* will not delve into the past nor into questions of innocence or guilt of the terrible crime for which he was convicted.

Will not delve into the past? That rendered the series a rather prison-grey affair, suitably bleak, occasionally nasty, but of interest chiefly to students of penology.

Yet Hansen also seemed to have intuited something about Kerr's need for dignity. As it is with most people, the opportunity to tell his personal story had probably seemed an appealing idea up to the moment he had to do it, when it became easier to deal in superficialities, descriptions, divagations.

'You say you are not bitter?' McKenna asked him at one point.

'Yes, that's correct,' Kerr replied. 'I am not bitter because I felt that if I became bitter I would only defeat my own purpose – because bitterness is like revenge. It's an emotion I can't afford.'

And Kerr knew better than most how expensive emotions could be.

***

Sydney was easier for Kerr – but still not easy. Owen McKenna visited him and Yolanda Kelly in a flat off Oxford Street; soon they moved to another apartment in Holdsworth Avenue, Woollahra, near the Lord Dudley

Hotel. McKenna liked Yolanda, who was charming and articulate; in a word, 'classy'. He met her children, fifteen-year-old Patrick and twelve-year-old Anna. They stayed in touch many years afterwards, the contact petering out when she retired to Port Macquarie. So it was that I found myself one day leafing through the Port Macquarie White Pages for Kellys, where there were no Ys but several Ps, which I ticked off with cold calls until a Patrick answered.

Patrick Kelly explained that his mother had passed away two years earlier, and he was loath to discuss John Bryan Kerr. But the dislike was clear. Could it have been otherwise towards someone who had broken up his family home? A teenage male confronted by an interloping rival for his mother's affection who happened to be a convicted murderer: This was also a dislike rooted in fear, for his mother, of Kerr. 'He was not a nice character,' said Patrick Kelly. 'Affable enough when sober; verbally aggressive verging on violent when drunk.' The proximity of the Lord Dudley was perhaps more problematic than it should have been.

Likewise, work. Yolanda took a job as a receptionist at the Rex Hotel in King's Cross; Kerr's only occupation was being John Bryan Kerr. On 24 July 1962, he signed a contract worth 180 guineas with Ronald Tarrant, editor of *Pix* magazine, for three articles 'in cooperation with one of my staff'.

This time rather more was expected, for he was cajoled into an account of the night he met Beth Williams. It was corny – 'Beth Williams called out to me. It was as if we were all pawns in some diabolical chess game, pushed hither and thither by capricious hands of fate' – but necessary. *Pix* introduced him as 'the most controversial figure in modern Australian criminology', claiming that 'the Kerr legend will probably never die'. But the legend needed ever more tending to keep alive. A fourth piece was commissioned, then a fifth. Capital punishment was back in the news with the death sentence passed in Victoria on Robert Peter Tait, a sexual psychopath who had killed a widow in a Hawthorn vicarage, with Bolte palpably reluctant to commute the sentence despite an anti-hanging movement now vocal and organised. Several figures were common to *The King v. Kerr,* including Sir Charles Lowe as judge, Sir Henry Winneke as solicitor-general and Pansy Wright as activist, organising a stirring open letter signed by academics and churchmen.

But Kerr's most thoughtful piece was the most understated, about the difficulty for former prisoners of making a fresh start. Doubtless it was the most personally pertinent at the time.

> The ceaseless controversy of my own case and newspaper notoriety publicising me as 'the most discussed figure in modern Australian criminology' has made it extremely difficult to re-establish myself and secure employment...

> Notoriety has allowed me to survive these first months of release by earning a living through writing newspaper and magazine articles.
>
> But what happens now?

Quite so. The unselfconscious quotation from his own series – 'the most discussed figure in modern Australian criminology' – betrayed his ambivalence. Kerr could not get over having been convicted of murder – it was all he had. For after about six months, the bloom was off the rose, and Yolanda was gone. She did not reconcile with her former husband, although they made a workable relationship, and Patrick Kelly could look back on his brush with John Bryan Kerr as an unfortunate interlude typical of his mother. 'My mother would pick up the bat for whoever was the underdog,' he said fondly. 'That was her nature.'

The struggle for work continued. To McKenna, Kerr made a joke of it. One day, he recounted, he was close to landing a sales representative job when one of the interview panel asked, 'This is just routine, so please don't take offence but have you ever been in trouble with the police?'

'Yes,' Kerr replied nonchalantly. 'For murder.'

Kerr told the story with a gusty laugh: he had thought 'those old blokes were going to faint'. But there was an underlying anxiety. He was a thirty-seven-year-old man with no qualifications who had never held a job longer than a year. How to put together a life so profoundly broken?

At last, in time for Christmas 1962, Kerr got lucky, applying successfully for the vacancy of assistant manager in the floor covering department of Cooper Brookes Pty Ltd, 316 Pitt Street, Sydney. Yes, he was selling carpet – and in the process began to sweep aspects of his old life under one.

13

MEET JOHN WALLACE

It was a Saturday afternoon at Kardinia Park in August 1984, a blustery day on the eve of the Victorian Football League finals. In the social club, Richmond FC coterie members were being hosted by their Geelong FC counterparts, the Pivotonians. Visitor Bruce Gough stood talking to the Pivotonians' president, Barry Solomon, and noticed his eyes wandering.

Solomon, a successful businessman, was the scion of the drapers who had sponsored 3GL's 'Solomons Family Quiz' in 1949. Scanning the room, he had just spied out the corner of his eye another of the visitors – a man he had last seen behind a radio microphone thirty-five years earlier.

'Who's that fellow over there?' he asked.

The Richmond man looked around.

'Oh, that's John Wallace,' Gough replied. 'A very keen supporter of the club.'

'But do you know his real name?' Solomon said. 'Because I tell you who he used to be: John Bryan Kerr.'

Later in the day, Solomon caught sight of the figure again, and couldn't resist introducing himself.

'Hello, I'm Barry Solomon,' he said. 'Do you remember me from way back, when you were at 3GL?'

The man looked back blandly.

'Yes, I do,' he said at last. 'I'm John Wallace now.'

He moved away.

Gough's mind, meanwhile, was racing. He remembered John Bryan Kerr. Everyone of a certain vintage remembered John Bryan Kerr. But, he reflected, what do you do under the circumstances of such a life, with a name so recognisable, and a reputation so uneffaceable? You might well live a lie or two for the sake of your hard-won peace.

***

In court, John Bryan Kerr had committed himself to a lengthy recitation of the events of a single night. When it came to constructing a past, he kept it robustly simple. Rummaging among his effects, I felt a frustrated admiration. The most poignant relic was a 1975 résumé where fifty-year-old John Bryan Kerr presented himself as forty-year-old John Wallace, accounting for his lost years in a couple of lines.

> 1953–56 Afton Nurses Agency, West St Kilda, family operated business, assistant account manager

> 1957–1961 Silicone Consolidated Industries, Market Street, Sydney, sales representative

Afton was self-explanatory, the name of the family home. And while Silicone Consolidated certainly existed, the reference in his personal effects was clearly a fake on a piece of the company's stationery. It was probably this reference that underpinned his 1962 job application to Cooper Brookes, explaining 'John Wallace-Kerr' as an unfortunate innocent in the wrong place at the wrong time – a role of which Kerr would have claimed some experience.

> May I introduce a former employee of ours by the name of John Wallace-Kerr who has been forced to leave our company through no action of his own.
>
> We are at present in state of retrenchment necessarily resulting in the reduction of staff.
>
> Mr Wallace-Kerr has proven himself a very loyal and able employee and I have no hesitation in recommending him for any type of employment.

So, within a year of his release from Pentridge, began the triple life of John Bryan Kerr, John Bryan Wallace-Kerr and and finally John Wallace, with little means for a researcher to tell where one ended and the others began. Was this glowing professional reference *really* written by his boss at Cooper Brookes?

> This letter will serve to introduce Mr J. Wallace-Kerr who was employed by this company ... During his employment with the company Mr Wallace-Kerr revealed a tenacity of purpose and attention to detail that has served him well in all his duties. Mr Wallace-Kerr's company-minded attitude is a rare attribute and he has shown outstanding qualities of loyalty and honesty.

And was this effusive personal reference *really* written by a partner at Freehill Hollingdale Page?

> I have known Mr John Wallace-Kerr for about two years, both professionally and personally. I have found him to be a man of great integrity, possessing a keen sense of what is fair and just. From my acquaintance with him, I have formed the impression that he is a man in whom one can place the highest trust, both in business and in a personal sense.

A keen sense of what is fair and just: yes, one might well place in such a man *the highest trust.* Actually, arranging Kerr/Wallace's work-related effects into a sort-of sequence told of a chequered history, thanks, almost certainly, to periodic discoveries of his identity.

There was an appointment letter dated 1 July 1964, for 'Mr John Wallace-Kerr' becoming a sales representative with Olympic Products in Pyrmont, earning £27 a week for selling rubber flooring and vinyl tiles. Then, soon after, a terse reference advising that 'Mr John Wallace-Kerr' had been 'terminated owing to retrenchment in his particular division'.

There was an appointment letter dated 21 August 1964 for 'Mr John Wallace-Kerr' becoming a sales representative of S.C. Johnson, selling cleaning products on £140 per month with a tax-free allowance of £70, company car, superannuation and profit share. But after six months he lost this job too. Strangest was an unaddressed, unexplained reference from what appeared to be a professional consultancy, Career Development in Sydney's Griff House, dated the following month, and reading in part:

> This will introduce John Wallace-Kerr.
>
> He is fundamentally strong for calling on the people you service, has wide sales and promotional experience, and is interested in joining a company with your stature in industry. His appearance and personal presentation speak for themselves...
>
> We have checked his references over the last ten years and are satisfied that if he is met halfway, he could handle efficiently almost any challenging sales position...
>
> He is flexible enough in his thinking to sell to ditchdiggers or executives ... His drive and strong sales ability have, on occasion, caused him to rub a few people the wrong way. And, due to his very

> rapid promotion in his last company, petty jealousies turned into the politics that occasioned his move. You will be able to judge for yourself the minor qualities he needs to improve and can best advise him according to your company policy.

We have checked his references for the last ten years: no need for you to ascertain whether he really does have *wide sales and promotional experience.* Meet him *halfway,* and there need be no risk of *politics* and *petty jealousies.* Neither Olympic Products nor S.C. Johnson was included in the aforementioned 1975 résumé; he listed himself instead in this time as having joined a company called Cretex Pty Ltd, a detergent manufacturer headquartered in Annandale, which he actually seemed to have joined in July 1965. Faithful reflections were hard to discern in this hall of mirrors. I was reminded of one of Denise Duncan's early comments: 'John spent his life looking over his shoulder wondering whether people had worked out who he was.' Quite a few assuredly did.

What began as a professional refurbishment became in time personal. In about March 1963, Brian Hansen from *Truth* came to Sydney to dig into the Bogle–Chandler mystery: the mysterious deaths of Dr Gilbert Bogle, a CSIRO physicist, and Margaret Chandler, a colleague's wife. No sooner had the journalist arrived than his hotel room telephone rang.

'G'day Brian,' said a familiar voice. 'Have a good flight? I think I can help you with your story.'

Hansen was astonished. How did John Bryan Kerr know where he was and what he was doing? Over dinner in the Australia Hotel restaurant, Hansen could elicit only enigmatic responses. Kerr explained instead that he was on the fringe of the circle that had attended the New Year's Party from which Bogle and Chandler absconded, bound for their terminal tryst. Thanks to a tabloid newspaper war between *The Sun* and the *Daily Mirror,* the party had been the subject of all manner of rumour and innuendo ('Weird Cults Tip In Deaths Puzzle'; 'The Beatniks Go For Cover'); Kerr provided Hansen with a Manly contact wishing to scotch such speculation. The subject of Kerr's own past never arose, and Hansen sensed that Kerr's attractive female companion knew nothing about it.

Jerry Hughes, a printing salesman whom Kerr encountered at the Lord Dudley round the same time, *was* taken into his confidence. I met Hughes and his charming partner Alison one afternoon in their secluded Dandenongs home. In old photographs round the room, he presented with a rogueish swagger. He had been a playboy in Potts Point, run an illegal key club in St Kilda, spent a lot of time with John Bryan Kerr and at one time fancied writing a book about him. Alas, a stroke had strafed his eighty-five-year-old memory. He reached for stories now like someone stretching for jars on a too-high shelf.

One recollection he regarded as important enough to repeat was of tackling Kerr earnestly about the Williams murder, 'C'mon John, enough fucking about,' he remembered asking his friend one day. 'In all seriousness, you did knock her off, didn't you?'

Kerr, Hughes remembered, returned his gaze inscrutably, 'That's for you to find out.'

Jerry and Alison now referred to their old friend fondly as 'The Murderer'.

Dennis Cameron-Kennedy, local representative for a Melbourne furniture company whom Kerr also met at the Lord Dudley but in 1967, never knew anything: the transformation into 'John Wallace' was by then all-but complete. I met Cameron-Kennedy one morning in a city cafe – a trim, alert figure with a dashing wing-commander's moustache. In hindsight, he was not quite sure what to think.

'I knew John a long time,' he said, a little sadly. 'But obviously I never *really* knew him.'

Only in hindsight was he aware how little his friend spoke of the past. 'One day he said he had a hyphenated name like mine – he was Wallace-Kerr – but didn't really use it. That was all I ever heard.'

Cameron-Kennedy often had Wallace over of an evening in Sydney – he was an excellent guest because, exhibiting the fetish for cleanliness that Owen McKenna had first noticed, he would insist on doing the dishes to an exactingly high standard. But Cameron-Kennedy could not recall a reciprocal invitation to Wallace's residences: either a house in Darling Point Road or the deco apartment he rented in Billyard Avenue, Elizabeth Bay. Strange now, Cameron-Kennedy reflected; at the time, somehow not.

And the death of Beth Williams – well, it never quite went away. It joined a continuum of crimes that unsettled Australians in their innocent embrace of seaside fun, alongside the Wanda Beach murders of January 1965 and the abduction of the Beaumont children a year later. In the twelve-year run of the landmark Melbourne-based police procedural *Homicide,* death on the beach was a subtly recurrent theme. The episode 'Bait' in May 1969 dealt explicitly with the strangled body of a young woman being discovered by a passerby – reflecting changed customs, the passer-by was not a morning walker but a jogging enthusiast. John Bryan Kerr might no longer be a face but he remained a name to conjure with. In the late 1960s, Graham Kennedy gave an interview in which he mischievously aired a Channel 9 rumour that Kerr was now masquerading as newsreader Kevin Sanders. Everyone laughed. But he had to be out there somewhere and doing something, didn't he?

'So John, tell us about yourself': it was John Bryan Kerr's lot that the simplest and politest of enquiries was the hardest to answer honestly. Best to present the smallest target – even, perhaps especially, in the matter of another life.

***

Kerrie Louise Williams put her younger sister Vicki in mind of Gidget, the vivacious and wholesome beach bunny played by Sandra Dee and Sally Field: she massed her long fair hair; she looked great in a bikini and wore vivid lipstick; she always seemed to have music playing. Those memories, and the photograph of a smiling Kerrie looking down from Vicki's wall in Goulburn for more than forty years, were all that remained.

It had been a story a long time in chasing down: the girlfriend whom John Bryan Kerr met in Sydney; the girlfriend who died. Brian Bourke and Denise Duncan knew aspects but neither dates nor details. Maybe, thought Denise, her name was Kerry. But looking for the untimely death of someone called Kerry sometime in the decade from 1965 is the kind of search that can lead protractedly nowhere – and for some days at the Public Records Office, it did me. I was perilously close to abandoning hope when it transpired that she had simply been misspelled on the inquest index as 'Kerri'.

When she met John Wallace, who was more than twice her age, Kerrie was twenty-two, raised in Orange, Walgett and Goulburn – too young and too countrified to remember his original notoriety, which may have been part of her appeal. The relationship spanned his return to Melbourne. In August 1970, Wallace left his job as sales manager at Debonair Carpet Cleaning Services in York Street, Sydney to become a sales representative in the food-sanitation division of Nightingale Chemicals in Ingles Street, Port Melbourne, moving into the spare bedroom in Chadwick Mansions. Kerrie worked not far away in a chemist shop on Toorak Road, and her youth and vivacity would have been a relief from the shadow of his parents' age and ailments. Like her father, Rose had drifted into dementia; as his son would later, Donald was suffering Parkinson's Disease. But then someone at Nightingale twigged who their new man was, and he was let go. And something happened, perhaps as a result, in the second bedroom of the groundfloor flat in Rockley Road, South Yarra into which Kerrie moved in July 1971.

Kerrie shared the apartment with a thirty-nine-year-old medical secretary, Anne Fairbairn. Although they 'never conversed about our personal lives', she found Kerrie 'a very honest person and of a very happy disposition' who was 'always very obliging and easy to get along with'. She was unaware that her flatmate had been prescribed both the sedative Mogadon (nitrazepam, a kind of benzodiazepine) and the sleep aid Dormal (chloral hydrate, an organic compound). But there was no real reason to ask, given Kerrie's manner up to and including her arrival home at 10.30p.m. on 21 October.

> She always said hello with a big smile, as she did on this occasion, and also commented on the weather being cold. This was common for Kerrie as she often felt the cold in Melbourne. Her appearance and actions were very normal in every

> respect ... Kerrie then went into the bathroom to shower and wash her hair. When she came out I said goodnight to her and she called out goodnight from her bedroom. As she walked from the bathroom to her bedroom I noticed that she was wearing her dressing gown and that she had her hair in rollers.

Fairbairn was briefly awoken in the night by a sound she took to be a possum at her window, but it was only after breakfast next morning she thought to call Kerrie through her slightly opened door.

> After calling to her several times and as it was getting close to 8a.m. I felt I should let her know what the time was. I opened the bedroom door to find Kerrie laying across the bed, dressed in the same dressing gown as I had seen her in the night before. The position I found her in indicated she had been sitting on the bed when something had caused her to fall backwards, falling onto her left side which caused her face to be downwards on the bed. Her legs and arms were bluish in colour.

For twenty-one-year-old Constable Michael Nemtsas and two members of Prahran CIB who arrived just before 9a.m., it presented a curious scene: the room was orderly and the bed clothes turned back; there was an empty bottle of Mogadon and a near-empty bottle of Dormal but no suicide note. They asked

Fairbairn about Kerrie's friends, and she offered the telephone number of John Wallace, who arrived soon after, 'insisted on seeing the body', and was 'shown the deceased'. Senior Detective Reg Baker from Homicide then appeared, wishing advice on 'the circumstances of the death of the deceased and the relationship with Wallace'.

For Kerr/Wallace, the possibilities needed no elaboration. He was in proximity to the untimely death of another girl in her twenties called Williams and answering questions from Homicide. It had ended badly once. None of his new friends would understand his predicament; it needed someone in the know. He hastened to the chambers of Brian Bourke, who heard the note of strain in his friend's smooth, well-modulated voice.

'I was with this girl until about 4a.m.,' he explained. 'And her body was found at 8a.m. in her unit. Is there anything you can do to help?'

'Did you have anything to do with it?' the barrister asked.

'I most certainly did not,' Kerr replied.

Bourke shared Kerr's alarm. It was only five years since his involvement in the defence of Ronald Ryan, whose unspoken presence lingered, as did the death penalty, not actually to be repealed for another four years.

'If there's any evidence to get you convicted of murder, you're in all sorts of trouble,' Bourke said. 'With the lunatics in charge of this state, they might hang you.'

He asked no further details. He never even knew Kerrie Williams' name. He contacted coroner Harry Pascoe and explained the turn of events: if the name John Bryan Kerr hit the headlines again, who knew where events might lead? Pascoe undertook to make enquiries.

Nemtsas noted in his report a phone call from Senior Detective Baker, 'who said that he had spoken with Wallace and had made other investigations and he was satisfied that all was correct'. And Pascoe advised Bourke he would avoid calling Kerr at the inquest, where he ruled that the death followed 'the effects of an overdose of chloral hydrate [Dormal] potentiated by alcohol, both self administered' – chloral hydrate is strongly associated with cardiac arrhythmias in overdose. 'John Wallace' was required only to sign a form, next to a guiding 'X', confirming identification of Kerrie's body.

Kerr/Wallace then ensured that even his own version of events did not survive. In February 1972, he gave an interview to Constable Nemtsas which yielded a written statement, but which he insisted on taking away for further perusal before adding his signature. He never returned it.

'I have interviewed all witnesses involved in this matter,' concluded Nemtsas. 'I am unable to find any suspicious circumstances involving the death of Kerrie Louise Williams, except it appears odd to me that she would go to the trouble of having a shower and then putting her hair in rollers if she was expecting death. It would appear she was preparing for the following day.'

It would, but when Nemtsas was posted to Mildura a few weeks later, nobody picked up the threads of his inquiries. And merely 'odd' fell short of 'suspicious' because of surrounding facts of reasonable durability. She had had a drink. She had taken a sleeping draught. She may have chased it down with sedatives. How it happened did not bring her back. Vicki Simons remembered Kerrie's death becoming a closed subject in her family.

'Our father had been to war,' she said. 'He didn't talk much.' Nearly forty-five years later, it was just something that happened, and she was happy to have the opportunity to remember her sister. She sent me the photograph.

'Please look after it,' she said. 'It's all we have left.'

***

I was able to trace Michael Nemtsas, who had left the police in April 1979, but his memory was dim. He had handled several such cases in his time, and they blurred in his mind. He could not remember 'John

Wallace' or their interview, nor could he be sure he ever knew 'Wallace's real identity. A former colleague of Nemtsas's, Peter Aldred, recalled policework in Prahran as being a little like this. 'Sergeants wouldn't leave the office,' he said. 'They just left us to our own devices. It was all pretty ad hoc.'

These were dog days in Victorian policing more generally, in a way that might have afforded John Bryan Kerr a sense of vindication. As he returned to Melbourne, his old nemesis Bluey Adam, retired nearly four years, had been thrust unwillingly into the limelight, one of a host of Homicide Squad members accused of accepting backhanders from illegal abortionists. Gross, frowsy, stricken with diabetes, he was a shadow now of 'Sir Blue'.

In September 1970 Adam was charged with multiple counts of attempting to pervert the course of justice, as were his close friends Superintendent Jack Matthews, also involved in *The King v. Kerr* as a young detective, and Detective Inspector Jack Ford, who had followed Matthews as Homicide chief. Imagine the scope for *schadenfreude* as Adam now retraced Kerr's steps by spending more than nine months on remand in Pentridge – and there was rather less sympathy for Adam's devoted son Max than there had been for Donald and Rose Kerr.

Growing up Adam's granddaughters had been colourful for Christine and Barbara. Sometimes Grandpa Blue would regale them with exciting stories of leading manhunts and raiding brothels. Other times voices would fall in their presences – once, a dead bird was left on their doorstep. Absences were left unexplained. Grandpa Blue never came for Christmas, sending a huge ham and a magnum of champagne in his stead. Arrivals could be correspondingly unexpected. One day the girls were splashing in their paddle pool when a florid figure in navy blazer and panama hat rolled out of a squad car accompanied by a police photographer. 'I haven't got a recent picture of the girls,' Grandpa explained as he scooped them up, posed long enough for the giant flash to go off, then just as quickly disappeared.

With Grandpa's troubles, their Niddrie home grew more fraught, more silent. One day, Max returned from work as a Melbourne City Council electrician with a black eye, having apparently been involved in an altercation with a colleague.

Barbara was actually sent to live with friends in Geelong; Christine saw her father age with each visit to her grandfather in D Division. Adam was luckier than his peers, Matthews and Ford, both of whom were convicted and gaoled. But the old warhorse felt the stain on his character too, expressing it in terms that one could imagine eliciting snorts of derision from John Bryan Kerr: 'It's not easy to feel the same after you've been accused of something you didn't do. I don't know that I will ever live down the shame and ignominy I have been put through.' Adam was right:

he had months to live, his steadfast son only a year longer.

Were Kerr/Wallace and Kerrie also undone by a collision of his old and new identities, whether because of his termination at Nightingale, or Bluey Adam's renewed notoriety? What might have been discussed between the pair that fateful night? Their future? His past? Both were overshadowed by his conviction for murder.

As such, perhaps it's not surprising that Kerrie's death became something else that John Wallace could discuss but guardedly.

'What happened to Kerrie?' Cameron-Kennedy asked his friend one day.

'She was found dead in bed,' Wallace replied.

Cameron-Kennedy listened for more; there wasn't any. I found but two relics: a generic card from Kerrie's family after the funeral, unmarked; and, in the *Goulburn Evening Post,* a memorial notice with verse from the Irish poet William Allingham, and a closing sentiment freighted with meaning.

> WILLIAMS, Kerrie Louise – Died suddenly and tragically, aged 25, on October 22nd, 1971: 'Scarcely a tear left to shed, Hardly a word left to say; the end of a summer day, Sweet Love dead.' Beloved sweetheart of John Wallace, Melbourne, Victoria. Only you and I understand the truth and need of our devotion.

And in this he was correct: only he and she could understand the need *exactly,* although the truth could only really concern the most material fact about him – the hybrid identity he was struggling to blend and conceal. But in this, he was just about to receive some help from a surprising source – the police.

Ten days after the muted inquest into Kerrie Williams' death, Bluey Adam died at last in a Kew private hospital. John Wallace celebrated, as was his wont, with a great deal to drink, was pulled over driving home, breathalysed and fingerprinted. When the prints turned up a match, watchhouse police realised that they had a celebrity guest.

The first person to tell me this story, former Justice Barry Beach, had heard a secondhand version, with Kerr/Wallace appearing before the magistrate and declaring defiantly when he was asked for previous convictions, 'My name is John Bryan Kerr, and I was sentenced to death for murder, having been convicted on the perjured evidence of Detective Adam'.

As Peter Aldred recalled, the hearing was conducted amid utmost discretion to minimise publicity. The prosecutor had the case brought forward to the morning because the magistrate concerned was notorious for being drunk after lunch, and handed the previous convictions up to the bench rather than reading them out.

Aldred watched the fuss around Kerr/Wallace with interested bemusement.

How did he seem?

'Like he was better than everybody else,' said Aldred. 'Like he had the jump on everyone.'

Old habits died harder than old names.

***

Life went on. On 26 August 1972, his mother Rose died of a heart attack. Forty-seven-year-old Kerr was listed on the death certificate as thirty-nine-year-old 'John Wallace'. On 24 October 1973, his father Donald succumbed to his various ailments. This time his son certified the death as 'J. Kerr', perhaps partly because it was under this name that he was sole beneficiary of his father's modest estate.

It was a confronting moment. With Kerrie Williams' death, they were all he had; he had been their lives. In later years they had been a concern to him. Perhaps because anyone meeting them would have intuited that John Wallace was far older than he claimed, he had tended to keep them out of sight. Dennis Cameron-Kennedy, who often called at Chadwick Mansions, never met them – they always seemed to be in another room, and his friend would want to go out. Yet when Wallace moved into a city apartment block, Lonsdale Heights, near the Comedy Theatre, he did not sell the family share in the old flat. It remained sealed up, its pantry full, calendars unchanging, a nagging loose end for a man who in daily life abhorred untidiness, while he drifted from job to job to an accompaniment of occasional backstage whispers.

'See that bloke?' law student Phil Brewin was told *sotto voce* in 1972 when he worked casually at the city clothing company, Fairway. 'He's a convicted murderer.' Brewin was too young to remember *The King v. Kerr:* all he could see was that the older man was the store's sharpest dresser and smoothest salesman. 'Nothing like owning a $500 suit to help you sell a $40 suit,' he thought.

Fairway was missing on that aforementioned résumé, like Olympic Products and S.C. Johnson earlier, and Nightingale and Hooker Chemicals, where he also worked briefly, later. Instead, John Wallace claimed to have been at Oxy Metal Finishing in Kilsyth from 1971 to 1974, and GD Searle Australia in Cheltenham from 1974 to 1975, although where he worked was less important than the pattern it formed of never staying anywhere long – or long enough to have his identity and backstory queried. The women came and went too, which may have been related. They certainly were when John Wallace applied for a new job at the beginning of 1976.

The local manager of pharmaceutical company Merck, Sharp & Dohme (Australia), Bob Dale, was impressed when Wallace visited his Carlton office to interview for a role as a sales representative. Confident, well-spoken, well-groomed: 'If only all the applicants looked like this bloke,' thought Dale. Wallace was flown to Sydney for the five-week training course at Merck's headquarters in Ferndell Street, South Granville, and made a similarly favourable impression. Then, on the last Friday morning, when the inductees were due to sit a final exam, he did not turn up, and Dale, who was visiting, was called out of a meeting to be told. 'What do you want me to do?' he asked. Sales manager John McGregor said that he intended to hang fire until he knew more.

Dale was in his office again on Monday when Wallace appeared, looking sheepish. 'I suppose I've lost my job before I started,' he lamented. Dale asked what had happened; Wallace explained that his girlfriend of the time, Sandy, had rung to say that she was moving out of Lonsdale Heights, and he had hurried back to Melbourne to dissuade her – to no avail. The decision finally resided with McGregor's head trainer, a former pharmacist and later a state supervisor, whose name was John Kerr. Not knowing, of course, that he held the future of a namesake in his hands, Kerr was lenient.

John Wallace sat the exam on his own, passed and got the job; Merck got an excellent, passionately loyal employee, and remained unaware for his twenty years at the firm of his burnished background and discounted age. What they *did* learn were his idiosyncracies. He was, now almost obsessively, clean. He washed his hands after virtually every interaction, with a person or product. He carried a cloth, an old petticoat, with which he brushed every chair he was to sit on; the boot of his company car was full of cleaning fluids; the floor of his company car he laid daily with fresh tea towels. But Wallace, with his sharp tailoring and dapper moustache, impressed everyone he met – including, in his first year on the road, Denise Mahoney, who worked behind the counter at Orrong Pharmacy on High Street in Prahran. She was twenty-four, born in Katoomba. He was fifty passing as forty, although Denise took him as younger still. They had a drink at the Robert Peel Hotel in Collingwood, whose licensees, Bill and Roma Burns, were friends, then dinner at the Melbourne Waiters' Club in Meyers Place. Within a few weeks of their relationship beginning, Wallace frankly laid out his past as John Bryan Kerr.

Why did he tell Denise what he otherwise treated as a secret? Was it to compensate for his not having told Kerrie Williams at first? Was it to demonstrate his bona fides now? In either event, it did not matter. Denise had never heard of the case, and John Wallace had in the meantime exerted the same instantaneous attraction as John Bryan Kerr had on women from Barbara Robertson to Yolanda Kelly – and Beth Williams too. They soon moved into an apartment on Albert Street in East Melbourne for probably the happiest and certainly the most contented years of his life. He worked hard, and was valued and rewarded at Merck. He forged a strong ring of new friends, mainly through the Richmond Football Club, where he was a member: Bill and Dawn Durham, Arthur and Jean Bonser, Bruce and Elaine Gough.

For Denise Mahoney, John Wallace, as he became at last by deed poll in 1980, was hardly a standard boyfriend. Like his workmates, she had to learn to live with his extreme fastidiousness, such as his polishing any cutlery he was about to use, and cleaning his shoes so assiduously that their condition improved with age. Before car journeys, he liked passengers to clap their feet together three times to dislodge any sand; after car journeys, he liked lap sashes to repose just so. On returning from the supermarket, he would insist on putting the shopping away, carefully wiped and where he liked it. On finishing a call, he would spend as long as ten minutes rearranging the telephone cord. Denise was never sure if John's anxiety to control the environment around him was innate, or a result of his years in gaol, or both. They once argued heatedly over her leaving the toilet paper with a ragged edge.

Privately, Denise forbore dark moods and phases of panic. The prospect of having to obtain a passport, his first, when Merck invited him to a conference in Singapore, incapacitated John for days, because of the possibility people might know his real birthdate. Publicly, she made light of it, joking of being a stranger to her kitchen because John so favoured pubs and restaurants. Besides, she said, it spared her housework. 'I don't do any cleaning,' she told Jean

Bonser one day. 'Because I know that whatever I did, it wouldn't be good enough for John.'

Only every so often would there be an incident, usually involving alcohol, when she had to grit her teeth. On one occasion, John had a long lunch in Hobart, missed a plane, then missed Denise at the airport. She had spent four hours wandering when John erupted drunkenly on the scene and harangued her so explosively that he was detained by security, who came back to check his story. Was he *really* who he said he was? Was he really *John Bryan Kerr?*

In the Richmond coterie, John Wallace was officially a character, an entertaining, gregarious, noisily one-eyed fan who didn't mind exchanging a few words with opposition supporters, and who liked to kick on of an evening, every so often to a fault. These were days when players would mingle with members at after-match functions, and on one occasion he came to blows with Richmond wingman Dennis Collins, to whose girlfriend he had made a flirtatious remark – it earned him a two-week suspension from the club. But this afterwards became a subject of merriment, earning him the nickname 'Johnny Holiday'. Nor did it stop Richmond making use of his stentorian tones at Thursday-night coterie functions. With a bell and a gavel, he would introduce chairman of selectors Alan Cook, who would then read out the weekend's teams.

John and Denise could not but stand out, by the gap in their ages, by being neither married nor having children – in fact, Denise had been told by a doctor she would not be able to conceive. Then one day, at a function at Melbourne Zoo hosted by Bill and Roma Burns, John turned confidentially to Bill Durham.

'Denise is pregnant,' he said.

Durham was delighted. 'Well, John,' he said jovially, 'you'll *have* to marry her now.'

He offered as a venue his property on Fraser Spur Road in Neerim East, and there the nuptials took place on 17 December 1983, Dennis Cameron-Kennedy acting as best man. Among the guests, only a handful had known the groom as other than John Wallace.

***

'You know,' her obstetrician told Denise Wallace when she left hospital with baby Kate in May 1984, 'John's not going to cope well.'

A friendly warning: fatherhood would for John not be a natural state, and maybe should not be allowed to happen again. The future was coming, ready or not. The following month saw the last public appearance of John Kerr qua John Kerr, at the funeral of Lee Murray, attended by a sizeable contingent of his alumni. Denise, meanwhile, continued coaxing her husband into domesticity, at last persuading him to sell Chadwick Mansions so they could afford a proper family home in Mount Waverley. And at first, John Wallace rather reveled in his late, unexpected fatherhood. At Kate's christening, he spontaneously broke into 'Beautiful Dreamer': 'Sounds of the rude world heard in the day/Lull'd by the moonlight have all passed away'.

But the rude world could not be entirely escaped. While Bruce Gough didn't feel he had to tell everyone after his shock at Kardinia Park, he needed to tell someone. Not long after, Gough met Bill Durham at Princes Park, where they were to undertake a tour of the Carlton Football Club's facilities.

'How well do you know John?' he asked confidentially. 'Because you know who he really is, don't you?'

'What do you mean?' asked Durham.

'Well, what's his *real* name?

Durham was bemused. 'He's John Wallace.'

'He's John Bryan Kerr,' Gough replied.

Durham was dumbstruck. Back in 1950, he had taken a strong interest in the Kerr trials, arguing over developments up hill and down dale with law student friends. He drove to East Neerim that night with his mind in a whirl, and roused Dawn to tell her. She, too, was amazed, and didn't quite know what to say when next she met Wallace. The Durhams also admitted the Bonsers to the secret, and a few other coterie members came to know.

At this point, in fact, unbeknownst to him, all Wallace's fictions were nearly penetrated. A coterie member met one of his work colleagues, Gillian Forbes, socially. Learning that Forbes worked for Merck, she asked if she was aware of her fellow salesman the convicted murderer. Forbes was shocked enough to confide in her boss John Thompson. Fortunately for Wallace, Thompson poo-pooed the story, and counselled her against spreading gossip. The Goughs, Durhams and Bonsers, meanwhile, had decided on a similar course. There was no need, they agreed, for anything to change.

Yet with the best will in the world, the awareness *did* change the dynamic of the friendships. One day, for example, Elaine Gough heard a radio announcer wonder aloud, 'Whatever happened to John Bryan Kerr?' Nobody rang in; if only they knew, she thought. Certain aspects of John Wallace abruptly made sense, or at least were interpreted in new light: reticence about his past, fussiness about his surrounds, the quiet conversations into which he would slip with men of Pentridge, former governor Ian Grindlay and chaplain Father John Brosnan, when their paths crossed at the football.

Also, it had to be said, his lightning bolts of bad temper, sometimes from trivial causes, like a waitress spilling a cup of coffee, or another diner taking something from his plate. Denise, reticent but intensely loyal and protective, impressed them. She was so tiny yet seemed to have her husband's measure. Then one Saturday night in North Melbourne, there was a public fight. John had wanted to visit a particular new restaurant with his friends. After a long day at the football, the party arrived late and the booking had been given away.

John exploded with rage. Denise raged back. They stood haranguing each other in the street. John stormed off to his car, performed a screeching U-turn, and drove off into the night. Their companions dispersed, wondering whether their exchanges went further in private. Jean Bonser told her husband she never wanted to see John Wallace again. The others strove to maintain the pretence of normality. But by the time Denise bore their second child, Nicholas, in January 1989, the group was drifting apart. So was Wallace's marriage.

***

How do you ask someone why their marriage ended? It seemed on my part both a tremendous intrusion and an unavoidable one. But sitting in her daughter's kitchen in Toolamba, Denise had a succinct and convincing answer.

'You know what they say about children changing you?' she said. 'John didn't change.'

Nicholas's birth made John a sixty-three-year-old man with two pre-school children. When they appeared *en famille,* he was often mistaken for their grandfather; he handled them stiffly, awkwardly, as though they were somebody else's, of whom he had been given unwilling temporary custody. Raised by emotionally reserved older parents, he had little example to draw on. His fierce desire for control and routine sat uneasily with parenthood's unconditional, unpredictable urgencies.

Before too long, Kate was too big to sleep under the table in restaurants, and Nicholas too needful to leave to babysitters. But John was grooved in his customs. The week was for work; Saturday was for the coterie; Sunday was for catching up with his Merck reports. So ten years after their belated marriage, they separated, although it would be another four years until they divorced, and in between times they found a workable rapport that shuttled the children between them.

Kate actually took her parents' parting as well as a child can. She was used to his absences on business; she enjoyed the one-on-one time they now had together. Her father was not emotionally effusive: there were no huge hugs or professions of love. But in his formal way – over lunch, over coffee – he made her feel special. She loved his voice, his presence, his nickname for her of 'Smokey'. Her school, Korowa in Glen Iris, insisted she have counselling. She sat through it quite composed – thanks, but she would be fine.

Then, aged eleven, she returned home with a class project: a family tree. It set off a chain of questions. Who were her father's parents? Where had her father come from? What had he done during his life? In the living room at their new East Malvern home, Denise sat Kate down for the first of many revelations – her father had been in prison for a long time. Herself not knowing the whole of the story, Denise invited Jerry Hughes over. Sifting his old friend's effects, Hughes explained to Kate how her father had been convicted of murder.

Kate, as she put it to me one morning in Melbourne, is 'a processor'. Rather than responding to news instantly, she decides at her own pace. 'If my father elected not to tell me about this,' she told herself, 'there must have been a reason he thought it was not my business to know.' But there seemed an unconscious reaction too. Over the next five years, her life unravelled: she became an incorrigible truant, then a sexually active teenager and a drug user. She drifted away from her father, and he from her. Because the years seemed to hit the former John Bryan Kerr hard and at once. Officially sixty years old when he retired from Merck but actually seventy, he suddenly suffered the full-blown ravages of Parkinson's disease. And predeceased by his past, suddenly his ex-wife and children were all he had. He would ring them late at night from his unit in Syndal suffering hallucinations caused by his medication – he was being followed; he was being spied on; once, he thought he was in an airport in Hawaii. Denise and Kate would talk him through these crises. But they were only worsening.

John Wallace had relinquished his identity, but not his pride. When his GP and friend Dr David Marsh pressed him to give up his drivers' licence, he seemed about to explode with rage. Then one evening in 1997 on Canterbury Road, John rear-ended another driver and panicked, careening down to Kew Junction where he sideswiped several cars before crashing. He spent several days in Royal Melbourne Hospital before Denise could be found. She became his medical power of attorney, and he moved into a series of accommodations, finally ending up in the Harcourt Nursing Home in Shierlaw Avenue, Canterbury.

Parallel stories blurred. Denise married again; Kate, aged sixteen, fell pregnant to her boyfriend; John declined swiftly and irrevocably; from a last photograph by Jerry Hughes, he stared gauntly, his hair a shock of white. The echoes of his former life never abated. A week before Christmas 2000, fifty years to the day the executive council had spared his life, John Wallace became a grandfather. He met his grandson Mason only once. Bed-ridden and barely lucid, he managed to greet Kate one last time as 'Smokey'.

When he died on 7 November 2001, Hughes helped Denise with the funeral. Two notices were placed: one for 'John Wallace'; one for 'John Bryan Kerr.' Nobody at the service in the Renowden Chapel at Springvale Crematorium a week later knew who knew what. At first, Brian Bourke was expected to say a few words. But when Bourke suggested mentioning how they had met at Pentridge in the mid-1950s, Hughes became protective of his old friend. 'You can't say that!' he exclaimed. Later he introduced Bourke to Kate as a 'long-lost uncle'. Left to speak, Hughes did so briefly and in diplomatic generalities. 'What can you say about a man who lived as many lives in one?' he began. Only a handful of the mourners understood the question's full weight. He confined himself to a single story, recounting a favourite 'Johnism'.

> It was during a difficult moment when John was asked about the apparel he had worn on a particular night. 'That dark suit,' John said, pointing to it.
>
> 'Were these the shoes?' the questioner asked, referring to a pair of brown shoes.
>
> The reply was an instant Johnism: 'Brown shoes with a dark suit? Don't be ridiculous.'

A 'difficult moment'? That was one way to put it.

14

A COLD CASE

'In a strange way, I felt like I was betraying him. I still do.' It was my first meeting with Tina,[5] over coffee one morning in an outlying suburb of Melbourne. She was well dressed, punctual, warily polite – and had promised to explain how, fifty-five years after the 'confession' of John Bryan Kerr, she had come to take down a willing second confession to the murder of Beth Williams.

The meeting had been long in the contemplation. I had been aware since earliest days of the Victoria Police's reawakened interest in the murder of Beth Williams, colourfully described in News Ltd tabloids in September 2012 and in November 2013: type in 'John Bryan Kerr' and they are where Google lead. From them dangled an enticing possibility: that Kerr had been demonstrably innocent after all, as Kevin Morgan proved of Colin Ross in *Gun Alley* and as Estelle Blackburn established of John Button in *Broken Lives.* Yet after digesting the articles, I did my best, at least for the time being, to lay them aside. I was anxious to discover rather than to prove, to work towards an

---

5 Tina, Bill, Sandra, Mary, Jim and Annabel are not their real names.

understanding of events rather than backwards from a foreordained conclusion. I felt loyal to Denise and Kate, who were excited by the *Herald Sun's* confident prediction of a 'posthumous pardon'. But there were other reputations to treat fairly too.

Now I was ready, and so was Tina. Up to a point, anyway. Because hers was another life disarranged by past events – in a way, this was integral to the story she was relating. There had been bad choices. There had been drugs and alcohol. There had been an on-and-off relationship with a partner, Jim. There had been misadventure with the law – she was loath to be explicit and I enquired no further.

By 2000, however, twenty-four-year-old Tina had begun reassembling her life by working at a café in Burke Road. A regular there was seventy-two-year-old Bill. He presented as polite, friendly and well-to-do – always a hat, tweeds and a tie. He had for many years worked as a tennis coach; now he was retired, and liked to have a coffee while his wife Sandra attended a nearby clinic, where she was undergoing treatment for a serious illness. Tina was estranged from her father, but idolised her doting grandfather, and had a fondness for older men: 'I always thought of them as wise and brave. They'd been to war. They could fix anything, build anything.' She looked forward to Bill's visits; so, it seemed, did he.

Then Tina moved on to study social work. In May 2002, she and Jim became parents, to Annabel. But later that year she had a call from her former boss at the café: 'The old boy wanted you to know his wife passed. Maybe you should pay him a visit.'

They lived close by, so she did, and Bill cradled Annabel on the front porch of his two-storey clinker brick family home. She had recently read *Tuesdays with Morrie,* Mitch Albom's classic intergenerational memoir. Bill's situation reminded her of that of the elderly college professor to whom Albom became carer, and who in turn imparted 'lessons in how to live'. She began doing him little favours: paying bills, going shopping, taking him for medical check-ups at Epworth Hospital, driving him to visit his wife's grave. He had a male carer who helped shower him and brought his Lite n' Easy. Tina addressed immediate needs, like a catheter bag needing to be emptied, and spontaneous desires, like buying a cat from the RSPCA.

The life lessons, however, did not come. Bill was lonely, grieving, almost a prisoner in his own dark and forbidding house, wracked by competing fears of confined spaces and of outsiders. He had security shutters on the windows. He kept tennis racquets in each room and would describe using them to defend himself from intruders. He was fearful of doctors, and of operations, because he might 'talk' under anaesthetic. He was averse to crossing the Bolte Bridge, because of Sir Henry's association with the death penalty on Ronald Ryan. He stockpiled pornography, which made Tina recoil. The most disturbing part of Bill's life was his relationship with several young prostitutes and drug users. They would extract money from him with stories of urgent financial needs, such as for essential surgery. Bill, recklessly generous, could not conceive of them spending his gifts on drugs. There was an aggravated burglary at the house, almost certainly related.

Bill's family, a son and two daughters, all professionals in their thirties, tried to rein him in, but Tina became a source of further tension by her availability as an unwitting sympathiser, and as a focus of his affections. Because her relationship with Jim was unsettled, Bill grew ever more solicitous. He called her 'darling' and 'dear'. He bought her expensive gifts. He wrote her florid letters, punctuated with effusions ('I want you to be able to ring me anytime 24 hours a day', 'I love you ringing me Tina. You are the person foremost in my thoughts').

Over the course of 2003, these missives grew ever more charged. She went from being a friend in January ('Thanks for being a wonderful friend to me. It has made me very happy'), to a treasure in April ('I am going to spoil you rotten as you are the only girl I believe in. It's no use trying to stop me. There is plenty of money coming in'), to a sole heir in June.

> I told them I was going to take them all out of my will. Seeing you are the only friend I have got I am going to rewrite my will and leave my whole estate to you Tina. If you want or not I am going to do it. I told them all I was going to

> leave everything to you. You are wonderful and the only person I can trust in the whole wide world. I love you terribly much ... I am on top of the whole thing and am proud of myself for tossing them all.

Bill had indeed 'tossed them all'. His anxious children had sought a guardianship order to take control of his affairs, fearful he would take out a second mortgage on his house to meet the various importunings. But required by the court to see a psychiatrist, Bill presented soberly and respectably, and the application was dismissed. In retaliation, Bill revoked his eldest daughter's power of attorney and asked Tina to act in the role.

This worried Tina. She said Bill should be aware of troubles she had had in her past. He heard her out and waved them aside. And in the spirit of mutual truth-telling, he had his own confessions to make. He divulged a macabre past, which she from memory later documented in a girlish script on two unlined A4 sheets.

> At first he told me that he was involved in a large jewellery robbery, that he was the driver and received a new black car for his efforts. He became involved with prostitutes down at the Trocadero, I think near the Yarra River in the city. He has said he was banned at one stage from this area for loitering and 'perving' on prostitutes. He claimed he was 'drugged' and coerced into this

> robbery. He subsequently hid the car from his father, whom [sic] didn't allow him to own one. Soon after this incident, he was at a party in Rye with these people when Shirley Collins said she was going to 'dob them in'. Bill purposely took her for a drive and fearful of confined spaces – especially jail – killed her. When I asked how he had to have a think – bludgeoned or strangled. He thinks he used something to bludgeon her to death – he left her dumped.

Tina was shocked, incredulous, conscious of being manipulated by the tale, but resolved to bear with the teller.

> Soon after this he returned to the National Bank in the City – Collins St, where he used to work. He had a girlfriend whom he loved very much called Barbara Cully. She had previous knowledge of his meeting with Shirley Collins and soon after she was found killed. They apparently where [sic] going to jump off the top of the Collins Street National Bank – together. When it came to the time, Bill pushed her off the top, he was afraid of height he said. When he was leaving by the stairwell, a man called Rex Call saw him and asked after Barbara, Bill bribed him with a car and said she just jumped. He thinks he sorted this out quite well.

> Bill was approximately 24 years old when this happened. He also said that Shirley Collins' brother Mousy Collins shot at him on old Bendigo Road. Bill said he had to punch out the front shattered window of his car, he pulled over after he thought he was safe and retrieved the bullet. He put this bullet in the compost around the ... side of the house.

Four years earlier, Bill had presented as a sweet old man – the kind who could be anybody's grandpa. Could he really have been prey to instincts so dark? Nor was he finished.

> After all of this confession, he had one more to tell me off [sic]. Her name was Maurine [sic] Williams, this happened when he was 21 and working at the National Bank and was influenced adversely by a group of boys from the bank – one in particular. They apparently introduced him to prostitutes, The Trocadero (don't know how to spell), how to pick them up etc. Though this was not the case with Maurine Williams. She and a friend had made acquaintance with Bill at a boat club – I'm not sure which one – Elwood, Elsternwick rings a bell. He said there were arrangements to meet Maurine under the clocks at Flinders Street station, but she stood him up for a sailor. He apparently saw her soon (days) after this time and 'she was up for it'. Bill said all his group of friends 'had sex with her', and

> he was getting more and more frustrated because it was his and he had to wait for it and he was very angry with her because she stood him up. This took place near the Yarra (Southbank?). He said he strangled her. He said someone yelled out and he 'ran for his life'. They all had to 'split up' and Bill ran to St Kilda. The next morning the 'ring leader' at the National Bank questioned Bill to see if the police had questioned him. No-one did. Bill told me John Brian Kerr [sic] was arrested and charged with this. He was apparently very good in jail – Bill followed his progress. Bill was happy and never felt guilty about this man going to jail.

Tina was now in way over her head. These crimes, these names. They made no sense. She was inclined to think of them as the ramblings of an unsound mind, noting other symptoms in an addendum: 'Bill is very scared of DNA testing, the death sentence, jail, having a general anaesthetic and "talking", scared of height, scared of confined spaces, obsessed with washing hands, security'.

She was conscious, too, of Bill studying her reactions, and of his being gratified that she did not pull away. Was this an elaborate test? If so, she passed, and Bill wanted to reward her. In April 2004, knowing her reluctance to be a beneficiary of his will, he sold a small property he owned and gave Tina the proceeds, which she put towards a two-bedroom flat in Oakleigh.

But she kept her notes. Maybe down the track they would make sense.

***

They started to after Bill died of prostate cancer in a hospice eighteen months later. His last conversation with Tina, a few hours earlier, had been about ice-cream, and she tried to preserve happy memories of the old man she had got to know while escorting him to the tram stop. But she returned to the issue of his apparent secret life after a conversation with her grandmother. Tina had asked if she had ever heard of John Bryan Kerr. Oh yes, said her grandmother, that had been big news in its day. And Shirley Collins? Goodness, that poor girl...

At about 7p.m. on 12 September 1953, fourteen-year-old Shirley Collins left her foster parents' Reservoir home bound for her first party, an eighteenth birthday at a house in Punt Road. She had been invited by a young colleague on the aluminium counter at the Coles in Bourke Street, Ronald Holmes, who had undertaken to collect her in his uncle's car. There was a misunderstanding. Holmes thought they were meeting at Richmond Station – not part of the line on which Shirley was travelling.

Shirley apparently got off at West Richmond station, nearby which she was seen at 8.15p.m. walking 'very slowly and doubtfully' towards a 'not ... very modern car' whose driver had tooted its horn at her. The eyewitness, a cutler's wife, Gertrude Orbe, was hurrying up the station ramp with her niece, but somehow 'did not think it [the encounter] was quite right', and before moving on stopped to observe 'the girl' in conversation with the fresh-faced forty-something driver.

About five hours later, Shirley's foster mother raised the alarm about the girl's failure to return home. But it was not until 9a.m. on Tuesday that a Mount Martha resident chasing his fox terrier up a driveway of a weekend cottage came upon her devastated body. She was sprawled on her back, skirt, blue cardigan, canary blouse and grey overcoat pulled up above her head. Underclothing and the shattered glass from three long-neck beer bottles, at least one of which had felled her, were scattered round. The death blows had been inflicted by a six-kilogram length of guttering, which had broken every bone in her face and skull.

Homicide tried every trick in the search for information. They persuaded *The Argus* to publish a full-colour photograph of the victim's face superimposed on a model wearing suitable clothing. They prevailed on radio stations to broadcast a dramatisation of events. Police eventually interviewed more than 2000 people – to no avail.

When Tina took a friend to the State Library to look into the crimes, certain details resonated. The Trocadero in the murder of Beth Williams: hadn't Bill gone dancing there too? The long-neck beer bottles in the murder of Shirley Collins: hadn't they been Bill's preference? There were also vague similarities in that these were slayings of young women in which the bodies were stripped but no sexual assault took place. She was unaware of a further concidence, that the investigating officer in each inquiry was Bluey Adam – the Collins case, as he told Tom Prior of the *Sun,* confounded and tormented him.

> When I have nightmares, and I do sometimes, I hear Shirley Collins screaming for help. And there's nothing I can do. I wake up in a sweat and start going over the case again in my mind...
>
> Shirley was a lovely, kind, innocent little fourteen-year-old girl, the sort of girl anyone would be proud to have as a daughter.
>
> I got to know Shirley as if she had been a member of my own family. If she had been, I think I'd've gone mad. As it was there were times I felt like crying – or running amok. I still do, when I think of it.

There was no trace of a 'Barbara Cully' but, for the moment, Tina's curiosity was satisfied. Not for more than eight years after the confession did Tina finally decide to do something about it, after a chance admission in a conversation about murders with a social work colleague, Mary.

'I know something about a murder,' Tina let slip.

Mary began asking questions, and did not stop as Tina backpedalled. This was an opportunity. No, this was an *obligation.*

'You have to do something about this,' Mary argued. 'You could change things. You could help people.' In January 2012, Mary agreed to contact Crime Stoppers on Tina's behalf.

The first attempt was an anti-climax. The female operative to whom Mary spoke was brusque and off-putting, especially about questions of anonymity, which Tina was anxious to maintain. Mary was barely able to impart the names of the victims: Beth Williams, Shirley Collins and Barbara Cully.

Mary and Tina rang off, disappointed. But when Mary rang again the next day, the operative was more engaged. Overnight, she had apparently googled the cases involved and twigged to their significance.

'I'm glad you called back,' she said. 'This is going to Homicide.'

***

'Hope lives ... because the evidence never dies' was the slogan of the American police procedural *Cold Case,* which introduced the American expression for unsolved crimes or reinvestigations of new evidence to the vernacular. Each week Philadelphian Detective Lilly Rush thawed an enigma frozen in time with new-fashioned technology and old-fashioned intuition.

In reality, evidence is hardly less mortal than people. It *can* be shaken loose, by the triggering of a memory or the collapse of an alibi with a change in personal circumstance. Where available, DNA evidence can then provide a *coup de grâce.* But it can also grow disarranged, go missing, be destroyed: in January 2015, *The Age* reported that Victoria Police had 'lost' evidence from 140 cold cases over fifty years during a 1994 relocation. In fact, despite its apparent glamour, Victoria Police have had a cold case capability only since July 1999. And in 2012, it owed its survival to the tireless commitment of one man: Detective Senior Sergeant Ron Iddles, a twenty-five-year Homicide veteran.

I first met Iddles in Brian Bourke's office. He was broad-shouldered, blue-eyed, watchful. His boyhood dreams of a police career were nourished by watching *Homicide* on his parents' dairy farm in Echuca, and he might almost have stepped from an episode, his crew-cut head being perfectly suited to a pork-pie hat. He also had a gruff warmth. Later, I watched the video of an interview with Iddles by the Victoria Police Museum in which he described his foundation of the cold-case unit as part of the Homicide Squad, following a study visit to New York and Washington. Victoria, he recalled, then had 243 unsolved homicides. I was struck by the precision of that figure. Not 'more than 200' or 'about 250': somehow it dignified each individual life lost. The focus of one of his first reinvestigations, he continued, followed a plea from a man, Denis Clarke, whose six-year-old daughter Bonnie had been brutally raped and murdered in December 1982, and who was now dying of cancer. On the video, Iddles spoke for a minute and a half about how newspaper publicity had dislodged the recollection of a schoolfriend of Bonnie's pointing to a new suspect – already, as it happened, in gaol.

Iddles found the story difficult to tell. He paused once, twice, a third time. His voice shook. But he did not stop. It would have been easy for him to ask that the interview be done again, or edited, or not be used at all – evidently, he didn't. Asked later a standard question about dealing with 'confronting situations', he gave what sounded like a standard answer: 'You can't get emotionally involved to the extent that it clouds your judgement'. But the inference, I noted, was that you *could* get emotionally involved to the extent your judgement remained unclouded.

Cold-case work, Iddles explained to me at a later meeting, was less popular than its recent telegenia implied. Young detectives wanted 'fresh homicides'; they were loath to toil away at something that might take six to eight months and go nowhere. Had Tina rung Crime Stoppers immediately after Bill's death, there would have been no place for her intelligence to go. After a 2005 Boston Consulting Group management review, the cold-case unit had been disbanded by Chief Commissioner Simon Overland. It had only been revived six months before Mary's call, with Iddles, a senior detective and three others.

When the memo from Crime Stoppers crossed Iddles' desk, he penetrated Tina's veneer of anonymity in a few keystrokes. Entered into the police's LEAP system, Bill's name produced a complaint from him that named Tina as his power of attorney. He rang Mary's number, speaking firmly and quickly. 'I want to meet your friend,' he said. 'I've already done my research. Power of attorney would be a good place to start.'

Mary gasped: he *knows.* She asked him to repeat his name.

'Ron Iddles,' he said. 'Google me.'

When he rang off, she and Tina did so, coming across his vital statistics: 230 murder investigations, 95 per cent clearance rate.

It was May 2012 before he called again, his tone similarly terse. He was in the area. He would visit. A meeting was arranged in an empty conference room at the women's office. Mutually favourable impressions were made.

The cold-case unit colour-coded its files. The murder of Shirley Collins, for all its infamy, was a red: basically, not to be looked at in the absence of significant new evidence. The murder of Beth Williams was not a cold case at all: officially, John Bryan Kerr had been convicted, and served his sentence. But Iddles' interest was pricked. The key was discerning something in the confession to which only a murderer would have been privy.

Who had Bill been before crossing Tina's path? He was born in Adelaide in January 1928. His father was at the time a chemical engineer with one of the antecedents of Drug Houses of Australia, his mother the daughter of a Methodist missionary. The family moved to Melbourne after World War II, buying the suburban home in which Bill ended up ekeing out his days. He *had* worked as a teller in the National Bank headquarters at 271–279 Collins Street. And, as it happened, there *had* been a mysterious fatality in that building in March 1954, although her name was *not* ' Barbara Cully'.

***

Susan Oyston was born in Melbourne to a theatre couple, Yorkshireman Roger Oyston and Australian Sheila Florance, in June 1935 – the family went to England at the end of that year. Roger, a member of the Second Derbyshire Regiment, was killed near Normandy two weeks after D-Day; Sheila then married John Balawaider, a Free Polish Air Force pilot, with whom she returned to Melbourne in March 1948. Their cottage in Raleigh Place, Windsor, was a swirl of constant visitors, numerous cats, bohemian parties and domestic stoushes, Balawaider being a dedicated lecher, Florance a born drama queen.

Susan, intelligent and sensitive, coped with the tumult by enjoying her own company and interests: art, poetry, music, philosophy. On leaving school she took a job as an office girl at National Bank. Then, at a dance in December 1953, aged eighteen, she met twenty-four-year-old Julius Krinski, a handsome, brooding Hungarian *émigré,* training as a jeweller. A fortnight later, they decided to get married at Easter.

At 8.50a.m. on St Patrick's Day 1954, Susan Oyston fell fifty metres from the bank's roof, landing 4.5 metres from the main entrance. The inquest files at Public Records Office contained a photograph of her carefully-folded pale coat inside the wire safety fence that ringed the top floor, and statements full of uncomprehending woe. Susan, it was recorded, had been typically 'bright and happy' on arriving at work that morning.

'I think it's going to be a nice day,' she said to the lift operator taking her to the ladies' lockers on the ninth floor; then, as the door opened, 'See you later'. Employees often visited the roof, accessed by a staircase; Susan, in particular, enjoyed writing verse in the sunshine. Coroner James Burke SM equivocated: he found that she 'either fell or jumped' to her death. The involvement of another party had never been considered – and perhaps with reason.

For Krinski, who was *not* called at the inquest, Susan's self-destruction would have made some sense. He kept a frank diary, of which, shortly before his death in Thailand in 2010, he published an edition with a tiny American imprint, chronicling his love life in somewhat indecorous detail, his amours ranging from Zoe Caldwell to Pamela Stephenson. Krinski's account of his relationship with Susan – or Szuzi, as he called her – was especially intense, culminating in their attending a performance of *Madama Butterfly* at the Princess Theatre on the night of Monday 16 March 1954 – the night before her death.

> The bell rings for the second act. I return to find Szuzi sitting stiffly, her head hanging, gazing despondently ahead. By the end of the second act, she links her arm with mine again: 'If someone kills herself she doesn't care how much pain she inflicts on others by her act.'
>
> I am taken aback by her utterance. I feign indifference. I'll try to soothe her nerves tomorrow, but definitely not today. The play is thankfully drawing to a close. Here's an example for her: Madam Butterfly has just committed suicide. Her death induces a relentless, excruciating soul-searching in her lover. She could express the depth of her love only by such a final, desperate act. We are walking along Bourke Street. She is grasping for my arm as if clutching at her very life. She slips on Exhibition Street. She is not in this world right now. She slips again. 'I can take care of myself when I am alone. Alone I can do it.'

Krinski, himself somewhat disoriented, walked Susan to the gate of her family home and left her there.

> Our love will survive a night like this. I am already living in tomorrow, full of plans of reconciliation. We walk side by side silently for a while. She draws closer. 'You don't love me like I love you.'
>
> I wave her off. I tell her repeatedly that I love her. We are walking slowly in the scant, washed-out aura of streetlights. Traffic is minimal. Her voice is soft but shrill: 'You'll see what happens tomorrow!'

Inside, Susan conversed earnestly with a young actor, Peter Batey, then occupying the cottage sleep-out.

'Could anyone love someone so much that they would die for love?' she asked him. Batey said he didn't know, but thought Puccini had probably granted himself some 'artistic licence'. She smiled faintly and returned inside.

The cold-case unit had its third death, a fall from atop the National Bank building, but what to make of it? If Susan Oyston *was* 'Barbara Cully', then Bill had chosen his victim well, in that suicide was a plausible explanation for her untimely death. And if Bill *was* a triple murderer, then he rapidly mended his ways – stopping immediately in order to marry, start a family, borrow money from his father to build a house with tennis courts, and set himself up as a coach. Iddles thought Tina a credible informant, but more was required to move the case on, and that had to come from elsewhere. His experience in the matter of Bonnie Clarke had been an early lesson in the power of publicity. Thus it was that on 16 September 2012, John Bryan Kerr was introduced to a new generation across two pages of the *Sunday Herald Sun* with six period photographs under the headline:

> John Kerr was jailed over a 1949 killing but now the real killer has said...
>
> INNOCENT MAN WENT DOWN FOR MY CRIMES

***

True crime, it has been said, is crime fact that resembles crime fiction – and crime fiction craves a satisfactory resolution. Weighing up the new confession to the murder of Beth Williams, I was reminded of a book I had read twenty years earlier: a collection, *Case Reopened,* in which editors Stuart Coupe and Julie Ogden had invited eleven writers to resolve a famous unsolved Australian crime by fictional means. They deployed reliable tropes from the novelist's repertoire: from a lone avenger and an unknown eyewitness to a mystery parcel and a box of recordings.

Jean Bedford, for example, had the killer of the Beaumont children found 'in a deserted shed on a dust-torn station out past Coober Pedy', with 'an apparently self-inflicted bullet in his brain' and 'an old revolver by his side', surrounded by thirty years of newspaper clippings 'all about missing children'. That was what the irruption of Bill recalled – a fictional *deus ex machina,* and the more compelling for being so.

For there is something uniquely powerful and innately persuasive about confession. We are socialised to believe that confessions are therapeutic. We teach our children that it is best to be honest and take responsibility for their actions. We counsel one another in times of stress to simply 'let it out'. Confession tends to trump all other evidences in law, and enjoys special honour in religion, notably in the Catholic Sacrament of Penance. Lachrymose admissions of culpability and transgression are staples of the mass media. We trust in them, above all, because of our difficulty in believing that someone would willingly incur the consequences of testifying against themselves.

But not all confessions are equal, and false confession is far from uncommon: history is strewn with them, the Salem Witch Trials being perhaps the earliest conspicuous example. The Boorn–Colvin case of 1819, in which brothers from Vermont gave contradictory confessions to a murder neither of them had committed, inspired perhaps the first legal thriller, Wilkie Collins' 1874 novel *The Dead Alive.* And the Ivens case of 1906, involving a recanted confession by a mentally disabled man to the murder of a Chicago housewife, was the first to draw psychologists into the fray of a murder, leading to two famous studies, J. Sanderson Christison's *The Tragedy of Chicago* and Hugo Münsterberg's *In the Witness Stand.* It was in the latter that Münsterberg drew the first taxonomic distinction between types of false confession, distinguishing between those arising from external influences, such as coercive interrogations, and those from internal impulses, including a 'need to be punished'. The latter, he said, abounded amid the 'helpful humanity of our hospitals of the insane':

> There is no judge and no jury, only the physician and the nurse, yet no torture of punishment can be harder than the suffering of the melancholic who feels remorse for sins which he never committed, for crimes of which he never thought before. Years ago his friend died; now arises the illusion that he has poisoned him. The last fire in the town was laid by him; he is guilty of the unpardonable sin. The slightest fault in his real past takes, in this illusory affective state, new and gigantic dimensions: long-forgotten mistakes awake with unproportionate feelings of anguish. The patient accuses himself of meanness and deceit, of diabolical plans, and with growing accuracy he elaborates the minute details of his imaginary crimes.

Münsterburg's classification has since been updated by another American psychologist, Saul Kassin. Most common still are a type Kassin has called 'coerced-compliant', given in face of stress or inducement: the phenomenon of 'you better come clean or this will get nasty', 'just tell us and this will all be over' or 'just cop to this and the judge will go easy'. At a certain point, these might teeter over into another type he has dubbed 'coerced-internalised' – that is, the subject of genuine belief, sometimes because of mental inadequacy, sometimes because a need the confession expresses has blurred the line between truth and fiction. The classic Australian example would be that of John Button, cajoled by West Australian police and swayed by his own sense of responsibility into confessing to driving the car that killed his girlfriend in a February 1963 hit-and-run when, as on multiple other occasions, serial killer Eric Edgar Cooke had been at the wheel.

Most haunting of all remain those confessions Kassin has designated 'voluntary', given unprompted, sometimes as a personal sacrifice to save another, sometimes as a means of winning attention and notoriety. The latter have been particularly prevalent in high-profile unsolved cases: 200 confessions were made to having kidnapped the Lindbergh baby in March 1932, 500 to the January 1947 'Black Dahlia' murder in Los Angeles; five black youths who confessed to the rape of the so-called Central Park Jogger in April 1989 had their convictions vacated on DNA evidence thirteen years later.

And while sometimes thought a concomitant of crime's modern glamourisation, they were a nuisance in Australia even in the days of Bluey Adam, who endured a plague of them while pursuing the killer of Shirley Collins. 'A dozen scoundrels or psychopaths have confessed that they murdered Shirley but none of them did,' he grumbled to Tom Prior. 'I questioned most of them myself.'

In the case of Shirley Butler, the young woman widely thought a victim of Leszek Kacprzak, there was also a vintage example. On 22 September 1954, the *Sydney Morning Herald* ran a front-page report of a swoop on Ingham in North Queensland by top Sydney detective Ray Kelly in response to an anonymous tip-off that a twenty-two-year-old man at the town's Central Hotel with a naked woman tattooed on his arm 'knew all about the Butler murder'. It turned out that the tattooed man *was* the caller, having simply accreted details from contemporary newspaper accounts.

There lies a challenge of false confession, perhaps leading to its underacknowledgement, that it fits no existing mass-media stereotype or convention, save perhaps that of the swaggering serial killer padding his statistics. In the absence of a satisfactory final accounting, a speculative one will suffice. But confession is not always an end; sometimes, it actually marks a beginning.

15

OUT OF THE PAST

If there is anything more to the taste of news media than an old murder, it is a new murder. A week after John Bryan Kerr's exoneration by the *Sunday Herald Sun* Melbourne was gripped by a modern version of the Beth Williams case: that of Jill Meagher, raped and murdered as she walked home along Sydney Road from a night at a pub in Brunswick. For weeks, it was inescapable – and made for a curious comparison with the earlier crime.

Not that the murders were doubles, but they were, perhaps, reliefs of one another. In 1950, it had been the murderer who had been out of the ordinary: handsome, well-spoken, well-educated media professional John Kerr. In 2012, it had been the victim: attractive, vivacious, popular media professional Meagher. Both brought homicide into the circles of polite society. In place of the swarms of courtgoers in 1950 were the numberless virtual rubberneckers of 2012.

A change could perhaps be glimpsed in the social attitudes around the respective victims. In 1950, the defence had shown no compunction about querying the morality of a young woman who dated sailors and attended dance halls on her own; there was no such censure in 2012, at least once the victim emerged as a happily married woman, and the killer a depraved sexual predator. Yet the profuse security camera footage of the doomed Jill Meagher in her short skirt and vertiginous heels seemed to make everyone a voyeur. I now noticed after walking under the clocks of Flinders Street station a flashing sign in the concourse, 'This station is under 24-hour video surveillance'. Today, the first encounter of John Kerr and Beth Williams would have been on the news the following night.

The other impact of the death of Jill Meagher was that it consumed Ron Iddles' next year, up to and including Adrian Bayley's conviction. Bill's confession had been sent to the Office of Public Prosecutions for review, but here joined a long queue of matters, many of them of higher priority, especially those involving living people.

In the meantime, 'INNOCENT MAN WENT DOWN FOR MY CRIMES' had attracted attention, not least from Denise Duncan, who had been following the 'True Crime Scene' cold-case series in the *Herald Sun.* She had always taken her late husband's claims of innocence on trust, and never had any cause to change her mind.

Why? Again, she had a succinct and logical reply. 'Because John's ego was greater than his self-discipline,' Denise explained. Many's the time she had seen him disinhibited by drink, boorish and even boastful. But nothing like even the hint of an admission ever slipped out. Denise contacted the *Herald Sun,* agreeing to be interviewed for a follow-up piece, and spoke to Tina on the telephone about her story, her relationship with Bill, and the circumstances under which she had documented his remarks.

The story continued to develop. In November 2012, the *Herald Sun* added Susan Oyston to the presumed victim list of the still unnamed Bill, dwelling on the burden of guilt borne by her mother Sheila Florance, subsequently made famous by her role as Lizzie Birdsworth in *Prisoner.* For those Susan left behind had borne her loss like a cross. Florance strove to suppress the memory, so that it manifested itself in odd superstititions – she cut her hair short, like a penitent; she never wore the colour green, which had been her daughter's favourite.

Her brother Peter kept a photograph of Susan in his wallet; Julius Krinski kept one on his desk. And for many years, stories had swirled in the volatile Windsor household. What had been troubling Susan so? Why had she dwelt on the idea of 'dying for love'? Peter Oyston suspected his flirtatious mother of having an affair with Krinski – and Krinski's diary suggested that she *had* made several clumsy efforts to seduce him, although after Susan's death. Sheila in her cups confided in a grandson a suspicion that her husband had raped Susan – yet she was also known to take on stories with evangelical zeal. For example, she told a tragic and vivid tale of losing a baby during a World War II air raid, swept from her arms by an exploding bomb. Yet when Helen Martineau, Peter Oyston's wife and Sheila's biographer, went looking for historical proof, she could find none, suspecting in the end it was another trauma in disguise. A miscarriage? An abortion?

The possibility that Susan's life had been taken rather than given, then, struck the family forcibly, coming, as it also did, a year after Peter Oyston's death. Helen and her second husband, Steven Cugley, belong to a branch of esoteric Christianity that credits the deceased with the power to influence everyday affairs. The sudden revelation of Bill's confession seemed to them like Peter's spirit at work. 'It was like a gift,' said Helen when I visited her one morning in Carlton.

For Bill's family, it was not a gift but a bane. When the *Herald Sun* approached them with the information that their father had confessed to murder, they were devastated. His middle daughter, contacted out of the blue, gave a fervent denial: 'That's absolute rubbish if you think my father's done something like that, absolute rubbish ... If he did make any claims there's probably no substance to them whatsoever. Dad wasn't violent. He would be absolutely horrified if someone said he was violent. He was scared of women'.

These quotes appeared in a new *Herald Sun* story on 8 November 2013, this time concentrating on Bill, who was described, again without his name being used, as a 'family man' – an expression whose conventionally solid, reassuring ring was in this context designed to maximise the horror. He was one of us; he could have lived next door to you, all the while harbouring his 'dark secret'.

There was now also a contrived air of exposé: 'The *Herald Sun* has spoken to a woman who handed over written documents detailing his "deathbed" confessions that he had killed three women and watched with fascination as he let an innocent man be sentenced to death over one of his murders'. Actually the *Herald Sun* had spoken to Tina for as long as it took her, on Iddles' advice, to decline an interview – quotes attributed to her in the article were remarks Denise remembered from their conversation. The headline was 'NO END TO MYSTERY', although it would actually be the end of the *Herald Sun's* interest.

Not quite three weeks later, it was suddenly Iddles in need of media advice. For years he had been maintaining a demanding regime of public speaking engagements in regional Victoria, helping local charities raise more than $1 million while spreading the word about crime and punishment. During a recent presentation to 400 people in Bendigo raising money for the Prostate Cancer Council, he had fleetingly displayed an image of Jill Meagher's body in her hastily dug grave.

Two people complained. Now the *Herald Sun* headline was 'TOP COP'S JILL INSULT'. The ladder of cringeing public apology ascended all the way to Premier Denis Napthine, who pronounced himself 'sickened' and 'shocked' by the news: 'Immediately my heart went out to the Meagher family. This sort of thing is just totally and utterly unacceptable'.

What sort of thing and to whom it was unacceptable were never abundantly clear: the presentation had, after all, been concerned with policework, often grueling, sometimes shocking; nor had the Meaghers any need of Napthine's heart, having already extended Iddles their unqualified support. Yet a few weeks later, in one of those inexplicable intramural manouverings that are characteristic of the Victoria Police, Australia's most decorated Homicide detective was moved on to the post of secretary of the Police Association. Among other things, that left in limbo everyone with a stake in the deaths of Beth Williams, Shirley Collins and Susan Oyston, and those who might, or might not, have been responsible. Including me.

***

I knew she was a doctor. I knew her first name and the suburb she worked in. There was really only one phonebook listing that could be her. But I picked up the telephone at least a dozen times before steeling myself to contact Bill's oldest daughter. For how do you open a conversation with somebody about the possibility of their father being a murderer?

First of all, you must get through. Dr Jones was with a patient, a receptionist said briskly when at last I called. Would she know what it was regarding? I recited the full name of the doctor's father. There was a silence. It seemed very long indeed. The receptionist came back on the line: 'She says she will call you back'.[6]

I had the right person at any rate. But what is the decent interval to leave before you call back someone who has promised to call you back so you can ask them about their father being a murderer, but then not?

By this stage, at least, I had serious doubts about the whole scenario. For all their chic, serial killers are incredibly rare. Their killings follow patterns. They do not commonly stop after a while and blend into society. Nor do they commonly mangle fundamentals such as names. Beth Williams was known as 'Maureen' only when newspapers used her full name; no 'Barbara Cully' fell off any building. The situation was consistent with a highly suggestible person who had absorbed three deaths into their personal narrative, the first two because of their high profile (Beth Williams and Shirley Collins), the third because of its proximity (Susan Oyston).

In the end, I gave Dr Jones a couple of days, cautiously called her surgery again, and got straight

---

6 Dr Jones is not her real name.

through. Yes, she knew why I was calling. No, the family had no faith in the 'confession'. They were reluctant to add more, but Dr Jones had a warm and pleasant voice, and the conversation flowed as I explained my purpose and she her family's position. We eventually spoke for about half an hour, at the end of which she said I could get back to her when she was less busy in a few weeks, and she had discussed the matter with her siblings.

After another couple of months of back-and-forth, she agreed to respond to a specific list of questions, which I duly sent. The family knew of the confession only what they had been told by the *Herald Sun* journalist. They had not been advised of it by Tina. They had never been contacted by police. Their own calls to the force had gone unanswered, Iddles having moved on.

Had anyone troubled to talk to Bill's family, they would have benefited from some pretty fundamental information about their father. Bill had a long and fraught psychiatric history, dating back to his early twenties when he was diagnosed schizophrenic. Thirty years on from poor Grace Kerr, this was not quite a life sentence, but it took him partway along the same route.

In 1954, around the time of Susan Oyston's death in the building where he worked, Bill was admitted to what was now the Royal Park Psychiatric Hospital suffering a delusional disorder where he incorporated daily news events into his own life. The hospital then had two standard treatments for schizophrenia. Its old standard had been hypoglycaemic therapy, where patients were pushed into comas of varying lengths by heavy doses of insulin. It had also recently introduced electroconvulsive therapy, the inducing of *grand mal* seizures by electric current, done intensively and repeatedly to cause 'maximum disruption', on grounds that allowing patients to recover tended to limit therapeutic benefit (a pioneer of 'regressive ECT' in Italy, Lucio Bini, had in a flash of candour actually called it 'annihilation therapy'). Gagged and tethered, then zonked into unconsciousness, patients were jerked around like rag dolls, foaming at the mouth, fouled by their evacuating bladders and bowels.

Bill received both treatments, intense and terrifying, and suffered their sequelae of excitation, irritability, loss of memory, impaired cognition – in this light, his fear of confinement was hardly surprising. It was only anti-psychotic medication that would render Bill's life livable, plus a generous if controlling father and a supremely forbearing wife who made almost all important domestic decisions. Even then, he would remain prone to relapses, undergoing a further period of institutional care after his father's death in 1972.

There was more – considerably more – about the family's travails in the last few years of Bill's life, for some of which they held Tina responsible. Bill was a frail, naïve, deluded, recently widowed old man who took Stelazine for his schizophrenia. Was it not obvious that the likelihood of his speaking the literal truth about events half a century earlier was somewhat less than total? In hindsight, it was perhaps not only Bill who had proven suggestible. Confession cuts through, connects, compels, appearing as the truth, shimmering with boldness in a world of untruth and half-truth. It is, among other things, a relief. We can set skepticism aside, bask in reality's glow, for *why would we be told this were it not true?* Yet there are reasons, always reasons – not least, I suspect, what confession engenders, the welcome and approbation of the respondent, the sense of a rapt audience, of sharing, of trust.

By now I was running out of time, for while stories can ramify indefinitely, books must be contained, ruled off, set down. Perhaps inconclusion had always been this one's fate, the events being so long ago, the key survivors so few, the doubts so appreciable. My fictional counterpart now seemed more something like Barbara Vine's *A Dark-Adapted Eye* with its partial resolution, one backstory remaining impenetrable, another in perfect equipoise with two identically cogent and entirely opposite explanations. But then I received a letter, and took a final unforeseen detour.

***

There is no single great guide or *passe-partout* to the records of the past. It can take a chance comment, lucky encounter or a random kindness to turn you in the right direction, from someone who knows how they kept the Petty Sessions Register in Colac way back when, or someone who knows someone who understands the personnel records at the Navy Office barracks in Albert Park. Early on in my travels, for example, it was recommended I visit Malcolm Feiner, a thirty-year veteran of Corrections Victoria with the wonderfully vague title of 'Manager, Research and Evaluation' – one of those invaluable public servants who bear in their head decades of institutional memory. He pulled out old annual reports of the Inspector-General of Prisons, old copies of *Stockade,* scrapbooks of clippings about Pentridge in the 1950s, publications and contact details for the Retired Prison Officers Association.

In passing, I asked what he knew about the history of the bureaucratic mechanics for capital crimes. From a rummage of his desk he produced a 1990 academic analysis of death sentences in the nineteenth century, citing as its sources two record series: VPRS 264 Capital Case Files and VPRS 1100 Capital Sentence Files.

I paused. If these existed in the nineteenth century, they almost certainly existed in the twentieth, which meant there must be holdings relevant to *The King v. Kerr.* Quite what they could be was not immediately obvious, but there would be something, and if there was something, I had to see it. But because what turned out to be VPRS 264/P1, unit 22 and VPRS 1100/P0, unit 16 related to the last seventy-five years, the challenge became determining from whom to seek permission to inspect them. The Public Records Office (PRO)? Apparently not. The Department of Justice? Not them either. The Department of Premier and Cabinet? Wrong again.

My carefully prepared applications under the *Freedom of Information Act 1982,* complete with search-fee cheque, fell each time on stony ground. At last I ended up back at my starting point, with another invaluable public servant, Charlie Farrugia, a thirty-year veteran of the PRO, now a senior collections adviser. He offered to help me prepare an application under the *Public Records Act 1973* – to be exact, under Section 9 (2) (b), through the Keeper of Public Records, Justine Heazlewood, to the Arts Minister, Heidi Victoria. I would simply need to be patient. The wheels of archival justice grind exceeding small.

And so months passed. No point was served waiting around – for all I knew, the files could consist of a manila folder with two yellowing-clippings. I checked in periodically with Charlie – no, no news – but otherwise roved elsewhere. Until, six months after the process began, a letter arrived from the Arts Minister approving my application.

First thing the following morning, I was escorted to a meeting room two levels below ground at the PRO where the files awaited. They were massive. No, better – they were comprehensive. Unlike the records with which I had begun at the Office of Public Prosecution so long before, whose extensive prior use was obvious, these had barely been handled.

They were also different. VPRS 1100/P0, unit 16 was concerned with the evaluation of the recommendation for mercy by Cabinet, with various trenchant views, such as Bluey Adam's: 'Kerr is possessed of abnormal sexual habits, and whilst being interviewed frankly discussed same. He is vain and egotistical and considers himself to be above other members of society'.

VPRS 264/P1, unit 22 covered Kerr's whole incarceration, the documents methodically secured in reverse chronological order, from 1962 back to 1949, so that the effect was like undertaking an archaeological dig. The file actually began with Kerr's pre-release assessment by psychiatrist Allan Bartholomew, who had joined the Pentridge staff in 1959 and over the next quarter-century assessed everyone from Robert Peter Tait and Ronald Ryan to Julian Knight and Derek Percy. Kerr was unlike any of them, apparently more like a talk-show guest than a long-term prisoner: 'Kerr immediately impresses as a man of above average intelligence and verbal facility. He rapidly becomes at ease in the interview situation and endeavours to take full command by talking incessantly – tending to freely associate so that the conversation ranges widely and occasionally gets close to being rambling'.

Bartholomew struggled with his appointed task of evaluating the likelihood of Kerr reoffending. Kerr steadfastly maintained his innocence but would 'not readily discuss it', denied he had 'ever indulged in any perverted sexual acts' but may suffer 'true amnesia' around his behaviours. He thought Kerr 'a typical psychopathic personality of the non-neurotic type' but obviously 'not grossly mentally disturbed', and that his 'intelligence and maturity' minimised his risk to the community. The enigma, then, remained unpenetrated to the end of Kerr's punishment.

With that, I began working my way through the layers of conflicting opinion. Asperities from prisons chief Alec Whatmore ('an exaggerated ego fostered by his activities in debating'). Approval from education officer John Ryan ('reliable', 'an excellent organiser', 'intense loyalty, precision and accuracy'). Pleas from Lee Murray ('Kerr would be far better engaged at home trying to bring some joy and happiness into the lives of his parents'). Rebuffs from Attorney-General Bill Slater ('It is no part of my function to set myself up as a court of appeal from the properly constituted court of justice'). Letters from Rose Kerr, handwritten but deferentially formal: 'Dear Sir, I have the honour of writing to you again ... I now have the honour to remain, Yours respectfully, Rose A. Kerr'. Letters from Ena Smith, chatty and cheery: 'Anyway I wondered if there was a chance of a free pardon. After all he did go and intend to give his life for us in war 2'. Then at around 1956, a thick stratum of claim and counterclaim, requests and ripostes, as the *Argus* campaign and the petition for clemency roiled, including something I did not at first recognise.

Friday, 9 March 1956, was the zenith of *The Argus* crusade, with its 'Yes' or 'No' voting form at the bottom of a full broadsheet page of pro-Kerr coverage: 'Having studied the new Kerr evidence made available to *The Argus* by Lee Murray, do you believe that there is now a reasonable doubt of Kerr's guilt; justifying a State Government review of the Kerr case?'

On that same day, a thirty-year-old off-duty constable, Maxwell Keetley, rang Bill Donelly at Homicide and made an appointment to see him the next day. He had, he explained, attended Scotch with Kerr twenty years earlier; he had reacquainted with him and met Betty Smith in the late 1940s while living in Toorak with his new wife Mary; they had then drifted out of contact while running a post office in Fitzroy, just before his joining the force. He had something he wished to say that went back to the day after Kerr was charged.

Reading about his old schoolmate's arrest in the newspaper, Keetley recalled, he had telephoned Afton and offered his help. The following morning he drove there and was met at the door by Donald and Rose.

> I was invited into the lounge where I noticed a large photograph of John Kerr in the room. I advised Mr Kerr that he should see a solicitor and I suggested that he should see a friend of mine

> named John McD Jones of 421 Bourke St, Melbourne. I offered to drive him in and we left the house and drove to the east end of the City somewhere in the vicinity of Bourke Street and Russell Street. Enroute to the city I told Mr Kerr that I was going to join the Police Force and that I was due to be called up in a fortnight. Mr Kerr informed me that he was to meet a man named Lee Murray in the City and that is where I drove him to in the first place. He met Lee Murray and he introduced him to me. We then went to Mr J McD Jones' office, where I introduced them to Mr Jones.

A nagging question had been answered. I had never been sure how Jones had come to represent Kerr. At the initial bail hearing, Kevin Anderson had been instructed by the Kerr's family solicitors, Alexander Grant, Dickson and King; Jones had then succeeded them. If nothing else, a tiny unknown had been eliminated. I read on. According to Keetley, he then drove Donald Kerr and Lee Murray to Pentridge, and accompanied them to their first meeting with Kerr. It was a meeting that Murray had described in print a couple of weeks earlier as part of *The Argus* campaign.

> John sent for me that morning. He greeted me with the words: 'Lee, I didn't kill Beth Williams. She was all right when I left her. She must have met someone else after she left me.'

> Throughout the years he has never varied, and it was on a recent visit to him that he said: 'If I live to be 100 it will always be the same. I did not kill her.'
>
> John has never lied to me. At all times, on all matters, it has been a question of 'cards on the table first.'

Keetley gave a stunningly different account.

> As Kerr walked up he was swaggering and had a smile on his face. Mr Kerr was upset. My memory is that he said: 'Good day, Dad. Good day, Lee. How are you, Max?' One of the first things he then said was 'Do you think they will hang me?' He had a smile on his face as he said this. Mr Kerr (senr) had a short conversation with him. I cannot remember what was said between them. I wasn't taking particular notice of their conversation. I did hear Kerr say that the food was lousy and he didn't eat his breakfast.
>
> John Kerr spoke to me and said 'I didn't think you would wind up a policeman.' He was grinning when he said this. He beckoned me a bit closer and said 'Have you seen the body?' I said, 'No I am not in the Police Force yet.' He said, 'They tell me that the nipple on her teat was bitten off.' I said, 'I don't know whether it was or wasn't.'

> He said, 'I know I knocked her around pretty badly but I don't remember doing that.'

I know I knocked her around pretty badly but I don't remember doing that: I read it over and over.

Was this the *real* 'certain admission', made not to a foe but a friend? Had Keetley, visiting Kerr before his story was straight and his defences raised, heard fourteen words tantamount to a confession of guilt? Had Murray then interdicted?

That was Keetley's take, for he next quoted Murray as saying to Kerr: 'You are to keep your mouth shut and not say a word to anyone in here. There will be a solicitor out to see you soon'. Indeed, as Keetley left with Donald Kerr and Lee Murray, he observed Jack Jones arriving. They exchanged nods.

Next stop was Keetley's residence, attached to the North Fitzroy Post Office, where he and wife offered their guests a cup of tea. According to Keetley, the conversation was, again, unguarded. Keetley recalled Lee Murray's scathing judgement of Beth Williams: 'She was only a troll (or some similar name) to be out on the beach with a fellow at that time of the night'.

Only a troll: only a whore, really. Was that it, then? Had it been a lie all along, justified, as so often in crimes against young women, that she *had it coming?* That was also the impression carried away by Keetley's wife Mary, who completed her own confirmatory statement.

> I remember my husband and two men coming to where I was living at North Fitzroy and they came inside and they were introduced to me. They were Mr Kerr (senr) and Mr Lee Murray, a radio announcer. They had a cup of tea. I cannot remember Mr Kerr saying anything. He sat with his head bowed. Mr Lee Murray talked, and one thing I remember clearly was that the girl victim of the murder deserved what happened to her. He did not seem sorry for her at all.

Keetley recalled one remark by Donald Kerr: 'If he had not broken up with Betty Smith he wouldn't have done this'. This surprised Keetley, as he knew from conversation with John and Betty that the Kerrs had always rather disapproved of the couple's pairing. But here was another allusion to gender norms – that one of a woman's tasks in couplehood was to moderate a man's extremities of behaviour, that without a woman a man was at risk of being passion's slave.

Keetley concluded his day with a final assistance and observation. 'I drove them to the city and dropped them. By their conversation and demeanour both Mr Kerr and Lee Murray did not seem to doubt that Kerr was guilty, but both appeared worried by the penalty.'

And then, he kept his own counsel. He joined the police on 12 January 1950. Later that year, remarkably, he would be one of the constables posted at the Supreme Court to control crowds at *The King v. Kerr.* But he and his wife said nothing, at least officially, until 10 March 1956, when they gave their statements to Superintendent Charles Petty of CIB, copies of which were forwarded to Chief Commissioner Selwyn Porter, Solicitor-General Henry Winneke, Crown solicitor Thomas Mornane and placed in VPRS 264/P1, unit 22.

***

Sixty years later, what did I have? A faithful mirror of events or another distorting lens? No sooner had I digested the Keetley statements than I was pondering grounds for disbelief – it had become habitual. Keetley misheard or misunderstood. Keetley had taken too long coming forward to be credible. Keetley was a policeman advancing himself. And who was he anyway?

Max Keetley was born a few months before John Bryan Kerr, in Cottlesloe, Western Australia. He did, indeed, attend Scotch in 1935 and 1936. He married Mary Farrell in Bairnsdale in February 1947, lived in Toorak then North Fitzroy. They had three sons. I searched for, located and contacted the eldest, Paul, who generously emailed photographs and a few recollections. Their father was a flamboyant man – a singer, a storyteller, an entrepreneur, who spirited his family west in 1958, where a love of automobiles drew him into a successful career selling cars, culminating in his running Keetley Motors in Leederville. He died, Paul told me, of emphysema aged forty-four in 1969, survived by their mother, who had passed away only recently.

About the remarks by the Kerrs and Lee Murray, first light-hearted then callous, there did not seem much ambiguity. Kerr's apparent lack of recall was consistent with the disassociated state he had described in his court martial; it was consistent, too, with the 'point of view' of Rose Kerr, as confided to parole officer Hyland in 1961, that alcohol had 'an inordinate effect' on her son, leaving him 'no recollections of his behaviour when he sobered up'.

The scenario of the conversation at Pentridge was also plausible. Kerr had been a prisoner barely twenty-four hours. Worlds had been turned upside-down. The search was on, raw and desperate, for explanations and excuses. Lee Murray was giving orders, Donald Kerr taking stock, John Kerr possibly mulling an insanity defence. But for the family, how shaming – it might even expose the 'hereditary defects' of the previous Kerr generation.

The situation chimed, too, with something else that had registered with me while poring over Kerr's prison correspondence – that his most fervent avowal of innocence, in September 1950 shortly after his sentencing, was in a letter to his mother alone, not to his father or them both.

> I know my own innocence of this dreadful crime. My conscience is clear – as anyone could have observed by watching my demeanor throughout all my trials. All my faith is in my God. He, alone, knows what I know, and shall guide me through this world. I have never until just now, as you know, proclaimed my innocence at length to you or to those around here. You have always known my innocence, and I couldn't care less what other people think about it at all.

Could it have been at this stage that while Donald Kerr knew their son's guilt, Rose Kerr did not – indeed, was protected from knowing? It was hard to believe that pious, moral Rose would have been capable of writing so passionately in defence of her son while knowing him to have murdered Beth Williams. It was less hard to believe that sane, intelligent Rose steadily and privately came to acknowledge her son's guilt as the simplest explanation, and forgave him, as mothers do.

Why had Keetley waited more than six years to come forward? Quite possibly for the reasons Tina had done the same – because admissions made in private settings and friendly contexts seem to entwine us in obligations. Had Keetley volunteered details of the conversation in 1950, he might well have condemned a young man and an only son to death. As he did so in 1956, he ran no such risk, and strictly speaking abrogated no word of honour or code of secrecy.

I was now bound to say it was adding up. And yet ... and yet ... there remained something anomalous about this evidence. Virtually all that year, *The Argus* inveighed against the Victorian Government on Kerr's behalf, a challenge to everyone from Premier Bolte down, endangering the reputations of the Victoria Police and the Crown Law Department. Here, on the face of it, was confirmation that Kerr was a sadist, Murray a phony, their whole campaign a sham. Why had authorities not flourished such an apparent confirmation of the system's virtue?

***

More was necessary to establish the authenticity of Keetley's statement. I surrendered to my ingrained habit of accreting as much publicly available information as possible. He had some go, this man. He enlisted in the army, underage, and was an anti-aircraft gunner when Japanese bombs fell on Darwin. He then flew 713 hours, mainly in Sunderlands, as part of 461 Squadron, Royal Australian Air Force, finishing the war a Flying Officer. On demobilisation in February 1946, he ran a cab company in Darwin. How he knew Jack Jones was unclear, but the similarities weren't far to seek: they were ex-servicemen and Catholics; both fight fans too, it would seem.

Then from Perth came the death certificate, registration 104441J/1969. It was not Keetley's emphysema that had carried him off. Rather had he booked into a motel room on Perth's Great Eastern Highway and overdosed on barbituates. Yes, confirmed his son, not happily: the suffering had been too much to bear. Max Keetley was, Paul protested, a 'good father', which I didn't doubt, but our email correspondence ceased. I could hardly blame him, an involuntary link to a long-forgotten story. But his father had knowingly inserted himself in another man's life, and it was too late to look away.

So the police personnel file for *Keetley, Maxwell Paul, Reg No 10829* arrived on my desk. It documented a career in the Wharf, Wireless and Special Patrols initially full of promise, beginning when he was graded first of thirty-six in his recruit intake, with the notation: 'A well-conducted, conscientious, intelligent student, who will make a good constable'.

There were exam passes. There were commendations for 'vigilance, zeal and ability' and for 'efficient execution of duty'. Then a complaint, from him, to the Police Classification Board, that three other constables had been promoted ahead of him – dismissed in October 1954. Then a further complaint, about him, three months later, for drinking with wireless colleagues in the Royal Terminus Hotel, Brighton Beach, while on duty – fined £1 in March 1955. Then, a year later, just three weeks after his phone call to Bill Donelly, the allegation of another visit to the licensee of the same hostelry. How about letting a starting-price bookmaker operate from there? After all, it might be good for business. At last, a month after that, recorded by several newspapers, the allegation of a 2a.m. visit with a colleague to the Hawthorn flat of a low-end crook, Graham Thompson, who had been refusing to honour a £100 debt. According to the testimony of a neighbour: 'One called, "Open up, Graham, it is the police" ... I heard some noises like somebody being beaten up. I heard somebody say: "If you don't I'll shoot you. I'll put the gun in your hand when you are dead".'

Keetley's suspension from duty was accompanied by a terse note, dated 10 July 1956: 'This member is unreliable. Charges are pending against him'.

And though Thompson kept conveniently mum, meaning the assault charge failed, the Police Disciplinary Committee found Keetley guilty of 'discreditable conduct', and dismissed him from the force just before Christmas. His County Court appeal against dismissal failed, as did his application for a private inquiry licence, opposed by his former employers on grounds that there had been 'more suspicion connected with him than with any other member of the police force'.

More suspicion than with any other member. That was the view of Homicide's Bill Donelly – the man whom Keetley had telephoned thirteen months earlier in order to turn on Kerr. No wonder the west beckoned. Max Keetley, embittered perhaps, errant certainly, had made Melbourne too hot to hold him.

None of the foregoing eliminated the possibility that every word of Keetley's statement, supported by his wife, was true. Paul Keetley's parting shot to me was resounding. 'I could not imagine him accusing anyone of murder if he felt they were not. Period.'

But what a painful dilemma for the Victoria Police, that the member who perhaps affirmed their most controversial conviction was the member they most urgently needed to be rid of. Had Keetley's statement ever been made public, what sport would Kerr's circle have made of discrediting a disgruntled, disgraced cop. I wondered had they ever had a clue.

***

I wondered then and wonder still. For while it did not feel like I had reached the end, I had reached *an* end. Here was a task that could stretch on until the crack of doom, but would in the meantime remain suspended between balanced disbeliefs. All that remained certain after this time was that a life in full bloom, Beth Williams, had been cut off. Ever since then, the rustlings of irreducible doubt had kept succeeding generations awake, their stirrings disturbing other crimes, other lives. No witness being quite unimpeachable, no document entirely unambiguous, no conjecture altogether persuasive, it would probably ramify forever.

For more than a year, I had gone forth to discover and report back to Denise and Kate about the history of perhaps the most important man in their lives, most of which they hardly knew, as it long predated their experience of him. It might almost have been of a different man, so long before had it been. Yet there was one artifact that always seemed to collapse the distance of the decades: a recording of the voice of John Bryan Kerr. The provenance of the vinyl disc was mysterious, although it was almost certainly prepared for the Pentridge Prison radio station 3PD, because the text was a sermon by Presbyterian preacher Peter Marshall, whose life story was popularised by his widow Catherine in a 1951 biography, *A Man Called Peter,* adapted by Hollywood four years later. 'Let's Keep Christmas', a traditionalist's lament of the modernisation of Christmas rituals, was also published in a small quarto in 1953, and quickly became a favourite reading on radio stations – on YouTube, you can hear it read by Dick van Dyke.

To listen to it, Denise and Kate had to plug in an old phonogram, place the disc on the spindle, gently lower the needle and, through the slight surface hiss, there he was. 'Changes are everywhere,' John Bryan Kerr began. The voice was deep and sonorous, the delivery carefully phrased and enunciated. 'Many institutions and customs that we once thought sacrosanct ... have gone by the board. Yet there are few that abide ... defying time and revolution.'

It was the voice that Lee Murray trained; the voice that Beth Williams heard; the voice that talked back to Bluey Adam and responded coolly to counsel in Court 4; the voice that wooed Denise and sang at Kate's christening. Not especially warm, although not cold; in this context rather didactic; but proud, self-possessed, arresting. For we each stood quite still as we listened: the human voice is such an intimate instrument, maker of first impressions, layer down of memories. 'The old message: "For unto you is born this day in the city of David a Savior, which is Christ the Lord" is still the heart of Christmas,' Kerr continued. 'It can be nothing else ... and this message can neither be changed ... nor quite forgotten ... although there are many things that tend to make us forget.' None of us were listening to the words, of course: only the voice, their loved one, my subject, continuing twelve minutes to its climax. 'So we will not "spend" Christmas ... nor "observe" Christmas ... we will "keep" Christmas ... keep it as it is ... in all the loveliness of its ancient traditions. May we keep it in our hearts ... that we may be kept ... in its hope.' At last, an announcer's voice: 'And so concludes *A Man Called Peter,* with John Bryan Kerr.'

John Bryan Kerr was not concluding. John Bryan Kerr endured in record, recollection and their intersection. Only my involvement with him was coming to an end. To my last meeting with Denise and Kate, at a Melbourne café, I arrived feeling slightly awkward, bearing what might have been deemed bad tidings about their former husband and father. I handed them each a copy of the Keetley statements, explaining their origin. They read quietly, reflectively, between sips of coffee.

Well, I asked presently, did their contents ring true? No, they said, calmly but firmly, not in their experience, and theirs, frankly, was an experience I did not and could never have. They had never believed John Bryan Kerr was Beth Williams' murderer; they still did not and maybe could not, for what nourishes us in doubt is our faith in and love for one another. And he was in their futures, not mine.

We adjourned to lunch with Brian Bourke, who regaled us again with tales of crims and coppers past and present. John Bryan Kerr? Why, you never met a fellow like him. And on the way home I threaded my way through the foot traffic around the entrance to Flinders Street station, those surging back and forth, those watching and waiting.

ACKNOWLEDGEMENTS

'John Bryan Kerr? Well, I can tell you quite a lot.'

That's how it started, over lunch, with the doyen of the Victorian criminal bar, Brian Bourke, and his friend Angela Nordlinger. He is, therefore, the very first person to whom I should express my gratitude, not only for a personal introduction to the subject, but for many subsequent entrées. Even at eighty-six, Bourkey is a busy man, yet he always makes you feel that he has all the time in the world, and cannot help you enough. He enlisted in this effort even his daughter Lisa, who kindly hosted me when I was sojourning in the name of research.

That was on my first visit to Denise Duncan and Kate Montgomery, John Bryan Kerr's former wife and his daughter, at Toolamba. There is always a risk in journalism of growing too close to one's informants. I was acutely aware of this while writing *Certain Admissions* because I grew to like them so much. At the same time, they asked of me nothing except simply to tell the story as I found it. And so I not only like but respect them also. My involvement with them has been a privilege.

Partly through Denise and Kate, I was drawn into John Bryan Kerr's circle of friends, whose frank and fond remembrances assisted me greatly: Arthur and Jean Bonser, Dennis Cameron-Kennedy, Bill and Dawn

Durham, Bruce and Elaine Gough, Jerry Hughes and Alison Cassidy, Dr David and Claire Marsh, and Walter Nash. Thanks also to my subject's former school contemporaries, Weston Bate, Harry Carruthers, David Cock, Harry Duncan, Mike Fitchett, John Gundersen, Jeffrey Kiddle, Keith Morgan, Pat Sutton, and Fred Thomas. Scotch College is blessed to have an archivist as steeped in its fact and folklore as Paul Mishura.

Owen McKenna, aged ninety-one, astonished me when we met with a vivid and finely written essay of interviewing John Bryan Kerr in 1962, and memories flowed trippingly from his tongue. He and his former *Truth* colleague Brian Hansen reminded me why there can be no trade more fun and fulfilling than journalism; likewise my exchanges with Michael Cannon, formerly of *The Age,* Peter Golding and Jim Usher, formerly of *The Argus,* and Garry Barker, formerly of *The Herald* (who also happens to be my father-in-law).

If I go into depth about each contact, alas, I'll write another book as long again. It will suffice here to present a rough-and-ready alphabetical list of others who helped me along the way, with a brief explanation of their relation to the story: Barbara and Christine Adam, granddaughters of Bluey Adam; David Anstice, Bob Dale, Diane Haigh, Doug James, Gillian McDonnell (formerly Forbes), John McGregor, Wal Mobilia, Jim Thirsk and John Thompson, former colleagues of John Wallace at Merck, Sharp & Dohme (Australia); Peter Batey, Helen Martineau and Stephen Cugley, who patiently fielded my enquiries about Susan Oyston; retired Justice Barry Beach, Kerr's debating colleague; Philip Brady, Bob Phillips, Maurie Service, Brian Smith, John Tinney and Mike Walsh, former pupils of Lee Murray; Vic Carroll, former colleague of Bob Nelson; Dennis Challinger, former colleague of Alec Whatmore and Eric Shade; Margaret Chick, sister of Patricia Street; Andrew Lumb, friend of the late Peter Coldbeck; retired Justice John Coldray, audience member at *The Caine Mutiny Court-Martial;* Valerie Currer, daughter of Cyril Currer; Jill Dickson and Suzanne Mason, daughters of Sir Kevin Anderson; Professor Mark Finnane and John Myrtle, researchers of the life of Sir Jack Barry; Sandy and Peter Gray, descendants of Reg Gray; Barbara and Merrin Hawking, friends of Barbara Robertson; Sam Holt, neighbour of the Kerrs; Patricia Jones, daughter of Jack Jones, and her husband Peter Dotchin; Paul Keetley, who forebore my questions about his father Max; Patrick Kelly, who tolerated my questions about his mother Yolanda; Brian and John Monahan, sons of Sir Rob Monahan, and their sister Di; Brian McCarthy, who worked at Galballys in the 1950s and remembered the Kerr trials as though they had taken place the previous week, and his wife Kathleen; Professor Peter McPhee, biographer of Pansy Wright; Richard Nelson, son of Frank Nelson; Noel Purcell, former legal partner of Jack Jones; Associate Professor David Ranson at the Victorian Institute for Forensic Medicine; Dr Mike Richards, biographer of Ronald Ryan; Victoria Simons, sister of Kerrie Williams.

For insights into the Victoria Police Force, thanks to former officers (and their kin) Peter Aldred, John Frame, Ron Iddles, Loris Knight, Bill and Rochelle Jackson, Michael Nemtsas, Alan Porter, Ralph Staveley and Bill Woodley. For information about the workings of Pentridge Prison, thanks to Norman Banner, Dr David Biles, Bob Herron, Hugh Jones, Mick Ryan, Rod Wise and, above all, Malcolm Feiner, at Corrections Victoria; also to Adam Ford and Marty Ryan from Shayher Group, my hosts on a fascinating tour of the site. I had the continuous assistance of two experts, as it were. Whenever the story posed a medical question, my friend Dr Penny Sheehan of The Royal Women's Hospital sent chunky advices studded with citations; whenever the story threw up a genealogical conundrum beyond my capabilities with Ancestry and Trove, I relied on Graeme Haigh of Grajohn Genealogical Services. In their own ways, they were indispensable to my enquiries.

Others I cannot thank by name as they wished to remain anonymous, but they will know who they are, and I hope I have reciprocated their trust.

The following, too, volunteered either recollections, connections or elaborations that proved invaluable: Professor Geoffrey and Ann Blainey, Associate Professor Frank Bongiorno, Phil Brewin, John Cain, Philip Dunn QC, Meyer Eidelson, Herb Elliott, Professor Bridget Griffen-Foley, Professor John van Groningen, Justice Elizabeth Hollingworth and her associate Darryl Slabe, Rob Hulls, Pam and Trevor Jennings, Gerald Murnane,

Norman O'Bryan SC, Peter O'Bryan, Philip Rowell, Margaret Scott Simmons, Barry Solomon, Frank van Straten, Kaitlin Thal, Nigel Tulloh, Ian Wilson, retired Justice Jack Winneke, retired Judge Tom Wodak and Associate Professor Clare Wright.

As hinted at intervals, a very great deal of *Certain Admissions* was researched hunched over boxes and files. I traipsed back and back mainly to three places, and was received with unending assistance in each. Above all, the Public Records Office of Victoria, the walk to which from my home I could now undertake blindfolded: special thanks to Graeme Hairsine, Jack Martin and especially Charlie Farrugia for their conscientiousness and courtesy. And while I guess the forces of law and order are not usually thought of as open and transparent, Bruce Gardner and Jenny Combes at the Office of Public Prosecutions and Caroline Oxley of the Victoria Police Museum were of enormous and unfailing help.

Everywhere I went in search of records, I was received with zeal and tact. Thanks in particular to the following officers of collecting institutions or other archival collections: Sean Bridgman of the National Film and Sound Archive; Des Cowley at the State Library of Victoria; Deena Diamandis from the Department of Human of Services, Victoria; Chiarah Edwards and Kristy Fisher of the Department of Premier & Cabinet, Victoria; Salli Glass and Mark Upton from the Department of Health and Human Services, Tasmania; Andrew Griffin of National Archives of Australia; Kathy

Maikousis of the Department of Justice, Victoria; Waverleigh Mainwaring-Clarke of the Coroner's Court, Western Australia; Alexander Parise from the Italian Historical Society; David Russell of Royal Australasian College of Physicians; Lucy Spencer of Melbourne's Performing Arts Museum; Pamela Wilson at Toorak Uniting Church. Thanks to Gabrielle Coyne, Ben Ball and Rachel Scully at Penguin Australia, and to my editor and friend Foong Ling Kong. Always a pleasure, FL.

Lastly, I had the benefit of much friendly but also acute advice from readers and thinkers. Philippa Hawker, as ever, was a caring and generous critic, while I chewed over aspects of the story and the text with Monica Attard, Kaz Cooke, Ed Cowan, Lisa Gorton, Sonya Hartnett, Russell Jackson, Gretel Killeen, Amber McMahon, Deborah Robertson, Stephanie Sturrock, Julie Szego and Sally Warhaft. I was buoyed by their interest, benefited from their insights, and was never made to feel guilty about conversations dominated by my consuming passion. That's true friendship. As my working life was filled with violent death, my home life could hardly have been more tranquil, thanks to my wife, Charlotte, and daughter, Cecilia. That's true love.

OTHER PRIMARY SOURCES

NEWSPAPERS AND PERIODICALS

The Age
The Argus
The Bulletin
Canberra Times
Goulburn Evening Post
The Herald
Herald Sun
The Listener-In
Medical Journal of Australia
Pix
Police Gazette
Police Life
Sunday Herald Sun
Sunday Press
The Sun News-Pictorial
Truth (Melbourne)
Truth (Sydney)

BIRTHS, DEATHS AND MARRIAGES

Birth Certificates

Donald Wallace Kerr (1893), Grace Lillian Kerr (1899), John Bryan Wallace Kerr (1925), Keith McKenzie

(1907), Rose Ann McKenzie (1884), Elizabeth Maureen Williams (1929)

Marriage Certificates

Frederick John Adam and Gladys Parry (1926), Donald Wallace Kerr and Rose Ann McKenzie (1921), Horace Mason and Esme Hollonds (1951), John Wallace and Denise Robyn Maloney (1983)

Death Certificates

Frederick John Adam (1972), Leslie Brandon (1980), June Lynette Clyne (1967), Lenna Eveline Gundersen (1959), Maxwell Paul Barrington Keetley (1969), Donald Wallace Kerr (1973), Grace Lillian Kerr (1974), James Dawson Kerr (1910), Rose Ann Kerr (1972), John McKenzie (1950), Horace Mason (1984), Frances Nash (1953), James Christopher Roberts (1965), Ena Mary Smith (1963), Jane Taylor (1950), Harold Robert Thom (1951), John Wallace (2001), Arthur Bernard Williams (1969), Elizabeth Maureen Williams (1950), Kerrie Louise Williams (1971)

DEPARTMENT OF ATTORNEY-GENERAL AND JUSTICE, NSW

Prison admissions card, Leszek Richard Kacprzak No 4654G

DEPARTMENT OF HEALTH, VICTORIA

Records of patient, Grace Lillian Kerr 1921–1974

DEPARTMENT OF JUSTICE, VICTORIA

Prison admissions cards, John Bryan Kerr, No 49194

Pentridge Prison scrapbooks 1950–1962

Reports of Inspector-General of Prisons 1940–1970

ITALIAN HISTORICAL SOCIETY

Records and relics of Mario's Restaurant, Melbourne

MITCHELL LIBRARY, SYDNEY

MLMSS 7043/4-5

Papers of Ivan Chapman, 1942, 1963–1982, concerning Private Eddie Leonski, subject of *Leonski: The Brownout Strangler* (1982)

NATIONAL ARCHIVES OF AUSTRALIA

Employment records

MT917/1 Box 93 DW Kerr, Albert Park Barracks

Immigration records

Sp908/1 Box 1249 Leszek Kacprzak

Services records

Courts martial

A471 John Bryan Wallace Kerr (149942), Leslie James Irwin (164552)

RAN

A6770 John Bryan Wallace Kerr (PM 6094) RAN

RAFF

A9300 Edward Cyril Buckland (430358), Maxwell Paul Barrington Keetley (430822)

A9301 John Bryan Wallace Kerr (149942) RAAF

PUBLIC RECORDS OFFICE VICTORIA

VPRS24

Inquest deposition files

Shirley Collins (1953), Grace Lillian Kerr (1974), James Dawson Kerr (1910), Susan Mary Oyston (1955), James Christopher Roberts (1963), James Allen Stevens (1951), Stewart Patrick (1951), Kerrie Louise Williams (1971)

VPRS28

Probate and administration files

Frederick John Adam (1972), Leslie Brandon (1980), Samuel Winter Cooke (1929), Donald Wallace Kerr

(1973), John Kerr (1932), Barbara Doris Robertson (2004), Ena Mary Smith (1963), Leslie John Wood (1968)

VPRS30/P0006/13-14

Proceedings in *The King v Kerr,* Court No 393 of 1950

VPRS 264/P0001/22

Capital Case File, John Bryan Wallace Kerr

VPRS 301/P0000/84

Colac Court of Petty Sessions Cause List Books and Registers

VPRS 1080/P0001/157

Minutes of the Executive Council 1950

VPRS 1100/P0000/16

Capital Sentence File, John Bryan Wallace Kerr

VPRS 7244/P0002/158

Rate Books Toorak Ward

VPRS 8003/P0001/5

Melbourne Harbour Trust

Alphabetical Card Register of Shipping: Overseas Vessels, *Cape Archway – Columbia*

SCOTCH COLLEGE ARCHIVES

Enrolment details and school reports of John Bryan Kerr, copies of *Satura* and *Old Scotch Collegian*

VICTORIA POLICE MUSEUM

Police service records

Frederick John Adam (8409), Christopher Alexander John Coe (7278), Cyril Currer (8369), Maxwell Paul Barrington Keetley (10829), William Wall Warner Mooney (8682), Michael Dimitrios Nemtsas (4565)

Interview with Ron Iddles
http://www.policemuseum.vic.gov.au/qr3

SELECT BIBLIOGRAPHY

Anderson, Sir Kevin, *Fossil in the Sandstone: The Recollecting Judge,* Spectrum, Richmond, 1986

Berman, Peggy with Kevin Childs, *Why Isn't She Dead!,* Gold Star, Melbourne, 1972

Blackburn, Estelle, *Broken Lives,* Stellar Publishing, Mosman Park, 1998

Bradshaw, F. Maxwell, *Selborne Chambers Memories,* Butterworths, Sydney, 1962

Burns, Creighton, *The Tait Case,* Melbourne University Press, Parkville, 1962

Butt, Peter, *Who Killed Dr Bogle and Mrs Chandler?,* New Holland, Sydney, 2012

Cannon, Michael, *The Woman as Murderer: Five Who Paid With Their Lives,* Today's Australia Pub. Co., Mornington, 1994

Chapman, Ivan, *Leonski: The Brownout Strangler,* Hale & Iremonger, Sydney, 1982

Christison, J. Sanderson, *The Tragedy of Chicago: A Study in Hypnotism, How an Innocent Young Man was Hypnotised to the Gallows, Denouncements by Savants,* William S. Hein, New York, [2008]

Clyne, June, *June Clyne,* Hawthorn Press, Melbourne, 1971

Coleman, Robert, *Above Renown: The Biography of Sir Henry Winneke,* Macmillan, South Melbourne, 1988

Collins, Wilkie, *The Moonstone,* Penguin, Harmondsworth, 1966

_____, *The Dead Alive,* Shepherd & Gill, Boston, 1874

Coupe, Stuart and Julie Ogden (eds), *Case Reopened,* Allen & Unwin, Sydney, 1993

Darian-Smith, Kate, *On the Home Front: Melbourne in Wartime,* Melbourne University Press, Melbourne, 2009

Davies, Jenny, *Beyond the Façade: Flinders Street, More Than Just a Railway Station,* self-published, Mt Macedon, 2008

Dower, Alan, *Crime Chemist: The Life Story of Charles Taylor, Scientist for the Crown,* John Long, London, 1965

_____, *Deadline,* Hutchinson, Melbourne, 1979

Duck, Colin and Martin Thomas, *Whose Baby?: The World's Most Intriguing Custody Battle,* William Collins, Sydney, 1984

Ellery, R.S., *The Cow Jumped Over the Moon: Private Papers of a Psychiatrist,* F.W. Cheshire, Melbourne, 1956

Featherstone, Lisa, *Let's Talk About Sex: Histories of Sexuality in Australia from Federation to the Pill,* Cambridge Scholars Publishing, Newcastle Upon Tyne, 2011

Finnane, Mark, *J.V. Barry: A Life,* UNSW Press, Sydney, 2007

Forth, Gordon, *Winters on the Wannon,* Deakin University Press, Geelong, 1991

Frame, Tom, *The Life and Death of Harold Holt,* Allen & Unwin, Crow's Nest, 2005

Galbally, Frank, *Galbally!: The Autobiography of Australia's Leading Criminal Lawyer,* Viking, Ringwood, 1989

Golding, Peter, *Just a Chattel of the Sale: A Mostly Light-hearted Retrospect of a Diverse Life,* self-published, Sydney, 2004

Gregory, Alan, *The Ever Open Door: A History of the Royal Melbourne Hospital,* Hyland House, South Melbourne, 1998

Griffith, Geoffrey, *Homicide: True Stories of Australian Crime,* Farleigh Books, Sydney, 1967

Grindlay, Ian, *Behind Bars: Memories of Jail Governor* Ian Grindlay, Southdown Press, Melbourne, 1976

Haigh, Gideon, *The Racket: How Abortion Became Legal in Australia,* Melbourne University Press, Melbourne, 2008

Haldane, Robert, *The People's Force: A History of the Victoria Police,* Melbourne University Press, Carlton, 1986

Hansen, Brian, *The Awful Truth: The Inside Story of Crime and Sport,* Brian Hansen Publications, Melbourne, 2004

Henderson, Kent, *The Masonic Grand Masters of Australia,* Ian Drakeford Publishing, Melbourne, 1988

Herman, Anton, *Alan Missen: A Liberal Pilgrim,* Poplar Press, Canberra, 1993

Houghton, Norman, *'Drink Up, Gents': A History of Hotels in Colac and District, 1841 to 2011,* Norman Houghton, Geelong, 2011

Hume, Fergus, *The Mystery of a Hansom Cab,* Text, Melbourne, 2006

Inglis, K.S., *The Stuart Case,* Melbourne University Press, Parkville, 1961

Johnson-Woods, Toni, *Pulp: A Collector's Book of Australian Pulp Fiction Covers,* National Library of Australia, Canberra, 2004

Johnson-Woods, Toni and Amit Sarwal (eds), *Sold by the Millions: Australia's Bestsellers,* Cambridge Scholars Publishing, Newcastle Upon Tyne, 2012

Kassin, Saul and Lawrence Wrightsman, *The American Jury on Trial: Psychological Perspectives,* Hemisphere Pub, New York, 1988

Knight, Stephen, *Continent of Mystery: A Thematic History of Australian Crime Fiction,* Melbourne University Press, Carlton, 1997

Krinski, Julius, *A Life,* Aviar Press, Seattle, 2005

Lamble, Lloyd, *Hi Diddle Dee Dee: An Actor's Life for Me,* unpublished ms, 1994

Lynn, Peter, *From Pentonville to Pentridge: A History of Prisons in Victoria,* State Library of Victoria, Melbourne, 1996

McLaughlin, Judith, *Nothing Over Half a Crown: A Personal History of the Founder of the G.J. Coles Stores,* Loch Haven, Main Ridge, 1991

Marshall, Catherine, *A Man Called Peter: The Story of Peter Marshall,* Chosen Books, Ada, 2002

Martineau, Helen, *On the Inside: An Intimate Portrait of Sheila Florance,* Australian Scholarly Publishing, Melbourne, 2005

Middle Park History Group, *Middle Park: From Swamp to Suburb,* self-published, Melbourne, 2013

Missen, Alan and Brian Bourke, *The Australian Debater: A Practical Training Guide,* Cheshire, Melbourne, 1963

Morgan, Kevin, *Gun Alley: Murder, Lies and Failure of Justice,* Random House, Sydney, 2005

Morton, James and Russell Robinson, *Shotgun and Standover: The Story of the Painters and Dockers,* Pan Macmillan, Sydney, 2010

Münsterberg, Hugo, *On the Witness Stand: Essays in Psychology and Crime,* Doubleday, Page & Company, New York, 1915

O'Bryan, Norman Michael, *'Kinkora': Recollections of the O'Bryan Family,* self-published, Melbourne, 1994

Peel, Geoff, *3CS: 50 Golden Years,* Associated Communication Enterprises Pty Ltd, Melbourne, 1989

Prior, Tom, *The Sinners' Club: Memories of a Walk-Up Man,* Penguin, Ringwood, 1993

Rattigan, Terence, *The Winslow Boy: A Play in Two Acts,* French, London, 1948

Richards, Mike, *The Hanged Man: The Life and Death of Ronald Ryan,* Scribe, Melbourne, 2002

Rosenthal, Newman, *Sir Charles Lowe: A Biographical Memoir,* Robertson & Mullens, Melbourne, 1968

Roughead, William (ed), *Trial of Mary Blandy,* Butterworth & Co, Sydney, 1914

Rubinstein, Bill & Hilary, *Menders of the Mind: A History of the Royal Australian & New Zealand College of Psychiatrists,* Oxford University Press, Melbourne, 1996

Rzepka, Charles (ed), *A Companion to Crime Fiction,* Blackwell-Wiley, New York, 2010

Sharpe, Alan, *Crimes That Shocked Australia,* Currawong, Sydney, 1982

Toorak Presbyterian Church: A Jubilee Record, 1875–1925, McKellar Press, Malvern, 1925

Vine, Barbara, *A Dark-Adapted Eye,* Penguin, London, 1986

Usher, Jim (ed.), The Argus*: Life & Death of a Newspaper,* Australian Scholarly Publishing, Melbourne, 1999

Wansell, Geoffrey, *Terence Rattigan,* Fourth Estate, London, 1995

Wilson, Paul, Don Treble and Robyn Lincoln, *Jean Lee: The Last Woman Hanged in Australia,* Random House, Sydney, 1997

Wouk, Herman, *The Caine Mutiny Court-Martial,* Doubleday, New York, 1954

Wright, June, *Remembering Melbourne: Circa 1950,* self-published, Melbourne, 1997

_____, *Murder in the Telephone Exchange,* Affirm Press, Melbourne, 2014

Printed in Dunstable, United Kingdom

91338353R00252